The SQL Workshop

Learn to create, manipulate and secure data
and manage relational databases with SQL

Frank Solomon

Prashanth Jayaram

Awni Al Saqqa

The SQL Workshop

Authors: Frank Solomon, Prashanth Jayaram, and Awni Al Saqqa

Reviewers: Tor Harrington, Pradeep Kumar Gupta, Aaditya Pokkunuri, Shubham Jain, Fiodar Sazanavets, Shashikant Shakya, and Trevoir Williams

Managing Editor: Manasa Kumar

Acquisitions Editors: Alicia Wooding and Karan Wadekar

Production Editor: Salma Patel

Editorial Board: Shubhopriya Banerjee, Bharat Botle, Ewan Buckingham, Megan Carlisle, Mahesh Dhyani, Manasa Kumar, Alex Mazonowicz, Bridget Neale, Dominic Pereira, Shiny Poojary, Abhishek Rane, Brendan Rodrigues, Mugdha Sawarkar, Erol Staveley, Ankita Thakur, Nitesh Thakur, and Jonathan Wray

First published: December 2019

Production reference: 3220221

ISBN 978-1-83864-235-8

Published by Packt Publishing Ltd.

Livery Place, 35 Livery Street

Birmingham B3 2PB, UK

Why Learn with a Packt Workshop?

Learn by Doing

Packt Workshops are built around the idea that the best way to learn something new is by getting hands-on experience. We know that learning a language or technology isn't just an academic pursuit. It's a journey towards the effective use of a new tool—whether that's to kickstart your career, automate repetitive tasks, or just build some cool stuff.

That's why Workshops are designed to get you writing code from the very beginning. You'll start fairly small—learning how to implement some basic functionality—but once you've completed that, you'll have the confidence and understanding to move onto something slightly more advanced.

As you work through each chapter, you'll build your understanding in a coherent, logical way, adding new skills to your toolkit and working on increasingly complex and challenging problems.

Context is Key

All new concepts are introduced in the context of realistic use-cases, and then demonstrated practically with guided exercises. At the end of each chapter, you'll find an activity that challenges you to draw together what you've learned and apply your new skills to solve a problem or build something new.

We believe this is the most effective way of building your understanding and confidence. Experiencing real applications of the code will help you get used to the syntax and see how the tools and techniques are applied in real projects.

Build Real-World Understanding

Of course, you do need some theory. But unlike many tutorials, which force you to wade through pages and pages of dry technical explanations and assume too much prior knowledge, Workshops only tell you what you actually need to know to be able to get started making things. Explanations are clear, simple, and to-the-point. So you don't need to worry about how everything works under the hood; you can just get on and use it.

Written by industry professionals, you'll see how concepts are relevant to real-world work, helping to get you beyond "Hello, world!" and build relevant, productive skills. Whether you're studying web development, data science, or a core programming language, you'll start to think like a problem solver and build your understanding and confidence through contextual, targeted practice.

Enjoy the Journey

Learning something new is a journey from where you are now to where you want to be, and this Workshop is just a vehicle to get you there. We hope that you find it to be a productive and enjoyable learning experience.

Packt has a wide range of different Workshops available, covering the following topic areas:

- Programming languages
- Web development
- Data science, machine learning, and artificial intelligence
- Containers

Once you've worked your way through this Workshop, why not continue your journey with another? You can find the full range online at http://packt.live/2MNkuyl.

If you could leave us a review while you're there, that would be great. We value all feedback. It helps us to continually improve and make better books for our readers, and also helps prospective customers make an informed decision about their purchase.

Thank you,
The Packt Workshop Team

Table of Contents

Chapter 11: Advanced SQL 223

Preface

About

This section briefly introduces the coverage of this book, the technical skills you'll need to get started, and the software requirements required to complete all of the included activities and exercises.

About the Book

Many software applications are backed by powerful relational database systems, meaning that the skills to be able to maintain a SQL database and reliably retrieve data are in high demand. With its simple syntax and effective data manipulation capabilities, SQL enables you to manage relational databases with ease. *The SQL Workshop* will help you progress from basic to advanced-level SQL queries in order to create and manage databases successfully.

This Workshop begins with an introduction to basic CRUD commands and gives you an overview of the different data types in SQL. You'll use commands for narrowing down the search results within a database and learn about data retrieval from single and multiple tables in a single query. As you advance, you'll use aggregate functions to perform calculations on a set of values, and implement process automation using stored procedures, functions, and triggers. Finally, you'll secure your database against potential threats and use access control to keep your data safe.

Throughout this Workshop, you'll use your skills on a realistic database for an online shop, preparing you for solving data problems in the real world.

By the end of this book, you'll have built the knowledge, skills and confidence to creatively solve real-world data problems with SQL.

About the Chapters

Chapter 1, SQL Basics, explains how to create a simple database and how to create tables within databases. We will also learn how to populate data within a table.

Chapter 2, Manipulating Data, guides us through how to alter tables and delete and update entries within a table.

Chapter 3, Normalization, explains how to normalize tables within a database such that data integrity is maintained.

Chapter 4, The SELECT Statement, covers how to write basic queries to retrieve data from the database.

Chapter 5, Shaping Data with the WHERE Clause, covers implementing conditional clauses within our queries such that we get fine-grained control over our data.

Chapter 6, JOINS, talks about retrieving data from multiple tables by performing various join operations.

Chapter 7, Subqueries, Cases, and Views, talks about ways to retrieve data from intermediary tables using views and then sub-queries to further filter down results.

Chapter 8, SQL Programming, talks about advanced SQL concepts such as the functions and triggers.

Chapter 9, Security, looks at providing and revoking access to users on tables and databases.

Chapter 10, Aggregate Functions, teaches how use SQL aggregate functions and how to solve problems with them. We will also look at advanced clauses, such as the GROUP BY and the HAVING clauses, and see how they can help us to fine-tune our results

Chapter 11, Advanced SQL, looks at functions in SQL and how they can be used as powerful filtering tools.

Conventions

Code words in text, database table names, screen text, folder names, filenames, file extensions, pathnames, dummy URLs, user input, and Twitter handles are shown as follows: "We'll start with the **Orders** table since the **Orders** table ties the orders together with the **OrderItems** table."

A block of code is set as follows:

```
USE PACKT_ONLINE_SHOP;
```

Before You Begin

Each great journey begins with a humble step. Our upcoming adventure in the land of SQL is no exception. Before you can begin, you need to be prepared with the most productive environment. In this section, you will see how to do that.

To Install MySQL

To install MySQL, follow the steps present in the following documentation: https://packt.live/2rxXXv1

To Install the Code Bundle

Download the code files from GitHub at https://packt.live/2QCKNqB and place them in a new folder called **C:\Code** on your local system. Refer to these code files for the complete code bundle.

1

SQL Basics

Overview

This chapter covers the very basic concepts of SQL that will get you started with writing simple commands. By the end of this chapter, you will be able to identify the difference between structured and unstructured data, explain the basic SQL concepts, create tables using the **CREATE** statement, and insert values into tables using SQL commands.

Introduction

The vast majority of companies today work with large amounts of data. This could be product information, customer data, client details, employee data, and so on. Most people who are new to working with data will do so using spreadsheets. Software such as Microsoft Excel has many tools for manipulating and analyzing data, but as the volume and complexity of the data you're working with increases, these tools may become inefficient.

A more powerful and controlled way of working with data is to store it in a database and use SQL to access and manipulate it. SQL works extremely well for organized data and can be used very effectively to insert, retrieve, and manipulate data with just a few lines of code. In this chapter, we'll get an introduction to SQL and see how to create databases and tables, as well as how to insert values into them.

Understanding Data

For most companies, storing and retrieving data is a day-to-day activity. Based on how data is stored, we can broadly classify data as structured or unstructured. Unstructured data, simply put, is data that is not well-organized. Documents, PDFs, and videos fall into this category—they contain a mixture of different data types (text, images, audio, video, and so on) that have no consistent relationship between them. Media and publishing are examples of industries that deal with unstructured data such as this.

In this book, our focus will be on structured data. Structured data is organized according to a consistent structure. As such, structured data can be easily organized into tables. Thanks to its consistent organization, working with structured data is easier, and it can be processed more effectively. Tables are collections of entities or tuples (rows) and attributes (columns).

For example, consider the following table:

Student	Subject	Score
John Smith	English	69
John Smith	Mathematics	54
John Smith	Physics	47
John Smith	Environmental Studies	72

Figure 1.1: An example student's database table

For each row, there is a clear relationship; a given student takes a particular subject and achieves a specific score in that subject. The columns are also known as *fields*, while the rows are known as *records*.

Data that is presented in tabular form can be stored in a relational database. **Relational databases**, as the name suggests, store data that has a certain relationship with another piece of data. A **Relational Database Management System** (**RDBMS**) is a system that's used to manage relational data. SQL works very well with relational data. Popular RDBMSs include Microsoft SQL Server, MySQL, and Oracle. Throughout this book, we will be working with MySQL. We can use various SQL commands to work with data in relational databases. We'll have a brief look at them in the next section.

An Overview of Basic SQL Commands

SQL (often pronounced "sequel") stands for **Structured Query Language**. A query in SQL is constructed using different commands. These commands are classified into what are called sublanguages of SQL. Even if you think you know them already, give this a read to see if these seem more relatable to you. There are five sublanguages in SQL, as follows:

- **Data Definition Language (DDL)**: As the name suggests, the commands that fall under this category work with defining either a table, a database, or anything within. Any command that talks about creating something in SQL is part of DDL. Some examples of such commands are **CREATE**, **ALTER**, and **DROP**.

  The following table shows the DDL commands:

Command	Description
CREATE	Creates a new database or a new table
ALTER	Modifies the structure of a database or a table
DROP	Deletes a database or a table
TRUNCATE	Removes all table records and the allocated table spaces
RENAME	Renames a database or a table

  Figure 1.2: DDL commands

- **Data Manipulation Language (DML)**: In DML, you do not deal with the containers of data but the data itself. When you must update the data itself, or perform calculations or operations on it, you use the DML. The commands that form part of this language (or sublanguage) include **INSERT**, **UPDATE**, **MERGE**, and **DELETE**.

DML allows you to work on the data without modifying the container or stored procedures. A copy of the data is created and the operations are performed on this copy of the data. These operations are performed using the DML. The following table shows the DML commands:

Command	Description
INSERT	Adds new rows to a table.
UPDATE	Updates the existing data or rows or records in a table.
DELETE	Deletes records from a table.
MERGE	This is also called UPSERT (as in UPDATE/ INSERT). MERGE is used to insert new records or update existing records based on conditions.

Figure 1.3: DML commands

- **Data Control Language (DCL)**: When we sit back and think about what the word *control* means in the context of data, we think of *allowing and disallowing actions on the data*. In SQL terms, or in terms of data, this is about authorization. Therefore, the commands that fall in this category are **GRANT** and **REVOKE**. They control access to the data. The following table explains them:

Command	Description
GRANT	Gives access privileges to a user for the data in a database
REVOKE	Takes away the privileges a user has on the specified data

Figure 1.4: DCL commands

- **Transaction Control Language (TCL)**: Anything that makes a change to the data is called a transaction. When you perform a data manipulation operation, the manipulation happens to data in a temporary location and not the table/database itself. The result is shown after the operation. In order to write or remove something from the database, you need to use a command to ask the database to update itself with the new content. Applying these changes to the database is called a transaction and is done using the TCL. The commands associated with this language are **COMMIT** and **ROLLBACK**. The following table explains these commands in detail:

Command	Description
COMMIT	Saves the changes permanently in the database
ROLLBACK	Restores the database to its original form until the last COMMIT
SAVEPOINT	Creates a point for later use in order to roll back the new changes
SET TRANSACTION	Sets transaction properties to make it read-only, for example

Figure 1.5: TCL commands

- **Data Query Language (DQL)**: The final part of this section regarding the classification of commands is the DQL. This is used to fetch data from the database with the SELECT command. It's explained in detail in the following table:

Command	Description
SELECT	Displays static data or retrieves data from a table, based on certain parameters

Figure 1.6: DQL command

We'll look at these queries in detail in later chapters.

Creating Databases

An interesting point to note is that the **create database** command is not part of the regular SQL standard. However, it is supported by almost all database products today. The **create database** statement is straightforward. You just need to issue a database name along with the command, followed by a semicolon.

Let's start by creating a simple example database. We'll call it **studentdemo**. To create the **studentdemo** database with the default configuration, use the following command:

```
create database studentdemo;
```

To run this statement, click the **Execute** button (shaped like a lightning bolt):

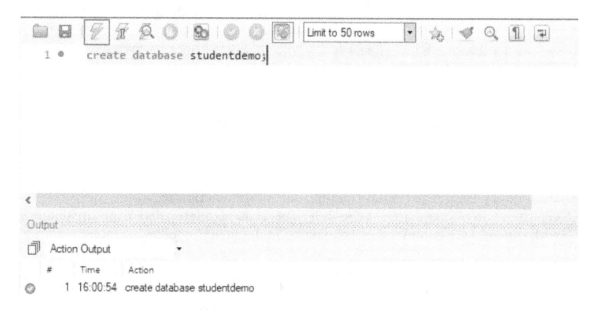

Figure 1.7: Creating the studentdemo database

In the `Action Output` pane, the successful completion of a command will appear. You will also be able to see the newly created database in the `Schemas` tab of the `Navigator` pane.

> **Note**
>
> SQL is not case sensitive. This implies **CREATE TABLE studentdemo;** is the same as `create table studentdemo;`.

We cannot have multiple databases with the same name. If you try to run the query again, you'll get the following error:

Figure 1.8: Error message displayed in the case of a database with the same name as another database

The Use of Semicolons

As you may have noticed, there's a semicolon, ;, at the end of the statement as an indication that that's the end of that statement. It depends on the database system you are using; some of them require a semicolon at the end of each statement and some don't, but you can still add it without worrying about the results.

> **Note**
>
> In general, it's good practice to use a semicolon at the end of a statement as it could play a significant role when we have multiple SQL statements or while writing a function or a trigger. This will be explained in more detail in the upcoming chapters. Throughout this book, we will use semicolons at the end of each statement.

Data Types in SQL

Like every other programming language, SQL also has **data types**. Every piece of data that is entered into a database must comply with the data types and their formats. This implies that any data that you store is either a number, a character, or some other data type. Those are the basic data types. There are some special data types as well.

For instance, "00:43 on Monday, 1 April 2019" is a combination of letters, numbers, and punctuation. However, when we see something like this, we immediately start thinking of the day. A data type is the type of value that can be stored in a system. Some examples of data types are `INTEGER`, `FLOATING POINT`, `CHARACTER`, `STRING`, and combinations of these such as `DATETIME`.

Since there's a large amount of data types, most languages classify data types. Here, we will go through some of the most common ones. The idea here is to get you acquainted with the data types, not to give you a complete rundown of them as this would overwhelm you with hardly any significant returns. Moreover, once the concept is clear, you will be able to adapt to the rest of the data types with little effort.

In the interest of better data integrity and modeling, it is critical to select the right data type for the situation. It may seem trivial when the database is small, but with a larger database, it becomes difficult to manage. As a programmer, it is your responsibility to model your data in the right way.

In order to keep this simple, let's broadly classify the data types into five categories:

- **Numeric data types**: Numeric data types include everything that involves numbers, such as integers (small/big), floating- and fixed-point decimal numbers, and real numbers. Here are some of the most common ones:

Data type	Lowest value of the range	Highest value of the range
Bit	0	1
Tinyint	0	255
Smallint	-32,768	32,767
Int	-2,147,483,648	2,147,483,647
Bigint	9,223,372,036,854,770,000	-9,223,372,036,854,770,000
Decimal	-10^38 - 1	10^38 - 1
Float	-1.79E + 308	1.79E + 308
Real	-3.40E + 38	3.40E + 38

Figure 1.9: Numeric data types

- **Fixed and varying length characters and text**: Performance is key when selecting either fixed- or variable-length characters. When you know that a certain piece of data will be of a fixed number of characters, use the fixed width. For example, if you know that the employee code will always be of 4 characters, you can use **CHAR**. When you are unsure of the number of characters, use variable width. If a certain column holds only six characters, you are better off specifying it so that space used will be limited. By doing this, you will get better performance by not using up more resources than required. If you are unsure of the width, you don't want to be limited by the total width. Therefore, you should ideally use character types of varying lengths. An example of this can be a person's first name, where the length of the name is not fixed.

> **Note**
>
> You can use **CHAR** with varying lengths of characters (**VARCHAR**) as well. For instance, in a field that accepts up to six characters, you can enter data that is three characters long. However, you would be leaving the other three-character spaces unused, which will be right-padded, meaning that the remaining spaces will be reserved as actual spaces. When the data is retrieved, these trailing spaces will be trimmed. If you don't want them to be trimmed, you can set a flag in SQL that tells SQL to reserve the spaces and not trim them during retrieval. There are situations where you would need to do this using the **TRIM** string function, for example, to enhance data security.

Unicode characters and string data types are different. They are prefixed with N, such as **NCHAR**, **NVARCHAR**, and **NTEXT**. Also, note that not all SQL implementations support Unicode data types.

> **Note**
>
> Unicode character data types consume twice the storage space compared to non-Unicode character data types.

The other character-based data type is **TEXT**. This can store textual data up to a certain limit, which may vary with the system. For instance, MS SQL supports text up to 2 GB in size.

- **Binary data types**: Binary forms of data are also allowed in SQL. For instance, an **IMAGE** would be an object of binary form. Similarly, you have **BINARY** and **VARBINARY** data types.

- **Miscellaneous data types**: Miscellaneous data types include most of the now-popular data types, such as **Binary Large Object (BLOB)**, **Character Large Object (CLOB)**, XML, and JSON. We have included **DATE**, **TIME**, and **DATETIME** as well in this class.

  Character and binary large objects include types such as files. For instance, a film stored on Netflix is a binary large object. So would be an application package such as an EXE or an MSI, or other types of files such as PDFs.

> **Note**
>
> SQL Server 2016 supports JSON. JSON Unicode character representation uses **NVARCHAR/NCHAR** or ANSI **VARCHAR/CHAR** for non-Unicode strings.
>
> MySQL version 5.7.8 supports a native JSON data type.

- **Proprietary types**: In the real world, there is hardly a pure SQL implementation that is favored by enterprises. Different businesses have different requirements, and to cater to these requirements, SQL implementations have created their own data types. For instance, Microsoft SQL has **MONEY** as a data type.

  Not all data types are supported by all vendors. For instance, Oracle's implementation of SQL does not support **DATETIME**, while MySQL does not support **CLOB**. Therefore, the flavor of SQL is an important consideration when designing your database schema.

As we mentioned previously, this is not an exhaustive list of all data types. Your flavor of SQL will have its own supporting set of data types. Read the documentation that comes with the product kit to find out what it supports–as a programmer or a SQL administrator, it is you who decides what is necessary. This book will empower you to do that.

The size limits illustrated in *Figure 1.9* are only indicative. Just as different flavors of databases may have different data types, they may have different limits as well. The documentation that accompanies the product you plan to use will have this information.

Creating Simple Tables

After creating the database, we want to create a table The **create table** statement is part of the SQL standard. The **create table** statement allows you to configure your table, your columns, and all your relations and constraints. Along with the **create table** command, you're going to pass the table name and a list of column definitions. At the minimum for every column, you must provide the column name and the data type the column will hold.

Let's say you want to add a table called **Student** to the previously created database, **studentdemo**, and you want this table to contain the following details:

- **Student name**: The student's full name.
- **Student ID**: A value to identify each student uniquely.
- **Grade**: Each student is graded as A, B, or C based on their performance.
- **Age**: The age of the student.
- **Course**: The course they are enrolled on.

To achieve this, we need to complete a two-step process:

1. To set the current database as **studentdemo**, enter the following code in the new query tab:

Figure 1.10: Switching from the default database to our database

You can open a new query tab, by clicking **File | New Query Tab**.

2. Create a table **Student** within **studentdemo** with the following columns:

```
create table Student
(
    StudentID      CHAR (4),
    StudentName VARCHAR (30),
    grade          CHAR(1),
    age            INT,
    course         VARCHAR(50),
    PRIMARY KEY (StudentID)
);
```

The preceding code creates a **Student** table with the following columns:

- **StudentID** will contain four character values. **'S001'**, **'ssss'**, and **'SSSS'** are all valid inputs and can be stored in the **StudentID** field.

- **grade** will just contain a single character. **'A'**, **'F'**, **'h'**, **'1'**, and **'z'** are all valid inputs.

- **StudentName** will contain variable-length values, which can be 30 characters in size at most. **'John'**, **'Parker'**, **'Anna'**, **'Cleopatra'**, and **'Smith'** are all valid inputs.

- **course** will also contain variable-length values, which can be 50 characters in size at most.

- **age** will be an integer value. **1**, **34**, **98**, **345** are all valid values.

StudentID is defined as the primary key. This implies that all the values in the **StudentID** field will be unique, and no value can be null. You can uniquely identify any record in the **Student** table using **StudentID**. We will learn about primary keys in detail in *Chapter 3, Normalization*.

> **Note**
>
> NULL is used to represent missing values.

Notice that we have provided the **PRIMARY KEY** constraint for **StudentID** because we require this to be unique.

Once your table has been created successfully, you will see it in the **Schemas** tab of the `Navigator` pane:

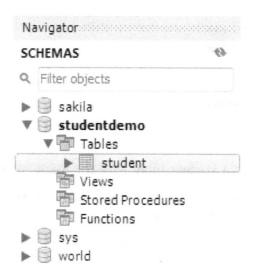

Figure 1.11: The Schemas tab in the Navigator pane

Exercise 1.01: Building the PACKT_ONLINE_SHOP Database

In this exercise, we're going to start building the database for a *Packt Online Shop*—a store that sells a variety of items to customers. We will be using the MySQL Community Server in this book. The *Packt Online Shop* has been working on spreadsheets so far, but as they plan to scale up, they realize that this is not a feasible option, and so they wish to move toward data management through SQL. The first step in this process will be to create a database named **PACKT_ONLINE_SHOP** with a table for storing their customer details. Perform the following steps to complete this exercise:

1. Create a database using the **create** statement:

```
create database PACKT_ONLINE_SHOP;
```

2. Switch to this database:

```
use PACKT_ONLINE_SHOP;
```

3. Create the **Customers** table:

```
create table Customers
(
      FirstName varchar(50) ,
      MiddleName varchar(50) ,
      LastName varchar(50) ,
      HomeAddress varchar(250) ,
      Email varchar(200) ,
      Phone varchar(50) ,
      Notes varchar(250)
);
```

> **Note**
>
> Similar to **varchar**, **nvarchar** is a variable-length data type; however, in **nvarchar**, the data is stored in Unicode, not in ASCII. Therefore, columns defined with **nvarchar** can contain values in other languages as well. **nvarchar** requires 2 bytes per character, whereas **varchar** uses 1 byte.

4. Execute the statement by clicking the Execute button:

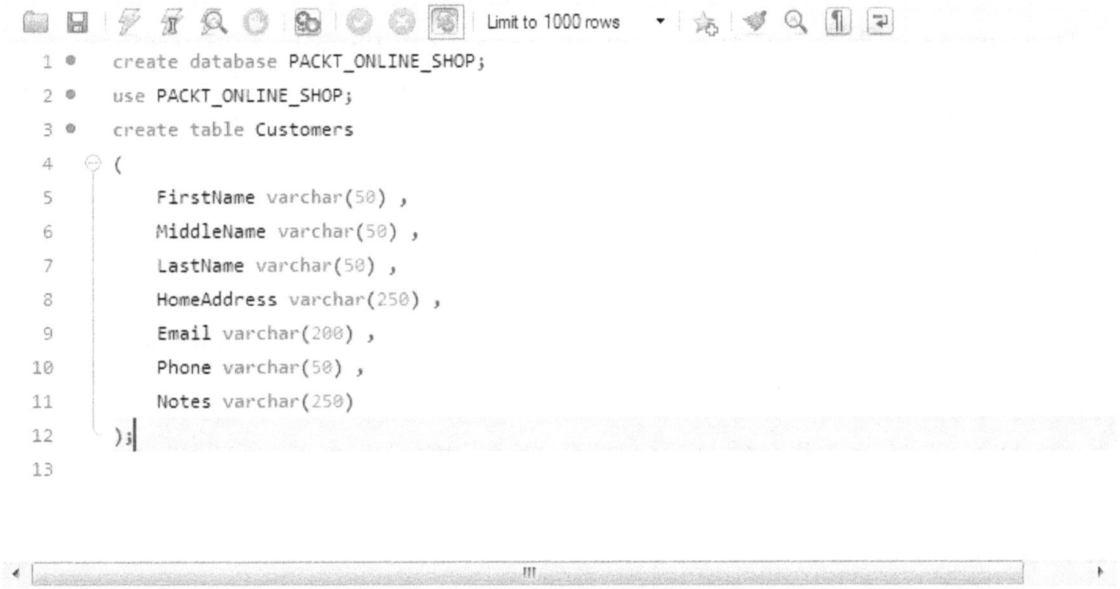

Figure 1.12: Creating the Customers table

5. Review the table by right-clicking the table in the **Schemas tab** and clicking **Select Rows - Limit 1000** in the contextual menu:

Figure 1.13: Column headers displayed through the SELECT query

This runs a simple **Select** query. You will learn about the **Select** statement in *Chapter 4, The SELECT Statement*. The top 1,000 rows are displayed. Since we have not inserted values into the table yet, we are only able to view the column headers in **Result Grid**.

> **Note**
>
> If you are working on Microsoft SQL Server, you can do this by right-clicking the table in the Object Explorer window and then selecting **Select Top 1000 Rows**.

In the next section, we will look at inserting values into tables.

Populating Your Tables

Once the table has been created, the next logical step is to insert values into the table. To do this, SQL provides the **INSERT** statement. Let's try adding a row of data to the **Student** table of the **studentdemo** database that we created previously.

Here is the SQL statement to achieve this. First, switch to the **studentdemo** database and enter the following query:

```
USE studentdemo;
INSERT INTO Student (StudentID, StudentName, grade, age, course) VALUES ('S001',
'Prashanth Jayaram', 'A', 36, 'Computer Science');
```

If you check the contents of the database after running this query, you should see something like this:

Figure 1.14: Values inserted into the database

> **Note**
>
> To see the contents of this database, follow the process you used in the earlier exercises. Right-click the table and choose **Select Rows - Limit 1000**.

Adding single rows like this in multiple queries will be time-consuming. We can add multiple rows by writing a query like the following one:

```
INSERT INTO Student (StudentID, StudentName, grade, age, course) VALUES ('S002', 'Frank
Solomon', 'B', 35, 'Physics'), ('S003', 'Rachana Karia', 'B', 36, 'Electronics'),
('S004', 'Ambika Prashanth', 'C', 35, 'Mathematics');
```

The preceding query looks like this on the Query tab.

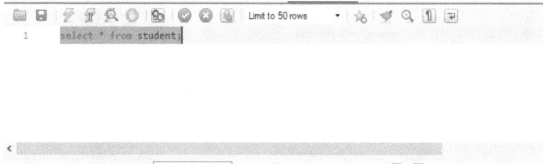

Figure 1.15: Adding multiple rows in an INSERT query

When you run the query, all three rows will be added with a single query:

StudentID	StudentName	grade	age	course
S002	Frank Solomon	B	35	Physics
S003	Rachana Karia	B	36	Electronics
S004	Ambika Prashanth	C	35	Mathematics
NULL	NULL	NULL	NULL	NULL

Figure 1.16: Output of multiple row insertion

Exercise 1.02: Inserting Values into the Customers Table of the PACKT_ONLINE_SHOP Database

Now that we have the **Customers** table ready, let's insert values into the table using a single query. We have the data from an already existing Excel spreadsheet. We will be using that data to write our query. Here is what the Excel file looks like:

	A	B	C	D	E	F	G
1	FirstName	MiddleName	LastName	HomeAddress	Email	Phone	Notes
2	Joe	Greg	Smith	2356 Elm St.	joesmith@sfghwert.com	(310) 555-1212	Always gets products home delivered
3	Grace	Murray	Hopper	123 Compilation Street	gmhopper@ftyuw46.com	(818) 555-3678	Compiler pioneer
4	Ada		Lovelace	22 Algorithm Way	adalovelace@fgjw54af.gov	(717) 555-3457	First software engineer
5	Joseph	Force	Carter	1313 Mockingbird Lane	judgecrater@ev56gfwrty.com	(212) 555-5678	Works everyday
6	Orville		Wright	80 Bicycle Lane	owright@sdg98.edu	(211) 555-4444	First pilot
7	Jacqueline	Jackie	Cochran	1701 Flightspeed Avenue	jackiecochrane@jryuwp8qe4w.gov	(717) 555-3457	Researcher
8		Paul	Jones	126 Bonhomme Richard A	jpjones@bonhommerichard.edu	(216) 555-6232	Admiral
9							

Figure 1.17: Source data in an Excel spreadsheet

> **Note**
>
> You can find the csv format of the file here: https://packt.live/369ytTu.

To move this data into the database, we will need to perform the following steps:

1. Switch to the **PACKT_ONLINE_SHOP** database:

```
use PACKT_ONLINE_SHOP;
```

2. Insert the values based on the Excel spreadsheet provided wherever we have blank data. We will use **NULL** to do this:

```
INSERT INTO Customers (FirstName, MiddleName, LastName, HomeAddress, Email, Phone, Notes)
VALUES('Joe', 'Greg', 'Smith', '2356 Elm St.', 'joesmith@sfghwert.com', '(310) 555-1212', 'Always gets products home delivered'),
('Grace', 'Murray', 'Hopper', '123 Compilation Street', 'gmhopper@ftyuw46.com', '(818) 555-3678', 'Compiler pioneer'),
('Ada', NULL, 'Lovelace', '22 Algorithm Way', 'adalovelace@fgjw54af.gov', '(717) 555-3457', 'First software engineer'),
('Joseph', 'Force', 'Crater', '1313 Mockingbird Lane', 'judgecrater@ev56gfwrty.com', '(212) 555-5678', 'Works everyday'),
('Jacqueline', 'Jackie', 'Cochran', '1701 Flightspeed Avenue', 'jackiecochrane@jryuwp8qe4w.gov', '(717) 555-3457', 'Researcher'),
(NULL, 'Paul', 'Jones', '126 Bonhomme Richard Ave.', 'jpjones@bonhommerichard.edu', '(216) 555-6232', 'Admiral');
```

3. When you execute the query and check the contents of the **Customers** table, you should see the following output.

FirstName	MiddleName	LastName	HomeAddress	Email	Phone	Notes
Joe	Greg	Smith	2356 Elm St.	joesmith@sfghwert.com	(310) 555-1212	Always gets products home delivered
Grace	Murray	Hopper	123 Compilation Street	gmhopper@ftyuw46.com	(818) 555-3678	Compiler pioneer
Ada	NULL	Lovelace	22 Algorithm Way	adalovelace@fgjw54af.gov	(717) 555-3457	First software engineer
Joseph	Force	Crater	1313 Mockingbird Lane	judgecrater@ev56gfwrty.com	(212) 555-5678	Works everyday
Jacqueline	Jackie	Cochran	1701 Flightspeed Avenue	jackiecochrane@jryuwp8qe4w.gov	(717) 555-3457	Researcher
NULL	Paul	Jones	126 Bonhomme Richard Ave.	jpjones@bonhommerichard.edu	(216) 555-6232	Admiral

Figure 1.18: The Customers table after inserting the values from the excel sheet

With this, you have successfully populated the **Customers** table.

Activity 1.01: Inserting Values into the Products Table in the PACKT_ONLINE_ SHOP Database

Now that we've migrated the customer's data into the database, the next step is to migrate the product data from the Excel spreadsheet to the database. The data to be entered into the database can be found at https://packt.live/2ZnJiyZ.

Here is a screenshot of the Excel spreadsheet:

	ProductID	ProductCategoryID	SupplierID	ProductName	NetRetailPrice	AvailableQuantity	WholesalePrice	UnitKGWeight	Notes
2	1	5	2	Calculatre	$24.99	100	$17.99	1	calculation application
3	2	5	5	Penwrite	$79.99	27	$49.99	2	word processing product
4	3	1	6	Vortex Generator	$2,499.99	1000	$1,999.99	0.01	space engine component
5	4	1	6	The Gourmet Crockpot	$24.99	72	$19.99	1.63	cookbook
6	5	1	6	Government Accounting	$14.99	26	$9.99	1.22	government accounting book
7	6	3	6	habanero peppers	$4.49	189	$2.99	0.009	hot peppers
8	7	2	1	10-mm socket wrench	$3.49	39	$1.89	0.018	important tool
9	8	3	4	tomato sauce	$1.19	1509	$0.89	0.232	bottled in glass
10	9	1	6	pure vanilla	$10.39	1509	$7.89	0.032	high-quality vanilla
11	10	3	2	keyboard wrench	$399.999.95	6128	$149.999.99	521.38	handle with care
12	11	2	1	power cell	$47.69	2346	$29.99	0.298	ten amp-hours per cell

Figure 1.19: Source data in an Excel spreadsheet

1. Create a table called **Products** in the **Packt_Online_Shop** database.

2. Create the columns as present in the Excel sheet.

3. Use the **INSERT** statement to input the required data into the table.

> **Note**
>
> The solution for this activity can be found on page 244.

Summary

In this chapter, we had a look at the different types of data and how data is stored in relational databases. We also had a brief look at the different commands available in SQL. We specifically focused on creating databases and tables within the databases, as well as how we can easily insert values into tables.

In the next chapter, we will look at how we can modify the data, the properties of tables, and databases, and build complex tables.

Manipulating Data

Overview

This chapter teaches you to implement the **INSERT**, **UPDATE**, and **DELETE** statements which help you keep the content present in a table up-to-date. We will also cover how we can use default values while updating the tables.

Introduction

In *Chapter 1, SQL Basics*, we learned the concepts that help set up a database. Although we did insert some data into the tables, we didn't quite get into the specifics of managing the data within the database. However, there might be circumstances where we might need to change the data inserted or present in the database. For example, an employee working for a company might want to change their official number from what was updated earlier. A product that is no longer manufactured needs to be removed from the list of products available. MySQL provides some commands we can implement to make changes to the database, which will be covered in this chapter. In this chapter, we will fill the tables we created in the previous chapter with data. We will also look at the **UPDATE** and **DELETE** operations that are part of **CRUD** (**Create**, **Read**, **Update**, and **Delete**).

The INSERT Operation

The **INSERT** operation inserts a record within a table. We have already used the insert operation in the previous chapter, however, in this chapter, we are looking at it in more detail. The following are some important points about the **INSERT** operation:

- It is not always essential to provide data for every single column when performing an **INSERT** operation. The columns can be left blank unless there is a constraint that forbids it. Some columns may even have default or system-generated values.

- You should not alter the system-generated values.

- The column values must match the order, data type, and size requirements.

- The values to be inserted into the table must be enclosed in quotes in the case of strings, date-time, and characters. Numbers should not be enclosed in quotes.

- If you do not specify the column names in the **INSERT** statement, your record should have a value for all the columns. Also, you should maintain the sequence of columns in the values.

- You can only insert values into one table at a time because **INSERT INTO** accepts only one table name as the table name argument.

Performing a Simple INSERT

As we have seen previously, the **INSERT** statement begins with **INSERT INTO**, followed by the table name. Next, you specify the names of the columns. It is mandatory to insert data into all the columns that require information (for example, columns that are specified as **NOT NULL**, or a column that is selected as the primary key).

Blank columns need not be provided with data using the **INSERT** statement. Also, there may be columns with default values; these don't need to be provided with data either, unless it's necessary.

After you've specified the names of the columns, you can use the **VALUES** clause to enter the values for those columns. In other words, you cannot specify the name of a column and then not provide it with data. If you do not wish to insert data into a column, then do not specify the column name in the **INSERT INTO** statement.

This process is as straightforward as it seems. This way, you insert one row or record into the table. However, in many cases, it is recommended to use the **UPDATE** operation along with the **SET** keyword to insert rows because the process is more efficient.

> **Note**
>
> We will discuss the **UPDATE** operation and its use with the **SET** keyword in detail in *The UPDATE Operation* section in this chapter.

Exercise 2.01: Inserting One Row of Data into a Table

In this exercise, we'll implement the **INSERT INTO...VALUES** SQL statement to add records to a table. First, we'll create an **EMPLOYEE** database and then we'll add a table to it. Next, we'll insert values into the table with the **INSERT** SQL statement and finally display the contents of the table. To do so, let's go through the following steps:

1. Create an **EMPLOYEE** database:

```
CREATE DATABASE EMPLOYEE;
USE EMPLOYEE;
```

2. Create a **department** table, with **departmentNo** as the PRIMARY key:

```
CREATE TABLE department (
    departmentNo INT PRIMARY KEY,
    departmentName VARCHAR(20) NOT NULL,
    departmentLoc VARCHAR(50) NOT NULL
);
```

> **Note**
>
> The syntax **PRIMARY KEY (departmentNo);** would also work.

3. Insert the values into the **department** table:

```
INSERT INTO department (
    departmentNo,
    departmentName,
    departmentLoc
)
VALUES (
    1,
    'Engg',
    'Texas'
);
```

4. From the **Navigator** pane, select the **Schemas** tab. Select **EMPLOYEE | Tables | department | Select Rows - Limit 1000**.

The expected output is as follows:

Figure 2.1: Adding values to a database table

Multiple Inserts

In *Exercise 2.01, Inserting Data into a Table*, we saw how simple it is to perform a single row insert within a table. You specify the names of the columns and the rows, and that does the job. However, you may want to insert more than one row in a single statement in the interest of efficiency. This can be done by either explicitly specifying the values for multiple rows in the **VALUES** clause or by using a **SELECT** statement. With the **SELECT** statement, you are essentially inserting values into one table by collecting data from one or more other tables. Again, we saw this previously when we wanted to populate table in *Chapter 1, SQL Basics*.

Let's go through another exercise to specify default values. Specifying a default value is simple; all you must do is use the **DEFAULT** keyword and specify the default value or a function that gets you the default value.

Exercise 2.02: Specifying Default Values

In this exercise, we will assume that all the departments of your company are centered at the headquarters in New Jersey, unless specified otherwise. We will also assume that every department has a record of the date that it was established. You are required to define your table accordingly. In this case, we will need a default value for the other columns in the database. Let's go through the following steps:

1. We already have a table called department, but it does not have a column to capture the established date. We will therefore drop the department table first and then create a new table. This allows us to overwrite it. The syntax for this is **DROP TABLE IF EXISTS**:

```
DROP TABLE IF EXISTS department;
CREATE TABLE department (
    departmentNo INT PRIMARY KEY AUTO_INCREMENT,
    departmentName VARCHAR(20) NOT NULL,
    departmentLoc VARCHAR(50) DEFAULT 'NJ',
    departmentEstDate DATETIME DEFAULT NOW()
);
```

Here we have provided default values for **deptartmentLoc** and **departmentEstDate**. The **departmentNo** column is an auto-increment column. This means that you do not explicitly control the values that go into the column. Your attempt to insert data into the column will raise an error in response. If you would like to control the values, you need to alter the table to reset the auto-increment value before inserting the values in the identity columns.

> **Note**
>
> The **NOW()** function will provide the system date and system time of execution. We will learn more about functions in *Chapter 8, SQL Programming*.

2. Let's set up a new department called **MyDepartment**, located in New Jersey. We will set the date the department was established as today. We do this by inserting a new value, **MyDepartment**, into the table:

```
INSERT INTO department (
    departmentName
)
VALUES (
    'MyDepartment'
);
```

3. From the **Navigator** pane, select the **Schemas** tab. Select **EMPLOYEE** | **Tables** | **department** | **Select Rows - Limit 1000**.

The expected output is as follows:

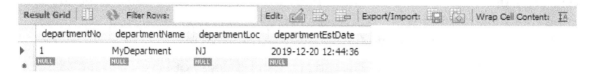

Figure 2.2: Adding a new department to the table

Similarly, you can add multiple rows to the table, and the default columns will pick their values accordingly. Say that you would like to add two more departments, Administration and IT.

4. Add multiple values to the **department** table:

```
INSERT INTO department (
    departmentName,
    departmentLoc)
VALUES
(
    'Administration',
    DEFAULT
),
(
    'IT',
    DEFAULT
);
```

5. Once you execute the command (by clicking the **Execute** button), inspect the contents of the table. The expected output is as follows:

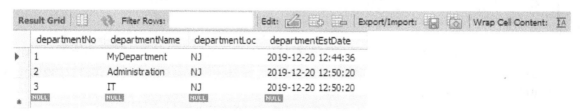

Figure 2.3: Default values added for the new inserts, Administration and IT, in the table

We can see from the output that the default values were automatically added. Also, if you would like to explicitly ask SQL to insert the default values, you could do that as well by using the **DEFAULT** keyword.

6. We can however, override the default value as well. To insert a department, Administration, that is in NYC, run the following command:

```
INSERT INTO department (
    departmentName,
    departmentLoc)
VALUES
(
    'Administration',
    'NYC'
);
```

7. View the contents of the **department** table, from the **Navigator** pane. The table will look as follows:

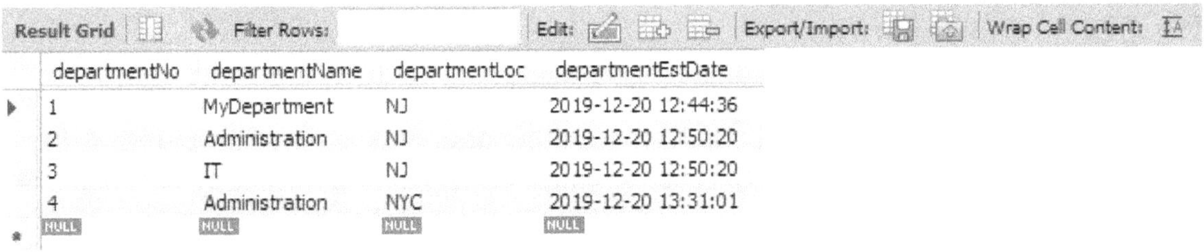

Figure 2.4: Overriding the default value

Using an INSERT Statement to Add Data from Another Dataset

Previously, we used the **SELECT** statement to fetch data from a table. That was only a basic way of doing this. This section will describe the other ways we can insert data from another dataset. The **SELECT** statements that will be used here can be either simple or multi-table complex **SELECT** statements.

Apart from **INSERT...SELECT**, you could use **CREATE TABLE AS SELECT * FROM**:

```
CREATE TABLE departmentdemo AS
    SELECT *
    FROM    department;
```

If we run the following query, we can see that the table **departmentdemo** has the following contents:

	departmentNo	departmentName	departmentLoc	departmentEstDate
▶	1	MyDepartment	NJ	2019-12-20 12:44:36
	2	Administration	NJ	2019-12-20 12:50:20
	3	IT	NJ	2019-12-20 12:50:20
	4	Administration	NYC	2019-12-20 13:31:01

Result Grid · Filter Rows: · Export: · Wrap Cell Content:

Figure 2.5: Inserting data from another dataset

Now, that we have an idea of how values are inserted in the table, in the next section we'll be learning about how we can delete values from the table.

The DELETE Operation

The **DELETE** statement deletes one or more rows within a table. Like the **INSERT** operations, **DELETE** also works only on a single table at a time. A deletion operation should be performed very carefully because deletion is permanent. Many database tools require you to add a **WHERE** clause to the **DELETE FROM** statement. When performing these deletion operations, which require a **WHERE** clause, and you would like to delete all the rows in a table, you could work around this by using a condition that is true for all the rows in the table.

For example, say you have an employee with **empno 1234** who is no longer associated with the company. In such cases your query would look like the following:

```
DELETE FROM employees
    WHERE empno = 1234;
```

If you would like to remove the top 5 rows from the **employees** table, we would use the following query:

```
DELETE FROM employees
    LIMIT 5;
```

Exercise 2.03: Deleting a record from a table

Consider that the product tomato sauce is no longer available in the **PACKT_ONLINE_SHOP** database. Therefore, our Products table should also reflect this data. To do this we will have to delete the entire row containing the details of the product tomato sauce. To do this, perform the following steps:

1. Inspect the contents of the **products** table, you should see the product tomato sauce present in there. Its product id is 8.

2. In the new query tab, enter the following query:

```
USE PACKT_ONLINE_SHOP
DELETE FROM products
    WHERE ProductName = 'tomato sauce';
```

> **Note**
>
> You might get an error here, because you are operating in Safe Mode. To disable Safe Mode, go to **Edit | Preferences | SQL Editor** and uncheck the **Safe mode** option. Once you do this, reconnect to the database, and the query should execute successfully.

3. Now, in the **Navigator** pane, go to **Schemas**, and then click **packt_online_shop | tables | products | Select Rows -Limit 1000**. You should get the following output:

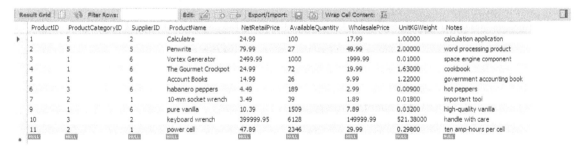

Figure 2.6: Deleting data from the products table

Notice that tomato sauce is no longer in the list.

The ALTER Operation

The **ALTER** keyword is used to make changes to the schemas present in the database. For example, if we want to add or delete columns in a table, we should be using **ALTER**. It can also be used rename to tables. For example:

```
ALTER TABLE departmentdemo RENAME TO departmentcopy;
```

This will rename the table **departmentdemo** to **departmentcopy**.

Now, let us look at solving one of the main issues we might encounter with auto-increment values using **ALTER**.

Exercise 2.04: Manipulating the Auto-Increment Values in a Table

In this exercise, we'll alter a table and manipulate the auto-increment values. We'll be continuing from where we left off in *Exercise 2.03, Specifying Default Values*. Let's go through the following steps:

1. Delete the rows where **departmentNo** is greater than 2; this will delete the two rows where **departmentNo** is 3 and 4:

    ```
    delete from department where departmentNo>2;
    ```

2. Select the **department** table to get a preview of the existing rows in the table:

departmentNo	departmentName	departmentLoc	departmentEstDate
1	MyDepartment	NJ	2019-12-20 12:44:36
2	Administration	NJ	2019-12-20 12:50:20
NULL	NULL	NULL	NULL

Figure 2.7: Existing rows in the table

3. Now, insert the sales department into the **department** table:

    ```
    insert into department(departmentname,departmentLoc)
        values('Sales','LV');
    ```

4. On selecting the rows, we can see that the **auto_increment** column starts at 5:

Result Grid		Filter Rows:		Edit:	Export/Import:	Wrap Cell Content:
departmentNo	departmentName	departmentLoc	departmentEstDate			
1	MyDepartment	NJ	2019-12-20 12:44:36			
2	Administration	NJ	2019-12-20 12:50:20			
5	Sales	LV	2019-12-20 15:13:07			
NULL	NULL	NULL	NULL			

Figure 2.8: The auto-increment column starting at 5

5. Delete the newly inserted **Sales** department:

```
delete from department where departmentNo=5;
```

6. Run the **ALTER TABLE** statement to reset the **auto_increment** column to **3**.

```
ALTER TABLE department AUTO_INCREMENT = 3;
```

7. Insert the **Sales** department:

```
insert into department(departmentname,departmentLoc)
        values('Sales','LV');
select * from department;
```

The output will be as follows:

	departmentNo	departmentName	departmentLoc	departmentEstDate
▶	1	MyDepartment	NJ	2019-12-20 12:44:36
	2	Administration	NJ	2019-12-20 12:50:20
	3	Sales	LV	2019-12-20 15:48:05
*	NULL	NULL	NULL	NULL

Figure 2.9: Sales department added

The UPDATE Operation

As we saw in the overview, **UPDATE** modifies data in one or more columns in a table. Just like the **INSERT** operation, the **UPDATE** operation can also only be performed against a single table using a single statement. In most situations, you will filter out the records you would like to update and update only them. This filtration is done using a **WHERE** clause in the **SELECT** statement. The **UPDATE** statement also contains a **SET** clause, which defines what needs to be modified within the table, along with the values.

In our demo, we'll update a table called **email**. You can set one column or more during an **UPDATE** operation. If you want to update multiple columns, separate the column names with a comma.

The database engine looks for the column that is specified in the statement and updates all the rows in it. If you would like to update only a certain row or a certain set of rows, you would use the **WHERE** clause. This way, you can identify only those intersections of rows and columns that you would like to update.

Suppose Ava-May changed her name to Ava-May Rodgers, and you had to update the table. You would use the following SQL statement:

```
UPDATE employees
SET
    Email = 'Ava-May.Rodgers@awesomenes.com'
WHERE empno = 3
```

From this simple example, we know that the **UPDATE** statement has the **UPDATE** keyword, followed by the table name, followed by the **SET** keyword, followed by the column names and values. If you would like to modify specific values, you would use a **WHERE** clause with the condition.

The Basic UPDATE Statement

Let's continue with a simple example. Suppose we have a table called **department** within a database. Imagine that you would like to set the modified date for each of the departments to the current date—in other words, we are going to change the modified date on all the rows. We do this using the following query:

```
update department set departmentEstDate=now();
```

If you query all the records within the table and see what **departmentEstDate** looks like for each record:

```
select * from department;
```

The **departmentEstDate** should be updated:

departmentNo	departmentName	departmentLoc	departmentEstDate
1	MyDepartment	NJ	2019-12-20 16:12:11
2	Administration	NJ	2019-12-20 16:12:11
3	Sales	LV	2019-12-20 16:12:11
NULL	NULL	NULL	NULL

Figure 2.10: Updating date in the department table

That was simple. Now, imagine you would like to set more columns. Imagine that you would like to update **departmentLoc** for all the departments in the table.

You would also like to set their **departmentEstDate** to the next day:

```
UPDATE Department
SET departmentLoc='GA',departmentEstDate  = Now()+INTERVAL 1 DAY;
```

> **Note**
>
> **+INTERVAL n DAY** is used to add days to the value returned by **Now()**.

When you run the query to see the contents of the table, you should see the following:

```
select * from department;
```

departmentNo	departmentName	departmentLoc	departmentEstDate
1	MyDepartment	GA	2019-12-21 16:19:32
2	Administration	GA	2019-12-21 16:19:32
3	Sales	GA	2019-12-21 16:19:32
NULL	NULL	NULL	NULL

Figure 2.11: Updated department table

ALIASING

In most situations in an enterprise environment, you are in a situation where you would use multiple tables, and multiple calls will be made to those tables. At that time, it would be much easier to use shorter aliases, especially when you would be referring to table names that contain other operators in them, such as **Company.department**. Would you like to write **SELECT * FROM Company.department**? Aliases help in these cases. For example:

```
UPDATE department D
    SET D.departmentLoc='NYC',
    D.departmentEstDate  = Now()+ INTERVAL 1 DAY
```

The output would be as follows:

departmentNo	departmentName	departmentLoc	departmentEstDate
1	MyDepartment	NYC	2019-12-21 16:30:37
2	Administration	NYC	2019-12-21 16:30:37
3	Sales	NYC	2019-12-21 16:30:37
NULL	NULL	NULL	NULL

Figure 2.12: Example of using shorter aliases

Conditional Update of Records

There are many instances where you need to accomplish something by simply modifying the existing data using conditional logic via the **WHERE** clause. For example, imagine that everyone in the sales team got a raise of 20%. Assume that you performed the calculation manually, that is, 1.2 times 8,000 is 9,600. You would like to set the salary of all the members of Sales to 9,600:

```
UPDATE E
SET Salary = 9600
WHERE Department = 'Sales'
FROM Employee E
```

Limiting the Records Using an UPDATE Statement

In this section, we will see how we can use the **LIMIT** clause in the **SELECT** statement to limit the number of rows to be updated using the **UPDATE** statement. As shown in the following code, the **LIMIT** clause accepts the offset and count arguments to limit the result set.

In the following example, we are limiting three records where we update the salary. These records are sorted in descending order and are getting the least commission:

```
UPDATE employees SET comm=1000
WHERE empno IN (
    SELECT empno FROM (
        SELECT empno FROM employees where comm<=500
        ORDER BY salary desc, comm ASC
        LIMIT 0, 3
    ) stg
);
```

> **Note**
>
> For now, don't worry too much about the syntax in the above code. A query nested inside another query as shown (where there's a **SELECT** statement inside another **SELECT** statement) is known as a subquery, and will be covered in detail in later chapters.

Exercise 2.05: UPDATE Using Computed Values

Consider the scenario where we are providing 10% off the net retail price of all the products in **packt_online_shop**:

1. Type the following query and execute the command:

```
UPDATE products
    SET
        NetRetailPrice = NetRetailPrice * 0.90;
```

2. Inspect the contents of the table products:

ProductID	ProductCategoryID	SupplierID	ProductName	NetRetailPrice	AvailableQuantity	WholesalePrice	UnitKGWeight	Notes
1	5	2	Calculatre	22.49	100	17.99	1.00000	calculation application
2	5	5	Penwrite	71.99	27	49.99	2.00000	word processing product
3	1	6	Vortex Generator	2249.99	1000	1999.99	0.01000	space engine component
4	1	6	The Gourmet Crockpot	22.49	72	19.99	1.63000	cookbook
5	1	6	Account Books	13.49	26	9.99	1.22000	government accounting book
6	3	6	habanero peppers	4.04	189	2.99	0.00900	hot peppers
7	2	1	10-mm socket wrench	3.14	39	1.89	0.01800	important tool
9	1	6	pure vanilla	9.35	1509	7.89	0.03200	high-quality vanilla
10	3	2	keyboard wrench	359999.96	6128	149999.99	521.38000	handle with care
11	2	1	power cell	43.10	2346	29.99	0.29800	ten amp-hours per cell
NULL	NULL	NULL	NULL	NULL	NULL	NULL	NULL	NULL

Figure 2.13: Updated products table using the computed values

The new price should now be reflected in the table.

The DROP Operation

We will now look at the **DROP** operation, to see how we can delete the schema altogether. The syntax is as follows:

```
DROP TABLE <table_name>;
```

To drop the **Customers** table in the **packt_online_database**, the query would be as follows:

```
DROP TABLE Customers;
```

If you now try to query the **Customers** table, it will no longer exist.

Activity 2.01: Inserting Additional values to the Products table

You notice that the following new products need to be added to the catalog:

- Pancake batter
- Breakfast cereal
- Siracha sauce

Write a query to add these items into the products table with Retail price as 5.99 and Wholesale price as 3.99. The product Category should be set by default as 1, and Product ID must be auto incremented.

> **Note**
>
> The solution for this activity can be found on page 246.

Summary

In this chapter, we looked at some advanced implementations of **INSERT** and how we can manipulate data using the **UPDATE**, **ALTER**, and **DROP** commands. It is very important to remember that the **ALTER** command is used to update the schemas, while the update command is used to make changes in the data contained in the schemas. However, changes in the data need to managed correctly, or they will result in inconsistent data. In the next chapter, we will look at normalizing data to ensure that data integrity is maintained.

3

Normalization

Overview

This chapter teaches you to maintain data integrity using the concepts of normalization and how you can connect tables together using keys and relationships. We will also look at some solid theory that back most database designs.

Introduction

In the previous two chapters, we looked at different aspects of a database. We provided an overview of the points to be considered while setting up a database. One of the key aspects we focused on was data integrity. We now know why data consistency is important. A step toward achieving better data integrity is database normalization. In this chapter, we will take a detailed look at achieving data consistency through normalization.

In the previous two chapters, we learned about the relational model of data. We saw that a database can contain any number of tables. These tables are connected to each other using a relation. This relation is usually established between the selected columns across tables using something called a **foreign key**.

Understanding that the relational model and data integrity are critical when working with data in business, we will take a look at the concept of normalization. Setting up the data model with constraints in mind and optimizing data management is more of an art than science. You can summarize the relational model as follows:

- A database server can contain many databases.
- Databases are collections of user-defined tables and system objects.
- Tables are collections of entities (rows) and attributes (columns).
- Tables can be used in conjunction with logical, mathematical, and summary operations.
- Tables can refer to other tables using a key.

In order to enforce data integrity, we use primary keys and foreign keys. These are called **referential constraints**. Referential constraints are important internal database objects that help maintain data integrity.

Primary Key Constraints

A primary key constraint on a column instructs the database engine to keep the entries in a column unique. For example, if we were to create a table with information about all the human beings on Earth, we could use the tongue print of human beings as unique identification. If tongue prints were in a column, it would be the primary key.

It is possible to have a duplicate tongue print; however, it is rare. In such a case, you could create a primary key across multiple columns. Therefore, you could combine the tongue print, fingerprint, and the retinal signature to make a primary key. In such a case, the *combination* of these values in these columns should be unique across the table. In other words, there may be a duplicate tongue print, a duplicate fingerprint, and a duplicate retinal signature in the table–the database engine will allow that. However, there cannot be a duplicate combination of all three. Alternatively, there can be no two human beings whose tongue prints, fingerprints, and retinal signatures exactly match. This is called a **composite primary key**.

Foreign Key Constraints

Let's look at this in the context of a primary key. When this primary key is referenced by a column in another table, this primary key becomes the foreign key of the other table. For example, consider the previously created database **PACKT_ONLINE_SHOP**:

```
DROP DATABASE IF EXISTS PACKT_ONLINE_SHOP;
CREATE DATABASE IF NOT EXISTS PACKT_ONLINE_SHOP;
USE PACKT_ONLINE_SHOP;
CREATE TABLE Customers
(
    CustomerID INT NOT NULL AUTO_INCREMENT,
    FirstName CHAR(50) NOT NULL,
    LastName CHAR(50) NOT NULL,
    Address CHAR(250) NULL,
    Email CHAR(200) NULL,
    Phone CHAR(50) NULL,
    Notes VARCHAR(750) NULL,
    BalanceNotes VARCHAR(750) NULL,
    PRIMARY KEY (CustomerID)
);
CREATE TABLE Orders
(
    OrderID INT NOT NULL AUTO_INCREMENT,
    CustomerID INT NOT NULL,
    OrderNumber CHAR(50) NOT NULL,
    OrderDate DATETIME NOT NULL,
    ShipmentDate DATETIME NULL,
    OrderStatus CHAR(10) NULL,
    Notes VARCHAR(750) NULL,
PRIMARY KEY (OrderID),
FOREIGN KEY FK_Customer_CustomerID(CustomerID) REFERENCES Customers(CustomerID)
);
```

Each customer can place one or more orders. Each order can be for one or more products. Each order belongs to *only* one customer. When the database is designed, the relationship is established between the customers and the orders with a one-to-many relationship. There is also a relationship between orders and products, with a cardinality ratio of many-to-many (because one order can contain many products, and many copies of one product can be sold through many orders). The **Orders** table contains the **CustomerID** column, which refers to the **CustomerID** of the **Customers** table. The **CustomerID** field (or column) in the **Customers** table is the primary key, but it is the foreign key for the **Orders** table. The **FOREIGN KEY** clause specifies the foreign key using the **REFERENCES** clause. In this context, **Customers** could be considered the parent table and **Orders** could be considered the child.

> **Note**
>
> MySQL automatically creates an index corresponding to the foreign key called **foreign_key_name**. SQL Server does not create a corresponding index when a foreign key constraint is created. SQL Server automatically creates an index when a primary key constraint is created.

Here are a few points that you need to remember:

- A foreign key always refers to a primary key.

- A table can have multiple foreign keys.

- The **INSERT** command only operates on those rows of the *child* table for which corresponding rows exist in the *parent* table.

- The **DELETE** command only operates on the rows from the *parent* table for which there are no corresponding records in the *child* table.

Consider a scenario where someone is purchasing a book or a course from the Packt store.

Let's look at the **OrderItems** table:

```
CREATE TABLE OrderItems
(
    OrderItemID INT NOT NULL AUTO_INCREMENT,
    OrderID INT NOT NULL,
    ProductID INT NOT NULL,
    Quantity INT NOT NULL,
    UnitPrice DECIMAL(10, 2) NOT NULL,
    Discount DECIMAL(10, 2) NULL,
    Notes VARCHAR(750) NULL,
    PRIMARY KEY (OrderItemID)
);
```

> **Note**
>
> The preceding code makes use of the **DECIMAL** data type. The syntax for this is **DECIMAL(p, s)**, where **p** is the precision (the total number of digits that can be stored in the number, before and after the decimal point) and **s** is the scale (the number of digits that can come after the decimal point). In the example, **DECIMAL(10, 2)** can store a total of 10 digits, including 2 after the decimal point.

There is **OrderItemID**, which represents the ID of the item within an order, which is automatically incremented. Then, we have **OrderID**, **ProductID**, **Quantity**, **UnitPrice**, **Discount**, and **Notes**.

OrderItemID is independent of this table in this case and could very much be the primary key since every item in an order is unique. However, there is a **ProductID**, which should ideally refer to the store inventory. This inventory could be called **Products** and would be a different table. Quantity is independent as well, but this is so arbitrary that no constraint could be placed on it other than **NOT NULL**. The **UnitPrice** field should also refer to the inventory because it changes with the product, and not with orders. **Discount** should also refer to another table altogether (you will see why when we discuss normalization).

Considering this, **ProductID** should be the primary key of the **Products** table as it is unique across the store. Given that, the **ProductID** within the **OrderItems** table should be the foreign key, referring to the **ProductID** within **Products**. Let's see how we can set this up in the table:

```
ALTER TABLE OrderItems
ADD FOREIGN KEY (ProductID) REFERENCES Products(ProductID);
```

To drop a foreign key, you can use the **ALTER TABLE** statement:

```
ALTER TABLE <table_name>
DROP FOREIGN KEY <constraint_name>;
```

In the context of our example, the syntax will be as follows:

```
ALTER TABLE OrderItems
DROP FOREIGN KEY ProductID
```

> **Note**
>
> You can have zero or more foreign keys in a table. Each foreign key in a table can refer to one or more columns in any arbitrary table in the database, depending on the requirements.

Preserving Data Integrity

Preserving data integrity is simpler than it sounds. If you set the data model correctly, it's not much of a challenge to preserve data integrity. Nothing in the real world is foolproof; however, a tight data integrity model will ensure minimal exceptions. Here is a little checklist:

- **Validate input**: Set up input validation in the fields that are critical to decisions and prone to errors. You can do this at the application level, of course, but it is good practice to set this up at the database level as well. Validate the input when it arrives.

- **Validate data**: Ensure that you check the data when performing any form of operations. Your data processes should not be corrupted themselves. Check that your processes are working as intended.

- **Remove duplicate data**: Sensitive data from a secure database can easily find a home in a document, an email, a spreadsheet, or in shared folders that more individuals than necessary have access to. It is important to check for these stray or duplicate entities and clean them up.

Types of Data Integrity

Let's look at the different types of data integrity:

- **Entity integrity**: This defines each row as unique within the table. No two rows can have the same name. To achieve this, a primary key can be defined. This field contains a unique identifier—no two rows can contain the same unique identifier.

- **Referential integrity**: Referential integrity is about relationships. When two or more tables have a relationship, we must ensure that the value of the foreign key always matches the value of the primary key, otherwise the record is orphaned.

  Referential integrity prevents adding records to a related table if there is no associated record in the primary or parent table, changing values in a primary table that can result in orphaned records in a related table, and deleting records from a primary table if there are matching related records.

- **Domain integrity**: This is primarily concerned with the validity of entries for a given column. It is important to select the appropriate data type for a column and set the appropriate constraints to define the data format or restrict the range of possible values.

- **User-defined integrity**: There are cases when you can apply business rules to the database. These rules may not have been covered by the three integrity types. User-defined integrity helps you to enforce your own rules to ensure data integrity.

Take a break now and let all the information you've looked at sink in a little. Next, we will dive into the concept of normalization and look at its different forms. We will see how normalization helps us achieve data integrity. We will work on a real-world example that we urge you to actively think about. You are here to learn about database management, and you came here on your own. It is time to show that passion in full.

The Concept of Normalization

Suppose we have a piece of software in our enterprise called *Enterprise Server Manager* that manages all the computers. The **Enterprise Server Manager** (**ESM**) has information about what computers we have, the operating system they run on, the version of the operating system, and so on.

Now, each server works for one or more teams. The respective teams have all the authority on these servers, along with being responsible for them. Imagine that you want the heads of the teams tagged as the owners of the servers. The server entries should contain the employee IDs, the names, the designations, and the department names of these owners. Here is an example:

ServerName	Operating System	EmployeeId	Name	Designation	Department
DBSVR001	W2012R2	67576	Jane Doe	Team Lead	Data Management
CXSVR001	W2012R2	78327	Jon Doe	Team Lead	EUC
MBSVR001	W2012R2	78327	Jon Doe	Team Lead	EUC

Figure 3.1: ESM Agent details

The preceding table has all the information we need and the data looks consistent for now, right? Jon Doe's information is being repeated, though. Is that an issue?

Imagine that Jon Doe leaves the organization and Jim Doe replaces him. Now, imagine that this table has 4,000 entries and Jon Doe owns 300 servers. To change the owner of the servers, you may think of replacing the names in the table using the following query:

```
UPDATE ServerInfo SET Name='Jim Doe' WHERE employeeName='Jon Doe';
```

Now, Jim Doe joins the organization, and four servers get assigned to him. He is part of the Network team. After you make the changes to the table, you realize that you did not update the employee ID, designation, or the department for the entries that had Jon Doe, and without looking at the data, someone unknowingly runs the following query:

```
UPDATE ServerInfo SET EmployeeId='79247' WHERE employeeName='Jim Doe';
```

Do you think there is a problem?

No: The designation for Jim Doe will be the same as Jon Doe, and so will the department. However, this is not true. There exists a problem.

Yes: There are two individuals with the name **Jim Doe**, and now, they both have the same employee ID, which is wrong. This second individual tries to fix this issue as follows:

```
UPDATE ServerInfo SET EmployeeId='79254', Designation='Network Specialist' WHERE
employeeName='Jim Doe' and Department='Network';
```

Did you observe how error-prone even this simple table is? What happens when you have 80 columns in a table and you try to update data this way? In the real world, the ESM Agent table has tens of columns, and so does the user information table in the Active Directory (an identity and access management system in an enterprise).

How about if we have one entry per person and have all the servers they own listed in one single column?

EmployeeId	EmployeeName	Designation	Department	ServerName	OperatingSystem
67576	Jane Doe	Team Lead	Data Management	DBSVR001	W2012R2
78327	Jon Doe	Team Lead	EUC	CXSVR001, MBSVR001	W2012R2

Figure 3.2: ESM Agent details

Do you think we still have a problem?

Yes: What happens when the number of servers Jon Doe owns is 300? It is not a problem yet. Consider that all the MBSVR servers (and there are 28 of them) are replaced by new MBSVR servers with new names. What would your update operation be like?

Let's summarize the disadvantages of above-mentioned scenario:

- Maintenance of the data becomes tedious, like all the activities we did when Jim Doe replaced Jon Doe.

- When we changed the name and nothing else in the table, and another Jim Doe joined the Network team, we observed an inconsistency in the data.

- When we had to go through three steps to fix data in a table with a mere six columns and four rows, imagine the work required when dealing with thousands of records of data. We had to update four columns when one individual replaced another.

- Most of all, four of the columns in two rows had the same data. What happens when the number of rounds is in the thousands and the size of the table grows more than necessary?

- One important aspect of this is that if you make the server information and owner information dependent on a single table, you will find empty values in the cases of users who do not own any servers.

- If you delete all the servers owned by an individual, you will also end up deleting that individual's information unintentionally.

Can you handle this situation better? Let's create two tables. The first one is the server information table:

ServerName	Operating System	OwnerId
DBSVR001	W2012R2	67576
CXSVR001	W2012R2	79247
MBSVR001	W2012R2	79247
EDSVR001	W2012R2	79254

Figure 3.3: Server information table

The second is the employee information table:

EmployeeId	Name	Designation	Department
67576	Jane Doe	Team Lead	Data Management
79247	Jim Doe	Team Lead	EUC
79254	Jim Doe	Network Specialist	Network

Figure 3.4: Employee information table

Let's assume that our IAM application manages the second table. If Hans Doe replaces Jim Doe, the Team Lead, at a later point, the second table will get all the necessary information about Hans Doe when the Human Resources team processes Hans' hiring. All you would have to do then is replace the **OwnerId** information in the server information table with a single query:

```
UPDATE ServerInfo SET OwnerId='79482' WHERE OwnerId='79247';
```

What if you need to get a table that's identical to the first table, as we saw at the beginning of this chapter? We can use the following query:

```
SELECT s.Servername, s.OperatingSystem, u.EmployeeId, u.Name, u.Designation, u.Department
FROM ServerInfo s
    JOIN EmployeeInfo u ON s.OwnerId = u.EmployeeId;
```

> **Note**
>
> You should recall the alias syntax from the previous chapter. **ServerInfo s** means that we can use the letter **s** to refer to **ServerInfo** (to save us having to type out the full name each time). **s.Servername** means that we're referring to the **Servername** column of the **ServerInfo** table.

We have circled back to the point where we spoke about relational databases and its importance in the world of data. If you look at the preceding two tables, you will see that they are two tables of a relational database, where there is a relationship established between the two tables based on the foreign key, which is `OwnerId` in the `ServerInfo` table. This refers to the `EmployeeId` in the `EmployeeInfo` table.

First Normal Form (1NF)

What we saw in the solution for this situation is called the **first normal form**. Why? Because it adheres to the following four rules:

- Every column must be single-valued
- The data type of all the data in any column should be uniform
- Every column should have a unique name
- The order in which the records are ordered does not matter

As you can see, the column names in our tables are unique. Every column has only one data type (in our case, all the values are strings—even the employee IDs are strings). There are no multi-valued cells in the tables. The fourth one gives us the freedom to put the data in any order.

Remember the situation where Jon Doe owned 300 servers, and the server names were all jammed in a single cell? This is not allowed in the first normal form because it makes update operations difficult. The normal form helps prevent such situations.

> **Note**
>
> The first normal form is considered the least requirement for any data in a relational database. If your data does not even adhere to the first normal form, you have a bad data model.

Second Normal Form (2NF)

Before you understand the second normal form, let's explore what dependency is with the help of the following scenario.

In an enterprise, it is important that the security updates are installed on every server. This process is known as *patching* the servers. Typically, updates get installed every month, and at the end of the month, many organizations check the percentage of servers that had been patched during the month. This number is calculated based on how many servers have how many patches in the *installed* and *not required* state. This calculation is done per server. Apart from the operating system updates, we would also like to install application updates. Therefore, based on what team we are talking about and what applications they own, the percentage of compliance can change.

For example, imagine that Microsoft released four updates to the Windows operating system. Citrix Systems, Inc, a multinational software company, released one update to their XenApp. We have the AwesomeFirewall application, provided by Awesomeness, Inc. They released two updates for AwesomeFirewall. Three Windows updates were installed on a server, CXSVR001, and one failed. The XenApp update was installed on the server, but only one of the two updates to AwesomeFirewall was installed on the server and the other failed.

Let's say that instead of individuals owning the servers, the teams own the servers. Let's assume that our organization enforces a compliance percentage on the team leads, saying that every team should have a patch compliance of at least, say, 92%, and that the score directly reflects on the person who leads the team. So, let's look at the two tables that we already have, which contain the server and the owner data.

Here is the list of servers:

ServerName	Operating System	OwnerId
DBSVR001	W2012R2	67576
CXSVR001	W2012R2	79247
MBSVR001	W2012R2	79247
EDSVR001	W2012R2	79254

Figure 3.5: Server list

And here are the details about the owners:

EmployeeId	Name	Designation	Department
67576	Jane Doe	Team Lead	Data Management
79247	Jim Doe	Team Lead	EUC
79254	Jim Doe	Network Specialist	Network

Figure 3.6: Owner details

We need to change the way we manage ownership. We need three tables:

- A table containing the server information
- A table containing the department information
- A table containing the employee information

Therefore, the revised setup would be as follows:

- The server information table:

ServerName	Operating System	DepartmentId
DBSVR001	W2012R2	DM
CXSVR001	W2012R2	EUC
MBSVR001	W2012R2	EUC
EDSVR001	W2012R2	NW

Figure 3.7: Server information

- The employee information table:

EmployeeId	Name	Designation	DepartmentId
67576	Jane Doe	Team Lead	DM
79247	Jim Doe	Team Lead	EUC
79254	Jim Doe	Network Specialist	NW

Figure 3.8: Employee information

- And finally, the department information table:

DepartmentId	DepartmentName
NW	Network
EUC	End User Computing
DM	Data Management

Figure 3.9: Department information

It is now time to establish relationships (given that we have made some drastic changes to the process that are used in tagging servers). Here are the four kinds of relationships we will have:

- A server may belong to one or more teams (because there can be different aspects of an application, and multiple teams may have ownership over the different aspects).

- A team can own multiple servers. Obviously, not all the teams can function with just one server.

- A team can have only one lead.

- A person can lead only one department (this has been enforced by the management).

As a corollary to this, it also means that a team lead can own multiple servers, and each server can be owned by multiple team leads.

To summarize, the cardinality ratios would be as follows:

Server - Department	Many-to-many
Server - Lead	Many-to-many
Department - Head	One-to-one

Figure 3.10: Cardinality ratios

Imagine that we created a table for the compliance percentage like so while keeping the patch numbers from the introduction to the second normal form in mind (operating system patches along with the application patches):

ServerName	DepartmentId	TotalReleased	Installed	Compliance
DBSVR001	DM	5	4	80.00%
CXSVR001	EUC	5	4	80.00%
MBSVR001	EUC	7	4	57.14%
EDSVR001	NW	6	6	100.00%
CXSVR001	NW	6	4	66.67%

Figure 3.11: Compliance percentage

How do you calculate the compliance percentage of each server per team? Remember that you need to be able to identify each record (or row) uniquely.

One way of doing this would be to have a `ComplianceId` as the primary key, like so:

ComplianceId	ServerName	Department	Compliance
CMP001	DBSVR001	DM	80.00%
CMP002	CXSVR001	EUC	80.00%
CMP003	MBSVR001	EUC	57.14%
CMP004	EDSVR001	NW	100.00%
CMP005	CXSVR001	NW	66.67%

Figure 3.12: Compliance percentage of each server

Typically, this is the first normal form and complies with all five rules that we listed. However, if you take a look at it, the server name and the department name together form a simpler primary key.

The simpler way to handle this would be to use the server name *and* the department as the primary key for compliance percentage—a composite primary key.

CXSVR001, in the context of the network team, has a compliance percentage of 66.67%.

Imagine, now, that you also add the team lead information to the table:

67576
79247
79247
79254
79254

Figure 3.13: Team lead information added

As you may have noticed, **LeadId** is dependent only on the department, and not the server name—it is not dependent on the entire primary key. This is *partial dependency* in database terms.

You must remove this partial dependency if you want your data to be in the second normal form, as per the requirements for the second normal form:

- The data should be in the first normal form.

- There should be no partial dependencies in the data.

To convert this data into the second normal form, you must get rid of the partial dependency brought in by **LeadId**. However, what if the patch compliance score is a key performance indicator for each of the leads? What if their yearly bonus depends on this aspect?

In other words, you need each of the servers to be tagged to the lead. The situation is that the servers belong to departments, not individuals. How do you achieve the second normal form while keeping this in mind?

One of the solutions is to alter the **Department** table to include the lead information:

DepartmentId	DepartmentName	LeadId
DM	Data Management	6757600.00%
EUC	End User Computing	7924700.00%
NW	Network	7925400.00%

Figure 3.14: Altered Department table to include lead information

Now, you can remove the **LeadId** column from the compliance table, and despite not having the **LeadId** in the table, you can calculate the compliance percentage of each of the leads.

Third Normal Form (3NF)

Consider a situation where a conflict arises between you and your colleague during the calculation of the compliance percentage. Your colleague states, "*Your way of calculating the compliance percentage is flawed! Look, one of Jon's servers gets four updates out of five and the other gets four out of six. You calculate individual servers, say 80% on one and 66.67% on the other. Then, you take an average and say the compliance percentage is 73.33%. Jon had to ensure the installation of 11 patches in all, out of which he installed only eight. His compliance percentage should actually be 72.73%, and not 73.33.*"

This situation has introduced a different level of complexity in our setup. Now, you need to look for a way to combine several aspects and introduce something that will allow for the calculation of the compliance percentage based on the total patches that are needed for a server *per application combination*, and the actual score for that combination.

Imagine you get lucky and find out that ESM has a way to combine applications into groups. Therefore, this can provide you with information regarding the total patches per group and the installed patches per group.

Here is the new table (we have included `ComplianceId` so that this table can independently have a primary key):

ComplianceId	ServerName	Department	Installed	ApplicationGroup	TotalUpdates
CMP001	DBSVR001	DM	4	OSDB	5
CMP002	CXSVR001	EUC	4	OSCX	5
CMP003	MBSVR001	EUC	4	OSEX	7
CMP004	EDSVR001	NW	6	OSFW	6
CMP005	CXSVR001	NW	4	OSFW	6

Figure 3.15: ComplianceId added to the table

For data to be in the third normal form:

- The data should already be in the second normal form.

- There should be no transitive dependency.

> **Note**
>
> Transitive dependency is a form of indirect linking between different attributes. For example, if A depends on B and B depends on C, then there is transitive dependency between A and C.

Now, to convert the data you already have into the third normal form, split all the data into the following four tables:

- A table that contains server information, called **Agent**:

EmployeeId	Name	Department	ApplicationGroup
67576	Jane Doe	Data Management	OSDB
79247	Jim Doe	End User Computing	OSCX
79254	John Doe	End User Computing	OSEX

Figure 3.16: Server information

- A table that contains employee information, called **Employee**:

EmployeeId	Name	Designation	DepartmentID	AppID
67576	Jane Doe	Team Lead	DM	1
79247	Jim Doe	Team Lead	EUC	2
79254	John Doe	Network Specialist	NW	3

Figure 3.17: Employee information

- A table that contains the department information, called **Department**:

DepartmentId	DepartmentName	DepartmentLoc
DM	Data Management	NewYork
EUC	End User Computing	Wisconsin
NW	Network	Texas

Figure 3.18: Department information

- A table that contains the patch information, called **PatchInfo**:

ApplicationId	AppName	ApplicationType
1	OSDB	OS
2	OSCX	Database
3	OSXE	Middleware
4	OSFW	VLDB

Figure 3.19: Patch information

You can further normalize data using the **Boyce-Codd normal form**, the **fourth normal form**, the **fifth normal form**, and the **sixth normal form** as well, but that would make your learning more complex. For now, take on board these three normalizations. Then, as you get more and more comfortable with these three forms, you can proceed to learn about the more advanced normal forms.

Denormalization

Denormalization of data is another important concept, especially when it comes to querying efficiency.

In an enterprise, everything is about balance. Most organizations that deal with data do not completely adhere to the complex form of normalization. The reason for this is simple: normalization may kill efficiency when you need to query a large amount of data. Therefore, while we gain in terms of data integrity when normalizing data, we pay a lot in terms of processing power if we ever have to query data.

For instance, consider the table in *Figure* 3.17. If a user has two email addresses, would you have a single column and add both email addresses to it? You could, but that would be non-compliant with the first normal form of data. How do you work around this issue? Create a new table with an employee ID and email address? But then, the employee would have two email addresses and cannot be uniquely identified. Therefore, you would need to add a primary key to that table and with this, the situation becomes much more complex than required.

In such a case, you could go for some minor denormalization and add a couple of columns to the existing `Employee` table, for instance, `PrimaryEmail` and `SecondaryEmail`. This way, your queries would be simplified.

Denormalization finds most of its use in data warehousing scenarios—situations where you query for a lot of data in a single shot. For instance, if you had to query 200,000 entries, referring to eight tables would consume much more processing power than your systems would support.

Therefore, data management is more of an art than a science.

Exercise 3.01: Building a Relationship between Two Tables

In your organization, you have been asked to present the employee and department data in two tables and build the relationship between the department and employee table.

The department table should contain the following data:

Column name	Datatype	Size	Key
dno	INT	4	PRIMARY KEY
dname	VARCHAR	30	UNIQUE NOT NULL
dlocation	VARCHAR	30	UNIQUE NOT NULL

Figure 3.20: Department table data

The employee table should contain the following data:

ColumnName	DataType	Size	Key	
eNo	CHAR	4	PRIMARY KEY	
eName	VARCHAR	30	NOT NULL	
eJob	VARCHAR	30	NOT NULL	
eManager	CHAR	4		
eJoinDate	TIMESTAMP		NOT NULL	
eGeneder	CHAR	1	M or F	
eSalary	DECIMAL	8,2	DEFAULT	0
eCommission	DECIMAL	8,2	DEFAULT	0
eDeptNo	INT		FOREIGN KEY	REFERENCES DEPARTMENT TABLE, dNo Column

Figure 3.21: Employee table data

Perform the following steps to achieve this:

1. Create a demo database called **employeedemo**.

    ```
    DROP DATABASE IF EXISTS employeedemo;
    CREATE DATABASE employeedemo;
    ```

2. Create a **department** table with the required data. Ensure there is referential integrity between the **department** and **employee** tables on the **dno** field:

    ```
    USE employeedemo;

    CREATE TABLE department
        (
            dno       INT PRIMARY KEY,
            dname     VARCHAR(30) UNIQUE NOT NULL,
            dlocation VARCHAR(30) UNIQUE NOT NULL
        )
    ```

3. Create an **EMPLOYEE** table with the required data, enforcing a check constraint on the **gender** field and default values on the **salary** and **commission** fields:

```
CREATE TABLE employee
(
    eno             CHAR(4) PRIMARY KEY,
    ename           VARCHAR(30) NOT NULL,
    job             VARCHAR(30) NOT NULL,
    manager CHAR(4),
    jdate           TIMESTAMP NOT NULL,
    gender CHAR(1) CONSTRAINT gender_chk
CHECK ( gender IN('M', 'F')),
    salary DECIMAL(8, 2) DEFAULT 0,
    comission       DECIMAL(8, 2) DEFAULT 0,
    deptno INT NOT NULL,
        FOREIGN KEY (deptno) REFERENCES department(dno)
)
```

As we can see, the foreign key constraints have been created between the department and employee tables. By using the **IN** keyword, we have added a check constraint on the **gender** field:

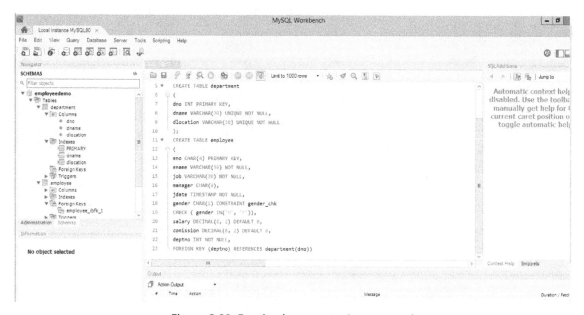

Figure 3.22: Foreign key constraints created

Activity 3.01: Building a Relationship between the Orders and the OrderItems table

To build the **packt_online_shop**, we need table to capture the data of all the order placed by customers. To do this, we need to create two tables: **Orders** and **OrderItems**. The **Orders** table must contain the details on who places the order, when the order is to be dispatched, and the current status of the order, while the **OrderItems** table should contain product specifics of the placed order, such as price, quantity, and so on. Build a normalized schema for the following scenario.

OrderItem must contain the following details:

- **OrderItemID**
- **OrderID**
- **ProductID**
- **Quantity**
- **UnitPrice**
- **Discount**
- **Notes**

Order must contain the following details:

- **OrderID**
- **CustomerID**
- **OrderNumber**
- **OrderDate**
- **ShipmentDate**
- **OrderStatus**
- **Notes**

> **Note**
>
> The solution for this activity can be found on page 247.

Summary

In this chapter, we referred to the different forms of constraints that we recapitulated from the previous chapter, but in a little more depth. We learned how these constraints help in maintaining data integrity. Later, we learned about the different forms of data integrity.

We then moved on and looked at the concept of data normalization and looked at the first three normal forms, namely the first, second, and third, using data from a fictitious enterprise setup we created. As an exercise, create your own database using the steps from the previous chapters and create the tables that were mentioned in the first section of this chapter.

Run the queries that you saw here and find out about the different ways in which you can normalize this data. If you are inclined to, go ahead and learn about the more advanced forms of normalization to build on the knowledge you've gained from this chapter. In the next chapter, we will look at querying normalized data.

The SELECT Statement

Overview

This chapter illustrates how to query data from a database, and how we can order them. By the end of this chapter, you will be able to select a specific number of columns, order and sort results, use naming aliases with the **AS** clause, filter your search results using the **LIMIT** and **DISTINCT** keywords, and combine and use **SELECT** with mathematical operations.

Introduction

So far, whenever we have wanted to see the results, we have used the `Select *` syntax either by entering that query directly, or by generating it using the appropriate option in the application's menu. This displayed the entire table. However, when we want to retrieve data from the database, we are often not interested in the entire dataset; we are only looking for specific details. For example, the Packt database contains details of all the books published by Packt. It might include columns such as **Book Name**, **ISBN**, **Author Name**, **Author ID**, **Author Email**, **Page Count**, and **Price**. But if we wanted to send out a survey to all the authors who have written for Packt, all we would require is the author's name and their email address:

Book Name	ISBN	Author Name	Author ID	Author Email	Page Count	Price
[...]	[...]	[...]	[...]	[...]		
[...]	[...]	[...]	[...]	[...]		
[...]	[...]	[...]	[...]	[...]		

Figure 4.1: A sample table containing all the details of a book

This is all we require:

Author Name	Author Email
[...]	[...]
[...]	[...]
[...]	[...]

Figure 4.2: The required details

Queries help us do just this. Using the **SELECT** statement, we can pick out specific columns from a table.

The syntax of a typical SQL query is as follows:

```
SELECT [COLUMNS LIST]
FROM [TABLE NAME]
WHERE [CONDITION]
ORDER BY [COLUMN NAME] [ASC|DESC]
```

Where:

- **[COLUMNS_LIST]** is replaced by the column names that you want to retrieve, separated by commas.

- **[TABLE_NAME]** is replaced by the table name in your database.

- **[CONDITION]** is the condition to narrow down your result.

- **[COLUMN NAME]** is the column that the result set will be ordered or sorted on.

- **[ASC | DESC]** is the order option, ascending or descending.

In this chapter, we will look in more detail at the different parts of a **SELECT** statement. We will cover the basics of writing a **SELECT** statement, customizing the query to achieve the desired results, and sorting the data based on various requirements. The **WHERE** statement, shown in the preceding snippet, will be covered in detail in the next chapter.

What Does the SELECT Statement Do?

The **SELECT** statement is used to select one or more columns from a table, thus defining what the columns of the output should look like. Therefore, whenever you are querying tables for data, it is mandatory to include the **SELECT** statement and the **FROM** statement in your syntax.

If the output requires all of the columns from the original table, instead of mentioning the entire list of columns, we can use the asterisk sign (*). This acts as a wildcard and selects all the columns in the **[TABLE NAME]** table specified. We will see some examples of what this means in practice.

> **Important**
>
> Before you work on any of exercises, please run the scripts present here: https://packt.live/2ZzYCss. This will set up the database for the chapters to come.

Retrieving All Columns of a Table

Consider the following scenario: A store manager wants to retrieve information about all the categories of items available in **PACKT_ONLINE_SHOP** in order to see where a new product fits in best. To retrieve a list of all the product categories, along with their details, run the following query:

```
use PACKT_ONLINE_SHOP;
SELECT * FROM ProductCategories;
```

After executing the preceding query, you'll see the following output:

ProductCategoryID	ProductCategoryName	Notes
1	condiments	melange, spices of all types and flavorings
2	tools	automotive, aviation, medical, and software repair / maintenance devi...
3	food	food products for humans and non-humans
4	airships	lighter-than-air aircraft
5	software	program products for execution on / by computers
6	books	bound, multi-page printed material
7	horse-drawn carriages	wheeled vehicles pulled by plant-eating non-human animals
NULL	NULL	NULL

Figure 4.3: The ProductCategories table

As shown in the preceding screenshot, the query has selected and retrieved all the records from all the columns of the **ProductCategories** table, which was taken from **PACKT_ONLINE_SHOP**.

> **Note**
>
> There are some cases where you can use the **SELECT** statement without needing to use the **FROM** part. For instance, to call a function, you only need to use the **SELECT** statement:
>
> **SELECT GETDATE();**
>
> We will discuss functions in further detail in the upcoming chapters of this book.

In the rest of this chapter, we will go through all the sections of the **SELECT** statement and demonstrate each of them, and we will combine all of them at the end of the chapter.

Selecting Limited Columns

When you only want to retrieve a couple of columns from the table, all you have to mention is the list of column names separated by commas in the **SELECT** clause.

Exercise 4.01: Selecting Columns from a Table

The store manager wants to check the **ProductCategoryId** field of all the categories in **PACKT_ONLINE_SHOP**. They need you to retrieve the relevant columns, **ProductCategoryId** and **ProductCategoryName**. To retrieve this data from the table, we need to perform the following steps:

1. Open a new query window.

2. Switch to the **PACKT_ONLINE_SHOP** database:

    ```
    use PACKT_ONLINE_SHOP;
    ```

3. Enter the following query:

    ```
    SELECT ProductCategoryID, ProductCategoryName
    FROM ProductCategories;
    ```

4. Execute the query. This query will result in the following output:

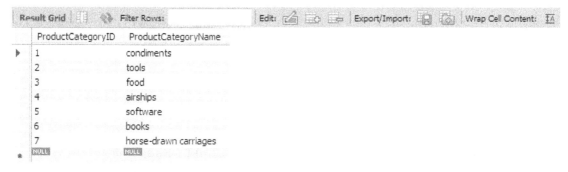

Figure 4.4: Selected columns from the ProductCategories table

Note that the columns are displayed in the exact order they were mentioned in the **SELECT** statement. So, if we want to show the name of the category first followed by ID, we use the following statement:

```
SELECT ProductCategoryName, ProductCategoryID
FROM ProductCategories;
```

This query will result in the following output:

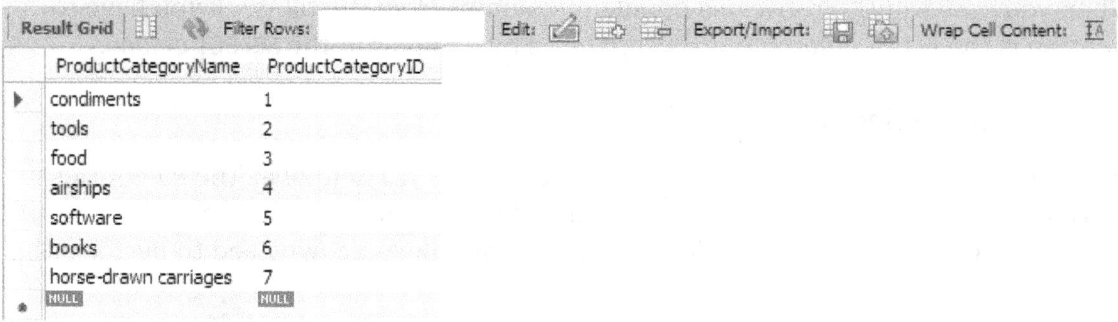

Figure 4.5: Columns in a different order from the ProductCategories table

Thus, we can filter the columns that are displayed in the output just by including them in the **SELECT** statement.

Using Naming Aliases

As you can see from the result sets we have so far, column names (column headers) match the column name/field name in the database. This is how it works by default. However, this is not always practical or user-friendly. When you extract data for the purposes of a report, you'll have various people looking at it, and so you might want to make the column heading clearer and more relatable. To provide the result set with a column header of your choice, use the **AS** keyword after the column name. The syntax for aliasing the column is as follows:

```
SELECT [Original name] AS [New name]
```

Exercise 4.02: Aliasing the Column Headers

While publishing a report, we want to rename the column headings of the previous query as **CATEGORY** and **ID**, respectively. To do this, perform the following steps:

1. Enter the following query:

```
SELECT ProductCategoryName AS CATEGORY, ProductCategoryID AS ID
FROM ProductCategories;
```

2. Execute the query. It will result in the following output:

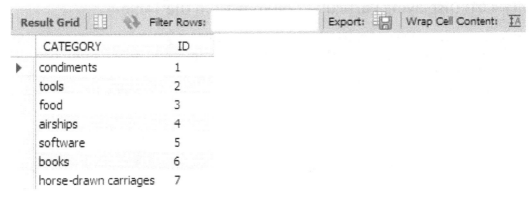

Figure 4.6: Renamed CATEGORY and ID columns

3. In cases where you want to use multiple words with spaces between them, use the full name between single quotes ' ', as follows:

```
SELECT ProductCategoryName AS 'PRODUCT CATEGORY', ProductCategoryID AS ID
FROM ProductCategories;
```

The output of the query would be as follows:

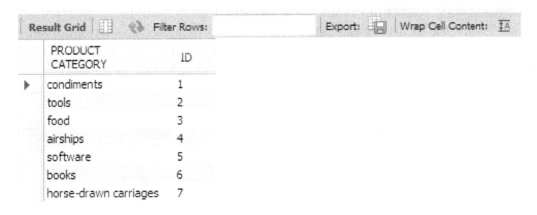

Figure 4.7: Data appended in the PRODUCT CATEGORY column

Activity 4.01: Displaying Particular Columns from the Table

To conduct a telephone survey for the customers of **PACKT_ONLINE_SHOP**, we require a report containing each customer's first name, last name, and contact number. The report should use the following column headers: **First Name**, **Last Name**, and **Phone Number**. Derive the required details from the **Customers** table of the **PACKT_ONLINE_SHOP** database.

1. Switch to the required database.

2. Use the **Select** statement to retrieve the required columns from the **Customers** table.

> **Note**
>
> The solution for this activity can be found on page 249.

Ordering Results

Often, we will want to sort our results in a way that makes them more user-friendly and readable. The **ORDER BY** part of the **SELECT** statement is designed to sort result set rows in either ascending or descending numerical order if the data is numeric, and ascending or descending alphabetical order if the data contains characters. By default, whenever the **ORDER BY** clause is used, rows will be sorted in ascending order unless specified otherwise.

The **ORDER BY** clause is placed at the end of the **SELECT** statement, and its general form is as follows:

```
ORDER BY [COLUMN1 NAME] [ASC|DESC], [COLUMN2 NAME] [ASC|DESC]
```

We can specify the column name or its alias along with the ordering type, which will either be ascending, with the **ASC** keyword, or descending, with the **DESC** keyword.

There are two main ways to order any result set. Let's have a look at them in detail.

Ordering Rows According to a Particular Column

Here, the rows will be sorted based on the selected column in ascending order. Columns that contain character values will be arranged alphabetically. Let's try to apply this to the **ProductCategories** table and sort the results by **CATEGORY NAME**, as follows:

```
SELECT ProductCategoryName AS 'CATEGORY NAME', ProductCategoryID AS ID
FROM ProductCategories
ORDER BY ProductCategoryName ASC;
```

The result is as follows:

CATEGORY NAME	ID
airships	4
books	6
condiments	1
food	3
horse-drawn carriages	7
software	5
tools	2

Figure 4.8: Product category names in alphabetical order

As you can see in *Figure 4.8*, the rows are now sorted alphabetically by **CATEGORY NAME** in ascending order. We can do the same exercise and sort them in descending order by using the **DESC** keyword as follows:

```
SELECT ProductCategoryName AS 'CATEGORY_NAME', ProductCategoryID AS ID
FROM ProductCategories
ORDER BY CATEGORY_NAME DESC;
```

The result is as follows:

CATEGORY NAME	ID
tools	2
software	5
horse-drawn carriages	7
food	3
condiments	1
books	6
airships	4

Figure 4.9: Product category names in descending alphabetical order

Ordering Rows According to Multiple Columns

Here, the rows will be sorted based on the first column. However, if there are multiple records with the same value, the value in the second column is used for ordering. Let's take a look at this with an example from the **Customers** table and select the **FirstName** and **CustomerID**:

```
SELECT FirstName, CustomerID
FROM Customers;
```

The result is as follows:

Figure 4.10: Table showing the FirstName and CustomerID columns from the database

You can observe that in the **FirstName** column, there are multiple entries with **NULL** as their first name. So, when we order our results by **FirstName** in ascending order and the **CustomerID** in descending order, we will notice the difference. Let's implement this as follows:

```
SELECT FirstName, CustomerID
FROM Customers
ORDER BY FirstName, CustomerID DESC;
```

The result is as follows:

Figure 4.11: FirstName in ascending order and CustomerID in descending order

As you can see in *Figure 4.11*, it's now sorted alphabetically by **FirstName** in ascending order, even though we didn't mention the ordering type explicitly in the statement (**ASC** being the default order). Where there are multiple entries in the name column that are the same (**NULL**), these are then sorted in descending order by ID.

> **Note**
>
> **NULL** is used to represent an empty or missing value. For this reason, **NULL** appears at the top of the sorted list in the output, rather than being sorted alphabetically according to the letter *N*.

A useful tip when using the **ORDER BY** clause is to use an integer abbreviation instead of the complete column name. Column abbreviations start with 1, which is given to the first column in your statement. 2 is given to the second column, and so on. Let's try to perform the same query as before, but we will now order the columns using their abbreviations and, this time, the second ordering column will be sorted in ascending order instead:

```
SELECT FirstName, CustomerID
FROM Customers
ORDER BY 1, 2;
```

The result is as follows:

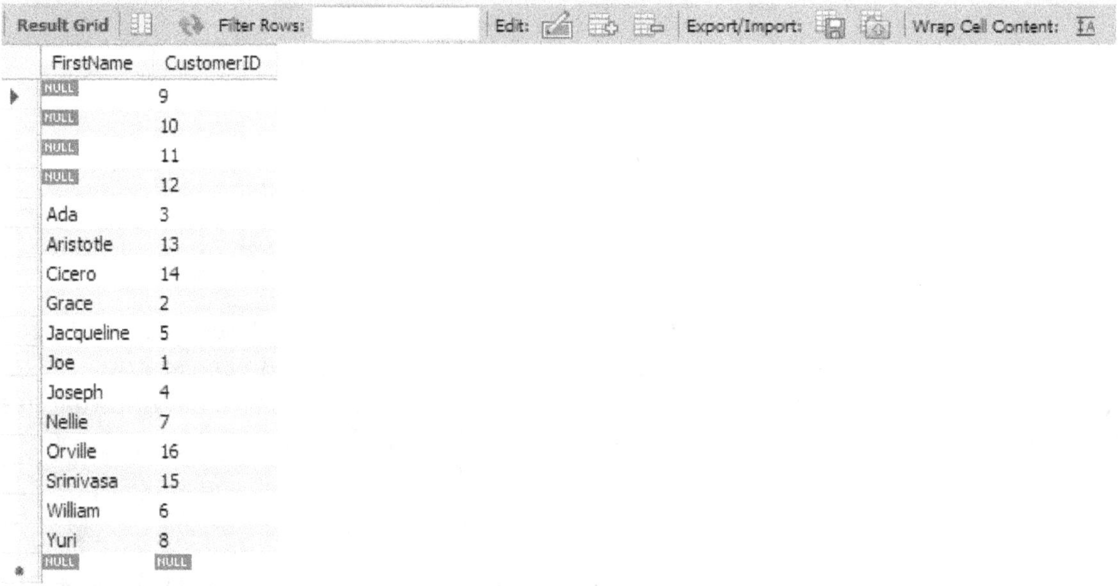

Result Grid | Filter Rows: | Edit: | Export/Import: | Wrap Cell Content:

FirstName	CustomerID
NULL	9
NULL	10
NULL	11
NULL	12
Ada	3
Aristotle	13
Cicero	14
Grace	2
Jacqueline	5
Joe	1
Joseph	4
Nellie	7
Orville	16
Srinivasa	15
William	6
Yuri	8
NULL	NULL

Figure 4.12: Sorting using integer abbreviations for the columns

As you might have concluded, the default ordering or **ASC** is applied here. If you need data in descending order, then the **DESC** keyword needs to be applied. The resultant SQL query will be as follows:

```
SELECT FirstName, CustomerID
FROM Customers
ORDER BY 1 DESC, 2 DESC;
```

The output for the query would be as follows:

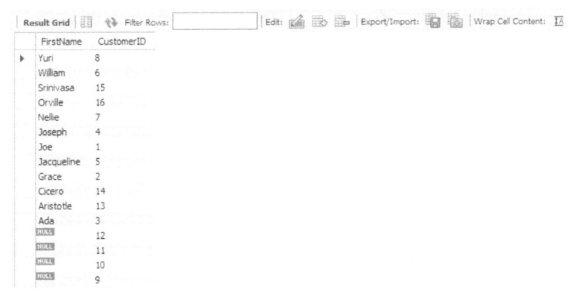

Figure 4.13: Output in descending order

Using LIMIT

We can limit the number of records displayed in the results by providing a specific number of records to be retrieved using the **LIMIT** keyword. It is an optional keyword and is used after the **SELECT** keyword in the following form:

```
SELECT [COLUMNS LIST]
FROM [TABLE NAME]
LIMIT [n];
```

[n] is the number of records you want to retrieve.

It is important to know that the **LIMIT** statement limits the number of records from the top row, working its way downward. It will execute based on the condition mentioned in the query. This implies that when the query is executed, the clauses with conditions (the **WHERE** and **ORDER BY** clauses) will be applied first, and then the top **n** rows will be retrieved.

> **Note**
>
> The equivalent SQL Server syntax for this would be:
>
> **SELECT TOP [n] [COLUMN LIST]**

Exercise 4.03: Using the LIMIT Keyword

The store manager wants to identify the five most expensive items from the product catalog. To obtain this report, we will need to do the following:

1. Type the following query:

```
SELECT ProductName, NetRetailPrice
FROM Products
ORDER BY NetRetailPrice DESC
LIMIT 5;
```

2. Execute the query. The result is as follows:

Figure 4.14: Top five most expensive items in the catalog

As you can see in *Figure 4.14*, the result table displays five records as per the **ORDER** clause used.

While if we used the same query and changed the number to **4** instead of **5**, your query would look like this:

```
SELECT ProductName, NetRetailPrice
FROM Products
ORDER BY NetRetailPrice
LIMIT 4;
```

The result should show four records instead of five, as shown in the following screenshot:

Figure 4.15: Top four most expensive items in the catalog

Using DISTINCT

Whenever we want to make sure we always retrieve distinct records (records with no duplication), we can use the **DISTINCT** keyword. The **DISTINCT** is an optional keyword that is used after the **SELECT** keyword in the following form:

```
SELECT DISTINCT [COLUMNS LIST]
FROM [TABLE NAME]
```

The **DISTINCT** keyword is commonly used with individual columns to make sure the retrieved column has unique values. When **DISTINCT** is used with more than one column, this means the complete set of selected columns should be distinct or unique, not only the first one. Let's see some examples to make this clearer.

For this example, we'll use the **Customers1.sql** script. It will create a new table called **Customers1** that contains duplicate values. The **Customers1** table will allow us to understand the functionality of the **DISTINCT** keyword. You can find the script set up for **Customers1** at https://packt.live/2Sv87rp. Run the query present in the **Customers1.sql**. You can see its contents by running the following query:

```
SELECT *
FROM Customers1;
```

The result is as follows:

FirstName	MiddleName	LastName	HomeAddress	Email	Phone	Notes
Joe	Greg	Smith	2356 Elm St.	joesmith@sfghwert.com	(310) 555-1212	Always gets products home delivered
Grace	Murray	Hopper	123 Compilation Street	gmhopper@ftyuw46.com	(818) 555-3678	Compiler pioneer
Ada	NULL	Lovelace	22 Algorithm Way	adalovelace@fgjw54af.gov	(717) 555-3457	First software engineer
Joseph	Force	Crater	1313 Mockingbird Lane	judgecrater@ev56gfwrty.com	(212) 555-5678	Works everyday
Jacqueline	Jackie	Cochran	1701 Flightspeed Avenue	jackiecochrane@jryuwp8qe4w.gov	(717) 555-3457	Researcher
NULL	Paul	Jones	126 Bonhomme Richard Ave.	jpjones@bonhommerichard.edu	(216) 555-6232	Admiral
Grace	NULL	Park	5 Hollywood	gpark@ftyuw46.gov	(310) 666-3678	Actor
Stephen	William	Hawking	4 Cambridge	stephenh@cambridge.gov	(454) 4444-9900	Professor of Mathematics
Stephen	NULL	Hillenburg	100 LA	shillenburg@la.gov	(454) 4433-9000	Director

Figure 4.16: Table with duplicate values

This is a standard **SELECT** query just to see results before we demonstrate our example. Take a careful look at the last row and the penultimate row; you will notice that they share the same first name, and so do rows 2 and 7. Let's see what will happen once we add the **DISTINCT** keyword to the statement:

```
SELECT DISTINCT FirstName, LastName
FROM Customers1;
```

The result is as follows:

Figure 4.17: Table after duplicate values are removed

We see that we get back the same number of records because there are no two rows that are identical across all the selected columns.

Let's use the same query but with the **LastName** column removed and see what happens:

```
SELECT DISTINCT FirstName
FROM Customers1;
```

Figure 4.18: After removing the LastName query from the previous table

In this case, we can see that there are only seven records. The duplicate **Grace** and **Stephen** entries have not been included in the results.

Using Mathematical Expressions

Sometimes, not all the information you need in a report is available in database fields. You often need to apply some mathematical expressions to your data to get the result you need. In this section, we are going to show you how you can use and build complex expressions and create your own calculated fields with the **SELECT** statement.

Mathematical expressions can be a combination of addition, subtraction, multiplication, and division, so your options in creating an expression are almost endless.

Please note that we are talking about mathematical expressions here, so all the fields involved in this expression should have a numeric data type. Otherwise, we will get an error.

Exercise 4.04: Calculating the Line Item Total

In the **OrderItems** table, we have the *quantity* and the *unit price* we need to get the *line item total*. The line item total will be the product of the unit price and the quantity. To do so, perform the following steps:

1. Type the following query with the additional column:

```
SELECT ProductID, Quantity, UnitPrice, (Quantity*UnitPrice) AS
   'Line Item Total'
FROM OrderItems;
```

2. Execute the query. Your result will be as follows:

Result Grid	Filter Rows:		Export:	Wrap Cell Content:

ProductID	Quantity	UnitPrice	Line Item Total
1	2	24.99	49.98
2	1	79.99	79.99
3	2	2499.99	4999.98
5	1	14.99	14.99
7	1	3.49	3.49
11	4	47.89	191.56
10	7	399999.95	2799999.65
2	2	79.99	159.98
6	1	4.49	4.49
5	1	14.99	14.99
10	2	399999.95	799999.90
7	1	3.49	3.49

Figure 4.19: UnitPrice and Line Item Total for products

As you can see, we used a multiplication expression to get the line item total. It's simple but can get complicated very easily, so we always recommend using parentheses whenever possible to make sure the expression is correct and clear.

Exercise 4.05: Calculating Discount

In the **OrderItems** table, there is a **Discount** field. We will use this field along with our last expression to get the line item price after the discount. Perform the following steps:

1. Write the following query:

```
SELECT ProductID, Quantity, UnitPrice, (Quantity*UnitPrice)
   AS 'Line Item Total', Discount,
   ((Quantity*UnitPrice)-(Quantity*Discount))
   AS 'Price After Discount'
FROM OrderItems;
```

2. Execute the query. You should get the following result:

ProductID	Quantity	UnitPrice	Line Item Total	Discount	Price After Discount
1	2	24.99	49.98	0.00	49.98
2	1	79.99	79.99	2.38	77.61
3	2	2499.99	4999.98	191.17	4617.64
5	1	14.99	14.99	0.00	14.99
7	1	3.49	3.49	0.91	2.58
11	4	47.89	191.56	0.88	188.04
10	7	399999.95	2799999.65	24999.95	2625000.00
2	2	79.99	159.98	2.17	155.64
6	1	4.49	4.49	0.00	4.49
5	1	14.99	14.99	1.89	13.10
10	2	399999.95	799999.90	25000.00	749999.90
7	1	3.49	3.49	0.00	3.49

Figure 4.20: Line item price after applying the discount

As you can see, we can use all math calculations effectively, and quickly retrieve data.

Activity 4.02: Extracting the Top Five Highest Priced Items

You are asked to generate a report showing the five highest value items in terms of the net retail price from **Packt_Online_Shop**. The report should contain the following columns:

- **Product Name**: This is the name of the product.

- **Product Retail Price**: This is the net retail price of the product.

- **Available Quantity**: This is the currently available quantity of the product.

- **Total Price of Available QTY**: This is the total net retail price of the available quantity.

Write a query that generates the requested report.

1. Use the **Select** statement to retrieve the required columns and use the AS keyword to provide aliases.

2. Order by the price.

3. Use the **LIMIT** keyword to obtain the top 5 products.

> **Note**
>
> The solution for this activity can be found on page 250.

Summary

In this chapter, we covered the **SELECT** query in detail, starting with its syntax and creating our own queries, customizing and limiting column names, and then creating our own calculated columns. We also saw how to control the ordering of the results we get, as well as how to limit the results using the **LIMIT** and **DISTINCT** keywords. In the next chapter, we will learn how to shape our statements and narrow down the results further using the **WHERE** clause.

5

Shaping Data with the WHERE Clause

Overview

In this chapter, we will see how to narrow down the records returned by a query according to specific requirements. We will also see how to search for **NULL** values. We'll also see how to use the **LIKE** operator to implement pattern matching. Handling **NULL** values and empty cells in the results is also covered in this chapter.

Introduction

In the previous chapter, we learned how to extract data from a specific table and sort it. However, in practice, we come across a lot of scenarios where we need to filter our results based on certain criteria and conditions. Consider the example of a table containing the details of all the books available from Packt, from which we want to find the names and ISBNs of all the books that cost more than $10. This scenario is illustrated in the following figures:

Price greater than $10

Book Name	ISBN	Author Name	Author ID	Author Email	Page Count	Price
[...]	[...]	[...]	[...]	[...]	[...]	[...]
[...]	[...]	[...]	[...]	[...]	[...]	[...]
[...]	[...]	[...]	[...]	[...]	[...]	[...]

Figure 5.1: Applying a filter to retrieve books that cost more than $10

The relevant columns are shown in the following table. The filtered result will look something like the second table in the following figure:

Price greater than $10

Book Name	ISBN	Author Name	Author ID	Author Email	Page Count	Price
[...]	[...]	[...]	[...]	[...]	[...]	[...]

Book Name	ISBN
[...]	[...]

Figure 5.2: Result after filtering and retrieving books that cost more than $10

In SQL, the **WHERE** clause allows us to apply the filter functionality. In this chapter, we will dig deep into using the **WHERE** clause in our queries by combining and adding different conditions to derive our results.

We will also look at handling **NULL** or empty values to ensure that our report is well controlled, precise, and based on our requirements.

The WHERE Clause Syntax

The **WHERE** clause is optional and can be added to any **SELECT** statement, usually after the **FROM** clause, as follows:

```
SELECT [COLUMNS LIST]
FROM [TABLE NAME]
WHERE [CONDITION]
ORDER BY [COLUMN NAME] [ASC|DESC]
```

As you can see in the highlighted line, this statement starts with the **WHERE** keyword followed by a condition.

Conditions in SQL are logical operators that can be used for comparison. Condition operators are listed in the following table:

Operator	Description
>	Greater than
>=	Greater than or equal to
<	Less than
<=	Less than or equal to
=	Equal to
Between… and	Between a specific range
!=	Not equal to
<>	Not equal to

Figure 5.3: Conditional operators in SQL

These operators can be used to compare two fields/values to achieve the desired results.

> **Note**
>
> The compared fields or values must be of the same data type for the statement to be successful.

A simple implementation of a **WHERE** clause is as follows:

```
USE studentdemo;
SELECT *
FROM Student;
```

The sample **Student** table looks like this:

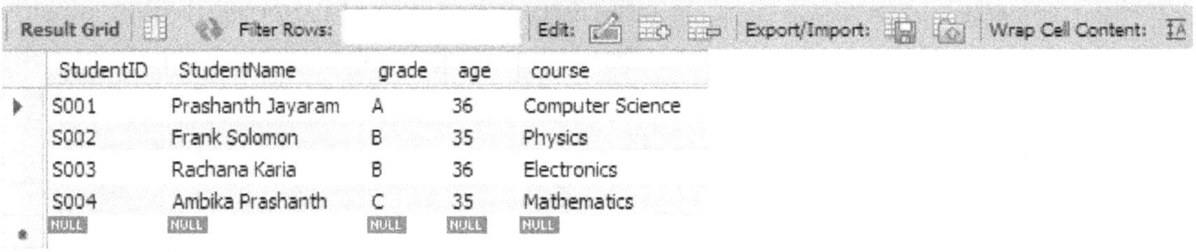

StudentID	StudentName	grade	age	course
S001	Prashanth Jayaram	A	36	Computer Science
S002	Frank Solomon	B	35	Physics
S003	Rachana Karia	B	36	Electronics
S004	Ambika Prashanth	C	35	Mathematics
NULL	NULL	NULL	NULL	NULL

Figure 5.4: Sample student table

Using the **Student** table of the **StudentDemo** database, say we want to retrieve the names and the IDs of those students who've enrolled in the *Electronics* course.

The SQL query to achieve this would be as follows:

```
SELECT *
FROM Student
WHERE course = 'Electronics';
```

The result would be as shown in the following screenshot:

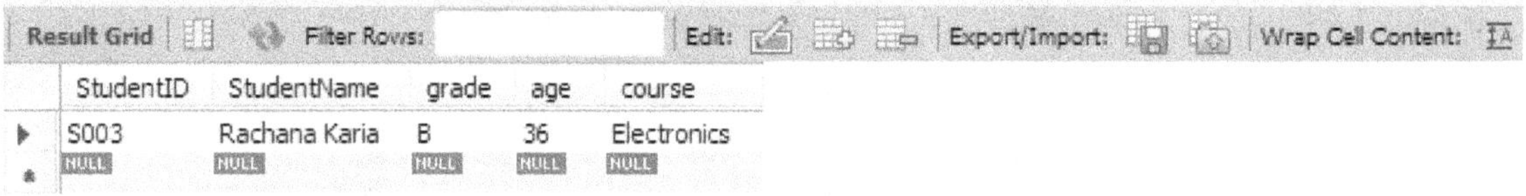

StudentID	StudentName	grade	age	course
S003	Rachana Karia	B	36	Electronics
NULL	NULL	NULL	NULL	NULL

Figure 5.5: Names of the students enrolled in the Electronics course

Exercise 5.01: Implementing Logical Operators in the WHERE Clause

The store manager wants a list of all the items that are priced over $14.99 and wants to label them as high-value products. To retrieve the list of all the products that are priced over $14.99, perform the following steps:

1. Open a new query window.
2. Switch to **PACKT_ONLINE_SHOP**:

```
use PACKT_ONLINE_SHOP;
```

3. Write a query to filter the products that are priced over $14.99:

```
SELECT ProductName AS 'High-value Products', NetRetailPrice
FROM Products
WHERE NetRetailPrice > 14.99
```

4. Execute the query; the result will be as follows:

High-value Products	NetRetailPrice
Calculatre	24.99
Penwrite	79.99
Vortex Generator	2499.99
The Gourmet Crockpot	24.99
keyboard wrench	399999.95
power cell	47.89

Figure 5.6: Products with NetRetailPrice greater than $14.99

As you can see in *Figure* 5.6, the result set is now showing 6 records out of 11, and all these products have a net retail price that's greater than $14.99.

5. To include products that have a **`NetRetailPrice`** of $14.99 in the previous results, use the >= operator as follows:

```
USE PACKT_ONLINE_SHOP;
SELECT  ProductName AS 'High-value Products', NetRetailPrice
FROM Products
WHERE NetRetailPrice >= 14.99
```

6. Execute the query, and you'll get the following results:

High-value Products	NetRetailPrice
Calculatre	24.99
Penwrite	79.99
Vortex Generator	2499.99
The Gourmet Crockpot	24.99
Government Accounting	14.99
keyboard wrench	399999.95
power cell	47.89

Figure 5.7: Products with NetRetailPrice greater than or equal to $14.99

We can control our results further by limiting our search to a specific range. We do this by using the **BETWEEN** operator. For example, if we were to filter students who have scored between **75** and **90**, our syntax for the **WHERE** clause would be:

```
WHERE SCORE BETWEEN 75 AND 90
```

Exercise 5.02: Using the BETWEEN Operator

The store manager now wants to list all the items in the range of $14.99 to $50 as *mid-priced items*. To derive a list of all items that are priced between $14.99 and $50, we will need to perform the following steps:

1. In a new query window, write the following query:

```
SELECT ProductName,NetRetailPrice
FROM Products
WHERE NetRetailPrice BETWEEN 14.99 AND 50
ORDER BY NetRetailPrice;
```

2. Execute the query. The result will be as follows:

Figure 5.8: Products with NetRetailPrice ranging from $14.99 to $50

Note that products with the price range ($14.99 and $50) will also be included in the results if they are available. In our case, you can see that the first record (which has a price value of **14.99**) is included in the results.

The Not Equal Operator

SQL supports the following symbols to denote the not equal operator: **!=** and **<>**. The not equal operator will exclude the conditions where values are equal in the results.

Exercise 5.03: Using the != and <> Operators

The store manager realizes that the tomato sauce received has gone bad, so he does not want to present it in the list of available items. To write a query to display all the products except the tomato sauce, perform the following steps:

1. Enter the **SELECT** statement, using the **WHERE** clause and the **!=** operator:

```
SELECT ProductName,NetRetailPrice
FROM Products
WHERE ProductName != 'tomato sauce'
ORDER BY NetRetailPrice;
```

2. Execute the query; you should see the following results:

ProductName	NetRetailPrice
10-mm socket wrench	3.49
habanero peppers	4.49
pure vanilla	10.39
Government Accounting	14.99
Calculatre	24.99
The Gourmet Crockpot	24.99
power cell	47.89
Penwrite	79.99
Vortex Generator	2499.99
keyboard wrench	399999.95

Figure 5.9: List of all products except tomato sauce after using the != operator

3. As an alternative, now replace the != symbol with the <> operator:

```
SELECT ProductName,NetRetailPrice
FROM Products
WHERE ProductName <> 'tomato sauce'
ORDER BY NetRetailPrice;
```

4.   Execute the query; your result should be the same as before:

ProductName	NetRetailPrice
10-mm socket wrench	3.49
habanero peppers	4.49
pure vanilla	10.39
Government Accounting	14.99
Calculatre	24.99
The Gourmet Crockpot	24.99
power cell	47.89
Penwrite	79.99
Vortex Generator	2499.99
keyboard wrench	399999.95

Figure 5.10: List of all products except tomato sauce after using the <> operator

As you can see, irrespective of the operator used, the results are identical and do not contain the product tomato sauce.

The LIKE Operator

Often, we come across situations where we need to retrieve data with a certain pattern. For example, you may want to get all customer names that start with an "A", or any customers with "Joe" in their name. This is where the **LIKE** operator comes in handy. Similar to the other operators we've seen in this chapter, the **LIKE** operator is used with the **WHERE** clause.

Let's implement it in our syntax:

```
SELECT [COLUMNS LIST]
FROM [TABLE NAME]
WHERE [COLUMN NAME] LIKE '[PATTERN]'
```

In the **LIKE** pattern condition, there are two wildcards that can be used together to create a pattern:

- % represents zero or multiple characters

- _ represents a single character

Figure 5.11 will give you a better understanding of how these wildcards can be used together to form a pattern:

Pattern	Description
'%x'	Any value that ends with the letter x
'x%'	Any value that starts with the letter x
'%x%'	Any value that has the letter x in any position
'x%z'	Any value that starts with the letter x and ends with the letter z
'_x%'	Any value the has the letter x in the second position
'x_%_%'	Any value that starts with the letter x and has at least three characters

Figure 5.11: Wildcard patterns for the LIKE operator

Let's see an example. To search for first names that have **o** in the second position, the following query can be run:

```
SELECT FirstName, LastName, Phone
FROM Customers
WHERE FirstName LIKE '_o%';
```

The output will be as follows:

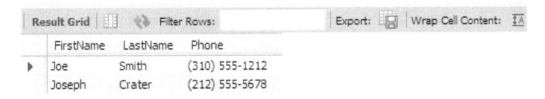

Figure 5.12: First names with an "o" in the second position

Exercise 5.04: Using the LIKE Operator to Check a Pattern at the Beginning of a String

To increase area-wide sales in LA, we want a list of customers from LA. We don't currently have any field specifically mentioning the state/country, but since we record the customers' phone details, we can filter the phone numbers that start with the code for LA (310), as follows:

1. Write a query implementing the **LIKE** operator in the **WHERE** clause to match the phone numbers that begin with **(310)**:

```
SELECT FirstName AS 'Customers from LA', Phone
FROM Customers
WHERE Phone LIKE '(310)%';
```

2. Execute the query. The result should be as follows:

Result Grid		Filter Rows:		Export:	Wrap Cell Content:

Customers from LA	Phone
Joe	(310) 555-1212
Yuri	(310) 555-5462
Aristotle	(310) 555-9182
Cicero	(310) 555-0822

Figure 5.13: List of customers with (310) in their phone number

Exercise 5.05: Using the LIKE Operator to Check for a Specified Length

We want to provide usernames to our customers so they can log into our system. We want to create each username from the customer's first name. However, our system does not allow three-letter usernames. The store manager will have to pull up a report on all the customers with three-letter usernames. To do so, perform the following steps:

1. Write the following query in a new query window:

```
SELECT FirstName, LastName, Phone
FROM Customers
WHERE FirstName LIKE '___';
```

2. The following records will be returned:

	FirstName	LastName	Phone
▶	Joe	Smith	(310) 555-1212
	Ada	Lovelace	(717) 555-3457

Figure 5.14: List of customers with three-letter usernames

Checking for NULLS

Before we learn to handle **NULL** values, let's define a **NULL** value. **NULL** equals nothing in SQL, so a field that has no value is considered **NULL**. Usually, **NULL** fields are the result of having optional fields in your tables.

Checking **NULL** values can be done using the following two special keywords, as it cannot be done using the logical operators:

* **IS NULL**

* **IS NOT NULL**

> **Note**
>
> An important point to highlight is the fact that fields with a value of **0**, or invisible characters such as spaces, are *not* considered **NULL**. **NULL** fields are fields that are left blank.

Exercise 5.06: Searching for NULL Values

Ideally, we want all customers' first names to be in our system. For any customer whose first name is missing from our data, we want to contact the customer and ask them about the missing information. To do this, we require a report of all the customers with missing first names:

1. Retrieve the middle name, last name, and phone number columns to check for all the customers with **NULL** values in the **MiddleName** field, as follows:

```
SELECT MiddleName, LastName, Phone
FROM Customers
WHERE FirstName IS NULL;
```

The result is as follows:

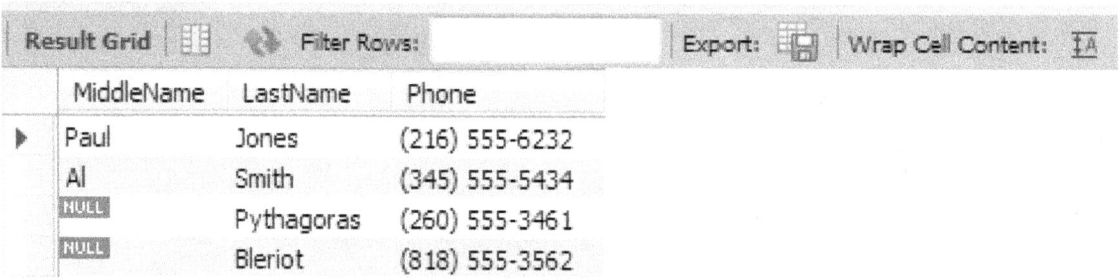

MiddleName	LastName	Phone
Paul	Jones	(216) 555-6232
Al	Smith	(345) 555-5434
NULL	Pythagoras	(260) 555-3461
NULL	Bleriot	(818) 555-3562

Figure 5.15: Customers whose first name is missing

We can now ring up people and ask them to enter their first names using this report.

Combining Conditions with the AND, OR, and NOT Operators

On many occasions, we may need to combine multiple conditions at the same time. The best way to do this in SQL is by using the following three operators, which can be used between conditions in the **WHERE** clause:

- **AND**: This operator makes sure both sides of the operator (both conditions) are true.
- **OR**: This operator makes sure one side at least of the operator is true.
- **NOT**: This operator makes sure that the condition following this operator is false.

Exercise 5.07: Querying Multiple Conditions

Joe, a customer from LA, has requested to speak to the store manager regarding a complaint. We are going to write a query to retrieve all of this customer's details. This will allow the manager to have all the required information to best help resolve the customer's complaint.

The state code for LA is (310). To pull the required information, perform the following steps:

1. Enter the query as follows:

```
SELECT *
FROM Customers
WHERE FirstName = 'Joe' AND Phone LIKE '(310)%';
```

2. Execute the query. This gives the following result:

CustomerID	FirstName	MiddleName	LastName	Address	Email	Phone	Notes	BalanceNotes
1	Joe	Greg	Smith	2356 Elm St.	joesmith@sfghwert.com	(310) 555-1212	A note	NULL
NULL	NULL	NULL	NULL	NULL	NULL	NULL	NULL	NULL

Figure 5.16: Customers with the name Joe with an LA code phone number

For clarity, we're also going to do a search for all customers who are either named Joe or who live in LA. This will help us to verify that we've got the right customer, rather than the wrong Joe, or the wrong person from LA. We will do this by using the **OR** operator on the same example:

```
SELECT FirstName, LastName, Phone
FROM Customers
WHERE FirstName = 'Joe' OR Phone LIKE '(310)%';
```

The result is shown in the following screenshot. As required, it displays all customers with either the first name Joe or a phone number that starts with (310):

FirstName	LastName	Phone
Joe	Smith	(310) 555-1212
Yuri	Gagarin	(310) 555-5462
Aristotle	NULL	(310) 555-9182
Cicero	NULL	(310) 555-0822

Figure 5.17: Customers with the name Joe or an LA phone number

There are no other Joes in our system, and there is nobody else in LA who has a similar name to Joe. So, we can be fairly confident we have got the correct person.

> **Tip**
>
> Whenever we combine conditions, it is always a good practice to use parentheses to group conditions together and make sure we are writing the correct query.

Now, say we have a scenario where we need to list all customers that have a first name starting with **Jo** and a phone number that starts with (310) or (210), but who don't have a last name of **Carter**. This is a perfect scenario to use all operators in one query:

```
SELECT FirstName, LastName, Phone,Notes
FROM Customers
WHERE FirstName LIKE 'Jo%' AND (Phone LIKE '(310)%' OR Phone LIKE '(210)%') AND NOT
LastName = 'Carter';
```

This returns the records shown here:

FirstName	LastName	Phone	Notes
Joe	Smith	(310) 555-1212	A note

Figure 5.18: Customers named Joe with a 310/210 phone code and without the surname Carter

As you can see, we used parentheses to separate the **OR** comparison and compare the full block with the first condition of the first name.

Activity 5.01: Combining Conditions to Extract Store Data

As store manager, you need to generate a report that shows the following columns: product name, product retail price, available quantity, and total price of available quantity.

However, you are asked to only include products that meet the following conditions:

- A net retail price that is lower than or equal to 24.99
- An available quantity that is at least 38 items
- A product name that doesn't start with 10

Generate the report as described.

> **Note**
>
> The solution to this activity can be found on page 251.

Summary

In this chapter, we have covered the **WHERE** clause in detail. We started with its syntax and then created conditions and compared data using wildcard symbols to form powerful patterns. We identified NULL values, and, at the end of the chapter, used certain operators to combine conditions. The next chapter will discuss how we can obtain data that is spread across multiple tables using Joins.

6

JOINS

Overview

This chapter will help you understand the functionality of the various joins and their implementation through examples. By the end of this chapter, you will be able to implement an **INNER JOIN** to retrieve overlapping data within multiple tables and write **LEFT** and **RIGHT JOIN** queries to filter the results that have been obtained from multiple tables. We will also be able to implement a **CROSS JOIN** to obtain a cartesian product of the table elements; and combine two queries using **UNION**.

Introduction

In the previous chapter, we saw how the **WHERE** clause can be used to filter elements and provide us with more control over the data we can retrieve from a table. However, in many cases, not all the data we require can be found in a single table. Having a single table to store all the data is also not feasible because its maintenance will be extremely difficult. One way of connecting tables and retrieving data from them is by using joins.

We can use the **JOIN** operation to extract data from multiple tables that have *common columns* using a single query. Based on the data that's required, there are various types of joins that are supported by SQL.

In this chapter, we will look at the following types of joins that are available in SQL:

- **INNER JOIN**
- **RIGHT JOIN**
- **LEFT JOIN**
- **CROSS JOIN**
- **UNION**

Each topic in this chapter will illustrate a type of **JOIN**. We will be working with the **PACKT_ONLINE_SHOP** throughout this chapter. First, we'll begin with the **INNER JOIN**.

INNER JOIN

The **INNER JOIN** is the default type of join that is used to select data with matching values in both tables. It can be represented with the following Venn diagram:

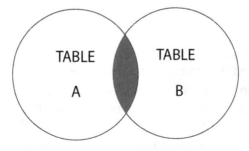

Figure 6.1: INNER JOIN

The **INNER JOIN** represents the highlighted section, which is the intersection between these two tables. Let's have a look at the **INNER JOIN** syntax:

```
SELECT [Column List]
  FROM [Table 1] INNER JOIN [Table 2]
    ON [Table 1 Column Name] = [Table 2 Column Name]
WHERE [Condition]
```

The syntax can also be written as follows:

```
SELECT [Column List]
  FROM [Table 1] JOIN [Table 2]
    ON [Table 1 Column Name] = [Table 2 Column Name]
WHERE [Condition]
```

> **Note**
>
> The use of **INNER** in the query is optional.

The **INNER JOIN** is one of the most commonly used type of joins. Let's implement this in an exercise.

Exercise 6.01: Extracting Orders and Purchaser Information

You are a store manager that needs to extract the details of all the orders, along with the customer details from the **PACKT_ONLINE_DATABASE**. To do so, follow these steps:

1. Look at the tables involved in obtaining the required elements and identify the common columns:

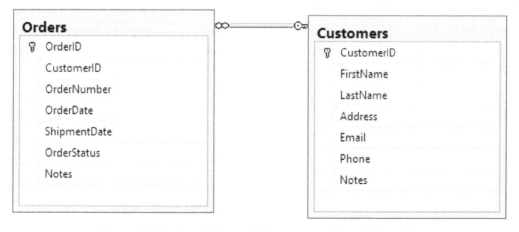

Figure 6.2: Orders table and Customers table relationship

As you can see, the **Orders** table and the **Customers** table both contain the **CustomerID** column. In order to join the two tables, we need to map the **CustomerID** columns of the **Orders** table to those of the **Customers** table.

2. Open a new query window, switch to the **PACKT_ONLINE_SHOP** database, and type the following query:

```
SELECT Orders.OrderNumber, Orders.OrderStatus, Orders.OrderDate,
    Customers.FirstName, Customers.LastName, Customers.Email
FROM Orders JOIN Customers ON Orders.CustomerID = Customers.CustomerID;
```

3. Execute the query. Your output should be as follows:

OrderNumber	OrderStatus	OrderDate	FirstName	LastName	Email
ABC123	shipped	2017-03-02 00:00:00	Grace	Hopper	gmhopper@ftyuw46.com
BCQ857	pending	2317-03-07 00:00:00	Ada	Lovelace	adalovelace@fgjw54af.gov
RST321	returned	1930-04-19 00:00:00	Joseph	Crater	judgecrater@ev56gfwrty.com
YQW672	shipped	2009-12-01 00:00:00	William	Shakespeare	wshakespeare@dyuioety4.gov
DTR321	shipped	2930-04-19 00:00:00	Nellie	Bly	nellie@fthw45asdgf.com
BCQ858	shipped	2317-03-18 00:00:00	Ada	Lovelace	adalovelace@fgjw54af.gov

Figure 6.3: Order and purchaser information

If you observe the naming convention that's used in naming columns, we started with the name of the table and a dot, ., followed by the name of the column. This is a great way to prevent ambiguity because sometimes, you may find the same column name being used in different tables. With this practice, your database management system will always know of the exact columns you want to refer to.

In the syntax, we have specified the join criteria by using **Orders.CustomerID = Customers.CustomerID**. This resulted in six records as output (which are the complete records of the **Orders** table), along with the fields from both tables.

The key element is to make sure that your join criteria are correct based on the shared columns between your joined tables. Next, we'll look at the next type of join, known as the **RIGHT JOIN**.

RIGHT JOIN

This type of join is used when you want to select records that are available in the second table and matching records in the first one. This can be visualized with the following Venn diagram:

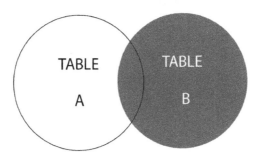

Figure 6.4: RIGHT JOIN

As we can see, the **RIGHT JOIN** represents the highlighted section, that is, **TABLE B**, and the intersected section of **TABLE A**. Let's look at the syntax for the **RIGHT JOIN**:

```
SELECT [Column List]
   FROM [Table 1] RIGHT OUTER JOIN [Table 2]
      ON [Table 1 Column Name] = [Table 2 Column Name]
WHERE [Condition]
```

The syntax can also be written as follows:

```
SELECT [Column List]
   FROM [Table 1] RIGHT JOIN [Table 2]
      ON [Table 1 Column Name] = [Table 2 Column Name]
WHERE [Condition]
```

> **Note**
>
> Writing **OUTER** in the query is optional.

Exercise 6.02: Implementing RIGHT JOIN

The store wants the list of customers, along with their orders, and also wants to include customers who haven't purchased anything from the store yet.

The challenge here is to show customers who haven't ordered yet—that's why, in this case, it would be perfect to use the **RIGHT JOIN**. As per the preceding diagram, this should result in an intersection area between table 1 (**Orders**) and table 2 (**Customers**), which indicates customers who have ordered something before, as well as the remaining area of table 2 (**Customers**), which indicates customers who have not ordered anything from us yet. Let's get started:

1. Open a new query window and enter the following query:

```
SELECT Customers.FirstName,
Customers.LastName,
Customers.Email ,
Orders.OrderNumber,
Orders.OrderStatus

FROM Orders RIGHT JOIN Customers ON
    Orders.CustomerID = Customers.CustomerID
```

2. Execute the query. You should get the following output:

FirstName	LastName	Email	OrderNumber	OrderStatus
Joe	Smith	joesmith@sfghwert.com	NULL	NULL
Grace	Hopper	gmhopper@ftyuw46.com	ABC123	shipped
Ada	Lovelace	adalovelace@fgjw54af.gov	BCQ857	pending
Ada	Lovelace	adalovelace@fgjw54af.gov	BCQ858	shipped
Joseph	Crater	judgecrater@ev56gfwrty.com	RST321	returned
Jacqueline	Cochran	jackiecochrane@jryuwp8qe4w.gov	NULL	NULL
William	Shakespeare	wshakespeare@dyuioety4.gov	YQW672	shipped
Nellie	Bly	nellie@fthw45asdgf.com	DTR321	shipped
Yuri	Gagarin	yuri@rheysdagf.edu	NULL	NULL
NULL	Jones	jpjones@bonhommerichard.edu	NULL	NULL
NULL	Smith	alsmith@dytsdrg.edu	NULL	NULL
NULL	Pythagoras	pythagoras@sdrg.edu	NULL	NULL
NULL	Bleriot	bleriot@wtrasf.gov	NULL	NULL
Aristotle	NULL	aristotle@ertyasdf.edu	NULL	NULL
Cicero	NULL	Cicero@ghyu45y.edu	NULL	NULL
Srinivasa	Ramanujan	srinivasa@imaginarynumber.edu	NULL	NULL
Orville	Wright	owright@sdg98.edu	NULL	NULL

Figure 6.5: List of customers with their orders and customers who haven't ordered anything

You may have noticed a similar result in *Figure 6.3*; however, you have some extra records with **NULL** values in the **OrderNumber** and **OrderStatus** fields.

3. To extract a list of customers who haven't placed any orders from the store, enter the following query:

```
SELECT Customers.FirstName,
Customers.LastName,
Customers.Email ,
Orders.OrderNumber,
Orders.OrderStatus


FROM Orders RIGHT JOIN Customers ON
   Orders.CustomerID = Customers.CustomerID
WHERE Orders.OrderNumber IS NULL
```

This results in the following output:

FirstName	LastName	Email	OrderNumber	OrderStatus
Joe	Smith	joesmith@sfghwert.com	NULL	NULL
Jacqueline	Cochran	jackiecochrane@jryuwp8qe4w.gov	NULL	NULL
Yuri	Gagarin	yuri@rheysdagf.edu	NULL	NULL
NULL	Jones	jpjones@bonhommerichard.edu	NULL	NULL
NULL	Smith	alsmith@dytsdrg.edu	NULL	NULL
NULL	Pythagoras	pythagoras@sdrg.edu	NULL	NULL
NULL	Bleriot	bleriot@wtrasf.gov	NULL	NULL
Aristotle	NULL	aristotle@ertyasdf.edu	NULL	NULL
Cicero	NULL	Cicero@ghyu45y.edu	NULL	NULL
Srinivasa	Ramanujan	srinivasa@imaginarynumber.edu	NULL	NULL
Orville	Wright	owright@sdg98.edu	NULL	NULL

Figure 6.6: Result table with only NULL values

In the syntax, we have specified the **JOIN** criteria by using **Orders.CustomerID = Customers.CustomerID**. This resulted in six records as output (which are the complete records of the **Orders** table), along with the fields from both tables.

Thus, we have seen how we can implement a **RIGHT JOIN** in the database.

LEFT JOIN

This type of **JOIN** is used when you want to select records that are available in the first table and match records in the second one. It can be represented with the following Venn diagram:

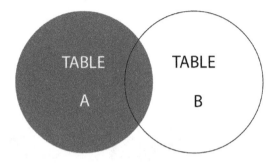

Figure 6.7: LEFT JOIN

The **LEFT JOIN** represents the highlighted section from **TABLE A** and the intersected section from **TABLE B**. Let's look at the syntax:

```
SELECT [Column List]
  FROM [Table 1] LEFT OUTER JOIN [Table 2]
    ON [Table 1 Column Name] = [Table 2 Column Name]
WHERE [Condition]
```

The syntax can also be as follows:

```
SELECT [Column List]
  FROM [Table 1] LEFT JOIN [Table 2]
    ON [Table 1 Column Name] = [Table 2 Column Name]
WHERE [Condition]
```

> **Note**
>
> The **OUTER** word in the query is optional.

This type of join is very similar to the **RIGHT JOIN**, with the only difference being that it executes the table on the opposite (left) side. Now that we have seen how we can implement **LEFT JOIN**, let's do an exercise to implement them and retrieve payment information from our **PACKT_ONLINE_SHOP** database.

Exercise 6.03: Implementing LEFT JOIN

The store manager now wants to analyze the payment data for the customers. Specifically, the manager wishes to retrieve only those orders that have payments with payment information. Here is how this information can be retrieved:

1. In the new query window, type in the following query:

```
SELECT   Orders.OrderNumber,
         Orders.OrderStatus,
         Payments.PaymentRef,
         Payments.PaymentType


FROM Payments LEFT JOIN Orders ON Payments.OrderID = Orders.OrderID
```

2. Run the query by clicking on the **Execute** button:

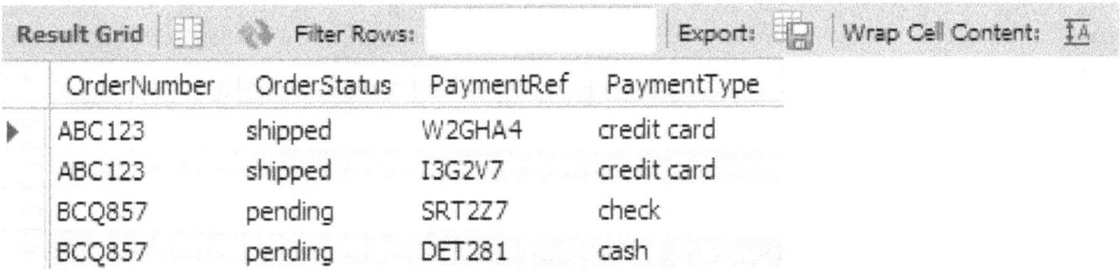

OrderNumber	OrderStatus	PaymentRef	PaymentType
ABC123	shipped	W2GHA4	credit card
ABC123	shipped	I3G2V7	credit card
BCQ857	pending	SRT2Z7	check
BCQ857	pending	DET281	cash

Figure 6.8: Result of the LEFT JOIN

Notice how we started the join with the payments table instead of the orders table to adapt the query with the **LEFT JOIN**. If we had put the orders table at the beginning, we would have got a list of all the orders instead of only the ones that have payments for them.

3. Execute the following query:

```
SELECT   Orders.OrderNumber,
         Orders.OrderStatus,
         Payments.PaymentRef,
         Payments.PaymentType


FROM Orders LEFT JOIN Payments ON Payments.OrderID = Orders.OrderID
```

This results in the following output:

OrderNumber	OrderStatus	PaymentRef	PaymentType
ABC123	shipped	W2GHA4	credit card
ABC123	shipped	I3G2V7	credit card
BCQ857	pending	SRT2Z7	check
BCQ857	pending	DET281	cash
RST321	returned	NULL	NULL
YQW672	shipped	NULL	NULL
DTR321	shipped	NULL	NULL
BCQ858	shipped	NULL	NULL

Figure 6.9: Result of the LEFT JOIN as per the order of join

As you can see, the order of how you join your tables together is important because it determines your result set.

CROSS JOIN

This type of join is used when you want to combine the elements of a particular column with the elements of another column. This implies that each record from the first table and each record from the second table are laid out in all possible combinations in one single table, just like in the case of a cartesian product. Here is how we can perform this task using the **CROSS JOIN** syntax:

```
SELECT [Column List]
   FROM [Table 1] CROSS JOIN [Table 2]
WHERE [Condition]
```

To understand this concept well, we will perform **CROSS JOIN** on simple tables and see how they work in the following exercise.

Exercise 6.04: Implementing CROSS JOINS

Consider that we have a table called **Facecards**, with a column called **suits**, and a table called **CardSuite** with a column called **cardvalue**. Now, we want to cross-reference all the suits with all the card values. To do this, perform the following steps:

1. Create a table called **Facecards** with the following values:

```
Create table Facecards (cardvalue varchar (50));
insert into Facecards (cardvalue) values ('King');
insert into Facecards (cardvalue) values ('Queen');
insert into Facecards (cardvalue) values ('Jack');
insert into Facecards (cardvalue) values ('Ace');
```

2. Create a table called **CardSuit** with the following values:

```
Create table CardSuit (suit varchar(50));
insert into CardSuit (suit) values ('Heart');
insert into CardSuit (suit) values ('Spade');
insert into CardSuit (suit) values ('Clubs');
insert into CardSuit (suit) values ('Diamond');
```

3. Implement the **CROSS JOIN** query to cross-reference the two columns:

```
SELECT Facecards.cardvalue,
       CardSuit.suit

FROM Facecards CROSS JOIN CardSuit
```

4. Execute the query:

cardvalue	suit
King	Heart
Queen	Heart
Jack	Heart
Ace	Heart
King	Spade
Queen	Spade
Jack	Spade
Ace	Spade
King	Clubs
Queen	Clubs
Jack	Clubs
Ace	Clubs
King	Diamond
Queen	Diamond
Jack	Diamond
Ace	Diamond

Figure 6.10: List of all combinations between products and their categories

As shown in the preceding screenshot, you will find a list of all possible combinations between the suit and **Facecards** values.

UNION JOIN

The **UNION** operation is used to combine two queries. Let's look at the syntax:

```
SELECT [COLUMNS LIST] FROM [TABLE NAME]
UNION
SELECT [COLUMNS LIST] FROM [TABLE NAME]
```

However, the most important point to remember when we use the **UNION** operation is to ensure the following:

- Both query columns have similar data types
- Both query columns are in the same order

Let's take a look at the following exercise to see how the **UNION** query functions.

Exercise 6.05: Implementing a UNION JOIN

The store manager wants a telephonic feedback survey from everyone who the store employees work with. This implies that there's a list of suppliers and customers and their full names, along with their contact numbers. To do this, perform the following steps:

1. In a new query window, write the following query:

```
SELECT CONCAT(Customers.FirstName,' ',Customers.LastName) as 'FULL NAME',
        Customers.Phone AS 'Phone Number'
   FROM Customers
   UNION
   SELECT    Suppliers.ContactPerson AS 'Full Name',
             Suppliers.PhoneNumber AS 'Phone Number'
   FROM Suppliers
```

Clearly, you can see that there are two queries separated by the **UNION** keyword. The first query provides the full names of all the customers, while the second query provides the full names of all the suppliers. The **UNION** join will ensure that these values are retrieved as a single table. Notice that in this query we have used the **CONCAT** function. This concatenates the first and last names, joining them together to give the full name of each customer.

> **Note**
>
> In cases where either the first name or the last name is NULL, the resultant name would also be NULL.
>
> To avoid such instances you can add a statement to the query:
>
> **IFNULL (Customers.FirstName, '_')**

2. Execute the query, you will get the following output:

FULL NAME	Phone Number
Joe Smith	(310) 555-1212
Grace Hopper	(818) 555-3678
Ada Lovelace	(717) 555-3457
Joseph Crater	(212) 555-5678
Jacqueline Cochran	(717) 555-3457
William Shakespeare	(213) 555-3421
Nellie Bly	(213) 555-8523
Yuri Gagarin	(310) 555-5462
NULL	(216) 555-6232
NULL	(345) 555-5434
NULL	(260) 555-3461
NULL	(818) 555-3562
NULL	(310) 555-9182
NULL	(310) 555-0822
Srinivasa Ramanujan	(211) 555-1111
Orville Wright	(211) 555-4444
Smith Johns	(818) 555-3456
Smith Johns	(415) 555-2347
Trippe Juan	(212) 555-3783
Allen Wight	(109) 555-4721
Horace Greeley	(213) 555-7567
Adam Osborne	(310) 555-3456

Figure 6.11: Supplier and customer information

As you can see from the preceding output, the **FULL NAME** column will contain the names of both the customers and the suppliers, while the **Phone Number** column will contain the contact numbers of both the customers and the suppliers.

This concludes all the different ways of combining tables using joins.

Activity 6.01: Implementing JOINS

The store manager notices that there are some complaints about incorrectly priced orders by customers. He wants a report that contains the order's details, along with the product prices, in order to investigate this issue. Write a query to obtain such a result.

> **Note**
>
> The solution to this activity can be found on page 252.

Summary

In this chapter, we learned all about joins and how we can get data from multiple tables, and we explored the different types of joins, along with the **UNION** operation. These essential skills will be your base moving forward so that you can get creative with mix and match joins to pinpoint the result set you are looking for. In the next chapter, we will look at some other ways we can retrieve data from multiple tables.

Subqueries, Cases, and Views

Overview

In this chapter, we will look at some techniques that will help us add logic to our existing queries using **CASE** statements. We will also query data present in multiple tables using subqueries. We will also create views using queries that allows us the flexibility to create a temporary table to run queries on.

Introduction

In the previous chapter, we saw how the various types of SQL joins can *connect* multiple tables in a single **SELECT** query. This powerful technique gives us fine-grained control over the data that our SQL queries return. However, SQL offers much more. In this chapter, we'll use the **PACKT_ONLINE_SHOP** database to see how subqueries, **CASE** statements, and views boost the flexibility and power of SQL in an efficient, intuitive way. Like joins, subqueries can relate different tables together in the same SQL query, but compared to queries involving multiple outer joins and unions, subqueries can offer a simpler, cleaner query structure. This can make the development and maintenance of the code easier. **CASE** statements offer a clean, efficient way for a query to handle decisions, depending on the defined conditions that occur in the query. Views provide an efficient, effective way to group multiple tables together in a *symbolic* table that's available for use by other queries. In this chapter, we will look at each concept in detail.

Subqueries

In a SQL statement, a subquery operates like a joined table. It gathers data in a structured way and makes that data available for its outer SQL query. Placed in parentheses, a subquery, or an *inner* query, nests inside a parent, or an *outer* query. A subquery can nest in the following clauses of the parent query or another subquery:

- **SELECT**

- **FROM**

- **WHERE**

A lot of the power of SQL products comes from their ability to link different tables in a single query. As we have seen already, we can link tables with inner and outer joins. In a query, we can also use a subquery to relate data from different tables. We can easily use the result of a subquery in the parent query without dealing with a join. Although queries with joins often have better performance, a subquery structure can seem a little more intuitive at first glance. Additionally, it's always good to have another option available when we build our queries. Both MySQL and SQL Server handle subqueries. Although a SQL subquery is a complete, standalone SQL statement, here, we'll focus on subqueries that return only one column to avoid unneeded complexity as we explore the concept of subqueries. A subquery can certainly return two or more columns, but if the outer query expects only one column, the subquery must return only one column.

Suppose a Packt manager wants a list of products that have zero sales. The **Products** and **OrderItems** tables probably have the information we need because **OrderItems** ties specific products to specific orders. Using what we've learned about SQL joins, we can build a query to answer this question:

```
USE        packt_online_shop;

SELECT     Products.ProductID, Products.ProductName,
           Products.ProductCategoryID
FROM       Products LEFT OUTER JOIN
           OrderItems
ON         Products.ProductID = OrderItems.ProductID
WHERE      OrderItems.ProductID IS NULL
ORDER BY   Products.ProductID;
```

The result will be as follows:

ProductID	ProductName	ProductCategoryID
4	The Gourmet Crockpot	1
8	tomato sauce	3
9	pure vanilla	1

Figure 7.1: A MySQL OUTER JOIN query

In this query, we placed the **Products** table columns we wanted in the **SELECT** clause. The **LEFT OUTER JOIN** matches the rows between the **Products** and **OrderItems** tables. The **LEFT OUTER JOIN** also combines those rows with the **Products** table rows that don't match the **OrderItems** table rows. Although an inner join would match those rows, an inner join will miss **Products** table rows that have no **OrderItems** table matches. In the **WHERE** clause, **IS NULL** filtered out the rows from the **Products** table that have a matching row in the **OrderItems** table. This makes sense because we want the **Products** table rows that don't appear in the **OrderItems** table. The **ORDER BY** clause sorts the result set by **ProductID**. We can also solve this problem with a subquery.

Try the following subquery:

```
USE        packt_online_shop;
SELECT     Products.ProductID, Products.ProductName, Products.ProductCategoryID
FROM       Products
WHERE      Products.ProductID NOT IN

(SELECT    ProductID FROM OrderItems)
ORDER BY   Products.ProductID;
```

You should get the following result:

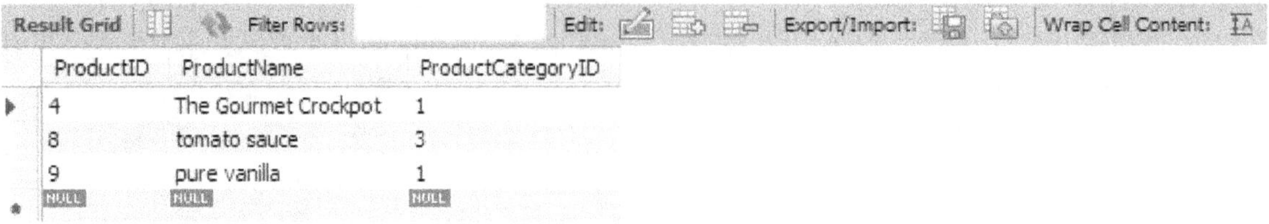

Figure 7.2: A MySQL subquery

We'll focus on the inner query–the subquery–first, and then work it out from there. In this query, we started with the following SQL query, which shows all the **ProductID** values in the **OrderItems** table:

```
SELECT ProductID FROM OrderItems
```

We placed this query inside parentheses to make it a subquery. In the outer query, the **SELECT** and **FROM** clauses have the columns from the **Products** table that we require. The outer query **WHERE** clause uses **NOT IN** to filter out the **Products** table rows that don't exist in the subquery. The **ORDER BY** clause sorted the result set by **ProductID**.

Exercise 7.01: Working with Subqueries

In this exercise, we will use a subquery to find the orders (as **OrderID** values) for the orders with no related rows in the **OrderItems** table. Let's get started:

> **Note**
>
> This exercise will work for both MySQL 8.0.15 and SQL Server 2014.

1. We'll start with the **Orders** table since the **Orders** table ties the orders together with the **OrderItems** table. Build a list of **OrderID** values for all the orders in the **OrderItems** table. Test it and put it aside for now:

```
USE packt_online_shop;

SELECT  OrderID FROM ORDERITEMS;
```

2. Build a list of all the **OrderID** values in the **Orders** table, as follows:

```
USE       packt_online_shop;


SELECT  O.OrderID
FROM    Orders O;
```

3. Add a **WHERE** clause to the query. Use **NOT IN** to filter the **Orders** table with the subquery that we built first. Sort the result set by **OrderID**:

```
USE       packt_online_shop;


SELECT    O.OrderID
FROM      Orders O
WHERE     O.OrderID NOT IN (SELECT OrderID FROM ORDERITEMS)
ORDER BY  O.OrderID;
```

The output is as follows:

Figure 7.3: Printing the ID that's not common for the order in the OrderItems table

In this exercise, we filtered out the order ID for the order that does not have a corresponding entry in the **OrderItems** table.

Activity 7.01: Finding the Product Category Name Using a Subquery

The Packt Online Shop management team needs to know the product category name for the **habanero peppers** product. You are asked to find the required information. Use a subquery to retrieve the requested data. The **Products** and **ProductCategories** tables have the data needed for the solution.

> **Note**
>
> The solution for this activity can be found on page 253.

Case Statements

As we build SQL queries and statements, often, we'll need a way to examine a set of conditions and then return a value based on one of those conditions. The MySQL and SQL Server **CASE** statement does exactly this. For example, we may need a **SELECT** query column that shows different values based on different, specific values or conditions that have been found in a specific database table column. We'll see an illustration of this in the next paragraph. A SQL **CASE** statement will step through a list of conditions and then return a result based on the first matching condition it finds. The **CASE** statements work in the **SELECT**, **UPDATE**, **DELETE**, **WHERE**, and **HAVING** clauses, and they operate a lot like simple **IF...ELSE** statements. Note that the **CASE** statement can't control execution flow in a SQL function or stored procedure. We'll look at functions and stored procedures in more detail later.

We can get *basic* product information from the **Products** table, but for now, we need a list of products that labels those products by **NetRetailPrice**. Specifically, we need to use these rules:

- If **NetRetailPrice** is less than or equal to **24.99**, then label it **Cheap.**

- If **NetRetailPrice** is more than **24.99** and less than or equal to **79.99**, then label it **Mid-price.**

- If **NetRetailPrice** is more than **79.99** and less than or equal to **2499.99**, then label it **Expensive.**

- If **NetRetailPrice** has any other price, then label it **Very Expensive.**

The query will look as follows:

```
USE        packt_online_shop;

SELECT     ProductName, WholesalePrice, NetRetailPrice,
           'Price Point' AS 'Price
   Point', UnitKGWeight
FROM       products
ORDER BY   ProductName;
```

The query will work as follows in MySQL:

	ProductName	WholesalePrice	NetRetailPrice	Price Point	UnitKGWeight
▶	10-mm socket wrench	1.89	3.49	Price Point	0.01800
	Calculatre	17.99	24.99	Price Point	1.00000
	Government Accounting	9.99	14.99	Price Point	1.22000
	habanero peppers	2.99	4.49	Price Point	0.00900
	keyboard wrench	149999.99	399999.95	Price Point	521.38000
	Penwrite	49.99	79.99	Price Point	2.00000
	power cell	29.99	47.89	Price Point	0.29800
	pure vanilla	7.89	10.39	Price Point	0.03200
	The Gourmet Crockpot	19.99	24.99	Price Point	1.63000
	tomato sauce	0.89	1.19	Price Point	0.23200
	Vortex Generator	1999.99	2499.99	Price Point	0.01000

Figure 7.4: Output for the MySQL query

The query returns the **ProductName**, **WholesalePrice**, **NetRetailPrice**, and **UnitKGWeight** columns from the **Products** table, plus a new column called **Price Point** to show the pricing label we want. This query will certainly work as is, but the **Price Point** column will literally show **Price Point** for every row. The SQL **CASE** statement will help with this. We can add the **CASE** statement to the query as follows:

```
USE        packt_online_shop;


SELECT     ProductName, WholesalePrice, NetRetailPrice,
           CASE
               WHEN  NetRetailPrice <= 24.99 THEN 'Cheap'
               WHEN  NetRetailPrice > 24.99 AND NetRetailPrice <=
                     79.99 THEN 'Mid-price'
               WHEN  NetRetailPrice > 79.99 AND NetRetailPrice <=
                     2499.99 THEN 'Expensive'

               ELSE  'Very Expensive'
           END AS 'Price Point',
           UnitKGWeight
FROM       products
ORDER BY   ProductName;
```

The code will look as follows in MySQL:

ProductName	WholesalePrice	NetRetailPrice	Price Point	UnitKGWeight
10-mm socket wrench	1.89	3.49	Cheap	0.01800
Calculatre	17.99	24.99	Cheap	1.00000
Government Accounting	9.99	14.99	Cheap	1.22000
habanero peppers	2.99	4.49	Cheap	0.00900
keyboard wrench	149999.99	399999.95	Very Expensive	521.38000
Penwrite	49.99	79.99	Mid-price	2.00000
power cell	29.99	47.89	Mid-price	0.29800
pure vanilla	7.89	10.39	Cheap	0.03200
The Gourmet Crockpot	19.99	24.99	Cheap	1.63000
tomato sauce	0.89	1.19	Cheap	0.23200
Vortex Generator	1999.99	2499.99	Expensive	0.01000

Figure 7.5: The output of the preceding MySQL case statement

The **CASE** statement starts with the **CASE** keyword and ends with **END**. It has one or more conditions—one for each rule that we want to test. Each condition starts with the **WHEN** keyword, then the condition to test, followed by the **THEN** keyword, and finally the result for that specific condition. As soon as the **CASE** statement finds a true condition, it will execute that condition and then leave the **CASE** statement. The **ELSE** keyword serves as a default if no conditions are true. In MySQL, a **CASE** statement column does not require a column name alias, but we should always include it. MySQL requires a **CASE** statement column name alias.

Exercise 7.02: Using Case Statements

The *Packt Online Shop* calculates its product shipping prices based on *NetRetailPrice * UnitKGWeight*. In a **SELECT** statement, we can place this in a **CASE** statement column to label each product by its shipping cost with the following rules:

- If **NetRetailPrice * UnitKGWeight** is less than or equal to **1.0**, then label it **Cheap**.

- If **NetRetailPrice * UnitKGWeight** is more than **1.0** and less than or equal to **35.00**, then label it **Mid-price**.

- If **NetRetailPrice * UnitKGWeight** is more than **35.00** and less than or equal to **100.00**, then label it **Expensive**.

- If **NetRetailPrice * UnitKGWeight** has any other price, then label it **Very Expensive**.

> **Note**
>
> This exercise will work for both MySQL 8.0.15 and SQL Server 2014.

Perform the following steps to complete this exercise:

1. We'll start with the **Products** table. First, let's build a basic list of products, their net retail price, and their unit kilogram values:

```
USE     packt_online_shop;


SELECT  ProductName, NetRetailPrice, UnitKGWeight
FROM    products;
```

2. Add a **Shipping Cost** column to the **SELECT** statement. Add only one condition to test the overall idea. Remember that we'll need a calculation. Ignore the **NULL** values in the **Shipping Cost** column:

```
USE     packt_online_shop;


SELECT  ProductName, NetRetailPrice, UnitKGWeight,
    CASE
        WHEN (NetRetailPrice * UnitKGWeight) <= 1.0 THEN 'Cheap'
    END AS 'Shipping Cost'
FROM    products;
```

3. Everything looks good, so add all the conditions. Remember the **ELSE** condition to cover the default:

```
USE packt_online_shop;


SELECT ProductName, NetRetailPrice, UnitKGWeight,
    CASE
        WHEN (NetRetailPrice * UnitKGWeight) <= 1.0 THEN 'Cheap'
        WHEN (NetRetailPrice * UnitKGWeight) > 1.0 AND(NetRetailPrice *
            UnitKGWeight) <= 35.00 THEN 'Mid-price'
        WHEN (NetRetailPrice * UnitKGWeight) > 35.00 AND
            (NetRetailPrice * UnitKGWeight) <= 100.00 THEN 'Expensive'
        ELSE 'Very Expensive'
    END AS 'Shipping Cost'
FROM products;
```

The output is as follows:

ProductName	NetRetailPrice	UnitKGWeight	Shipping Cost
Calculatre	24.99	1.00000	Mid-price
Penwrite	79.99	2.00000	Very Expensive
Vortex Generator	2499.99	0.01000	Mid-price
The Gourmet Crockpot	24.99	1.63000	Expensive
Government Accounting	14.99	1.22000	Mid-price
habanero peppers	4.49	0.00900	Cheap
10-mm socket wrench	3.49	0.01800	Cheap
tomato sauce	1.19	0.23200	Cheap
pure vanilla	10.39	0.03200	Cheap
keyboard wrench	399999.95	521.38000	Very Expensive
power cell	47.89	0.29800	Mid-price

Figure 7.6: Output from using the CASE statement

In this exercise, we saw how we can use **CASE** to print different values depending on different conditions.

Activity 7.02: Categorizing the Shipments Using CASE Statements

You have been asked to build a list of order shipment date categories for a report dated December 15, 2019.

The business rules define shipment dates before December 15, 2010 as *Past Shipment Dates*. A shipment date on or after December 15, 2010, but before December 15, 2019, is defined as a *Recent Shipment Date*. Anything else is defined as a *Future Shipment Date*

Use a **CASE** statement to build the required list, implementing a YYYY-MM-DD format for the date values. The result set should contain the order number, shipment date, and shipment date category columns.

The **orders** table has the raw data that you will need.

> **Note**
>
> The solution for this activity can be found on page 253.

Views

As a business grows, its financial management and reporting needs will probably grow as well. Management will turn to the database for answers. Every database query will be different, but eventually, it will become clear that the same, or very similar, **SELECT** statements seem to come up again and again. The same **SELECT** statement could show up in a subquery, or maybe in a stored procedure, which is something we'll learn about soon. That statement could become really complicated, with a lot of tables, outer joins, **CASE** statements of its own. If we could somehow save that **SELECT** statement and then use it like a table as a basis for other SQL statements and queries, we could save a lot of time and effort. SQL views will help solve this problem.

SQL views can encapsulate complex queries, exposing the columns in a much cleaner way for use by other queries. In other words, a view can join multiple tables together in a defined, structured way, and substitute all of that complexity with a view name that operates just like a table name. Views can also limit access to their component tables, which increases security. We can assign access to a view to different users in a secure, granular way. Additionally, a SQL view can make database maintenance easier if different queries and resources throughout the database use that view.

One change in one view could save us having to make the same changes in potentially hundreds of other database queries. Note, however, that we should avoid **UPDATE** operations with views because the security aspects of even simple views can make this really difficult, and views of even moderate complexity won't support updates.

Think of a SQL view as a predefined **SELECT** statement with one or more tables, and at least one column from one table. A view returns only table columns. Once defined, other SQL queries and statements can use that view as another table. A SQL view can isolate tables and columns securely, thus exposing only those data resources that other stakeholders may need. Additionally, if multiple database resources use the same view and the tables behind the view change, we would only need to change the view itself, that is, in a one-to-many way. Nothing that relies on the view would have to change. Without a view, we would have to change each of those resources, which would become a major pain point. The following code will convert the query into a view named **CUSTOMER_PRODUCT_VIEW**:

```
USE     packt_online_shop;
GO  --  Include for SQL Server; remove for MySQL


CREATE VIEW CUSTOMER_PRODUCT_VIEW
AS


SELECT  CONCAT(customers.FirstName, ' ', customers.LastName) AS
        'CustomerName', orders.OrderDate, products.ProductName
FROM    customers INNER JOIN orders ON
```

```
      customers.CustomerID = orders.CustomerID
    INNER JOIN orderitems ON
      orders.OrderID = orderitems.OrderID
    INNER JOIN products ON
      orderitems.ProductID = products.ProductID;
```

The query will return the following output on its successful execution:

100	19:57:26	CREATE VIEW CUSTOMER_PRODUCT_VIEW AS SELECT CONCAT(customers.FirstName, ' ', customers.LastName) AS 'CustomerName', orde...	0 row(s) affected	0.687 sec

Figure 7.7: A MySQL view

Enter the following query:

```
SELECT  CustomerName, OrderDate, ProductName
FROM    customer_product_view;
```

The output will look as follows:

Result Grid | Filter Rows: | Export: | Wrap Cell Content:

CustomerName	OrderDate	ProductName
Grace Hopper	2017-03-02 00:00:00	Calculatre
Grace Hopper	2017-03-02 00:00:00	Penwrite
Grace Hopper	2017-03-02 00:00:00	Vortex Generator
Ada Lovelace	2317-03-07 00:00:00	Government Accounting
Ada Lovelace	2317-03-07 00:00:00	10-mm socket wrench
Joseph Crater	1930-04-19 00:00:00	power cell
Joseph Crater	1930-04-19 00:00:00	keyboard wrench
Nellie Bly	2930-04-19 00:00:00	Penwrite
Nellie Bly	2930-04-19 00:00:00	habanero peppers
Nellie Bly	2930-04-19 00:00:00	Government Accounting
Ada Lovelace	2317-03-18 00:00:00	keyboard wrench
Ada Lovelace	2317-03-18 00:00:00	10-mm socket wrench

Figure 7.8: Displaying the values in a view

Exercise 7.03: Building a View

Build a SQL view that shows *Packt Online Shop* customers and their per-product spending by returning the **CustomerID**, **OrderDate**, **ProductID**, **ProductName**, and **PerProductSpending** columns. Let's get started:

1. First, build and test a basic SQL query for the list we need:

```
USE      PACKT_ONLINE_SHOP;

SELECT   customers.CustomerID, orders.OrderDate, products.ProductID,
         products.ProductName, orderitems.Quantity *
         orderitems.UnitPrice AS 'PerProductSpending'
FROM     customers INNER JOIN orders ON
             customers.CustomerID = orders.CustomerID
         INNER JOIN orderitems ON
             orders.OrderID = orderitems.OrderID
         INNER JOIN products ON
             orderitems.ProductID = products.ProductID;
```

2. Add some statements to build a view around this tested SQL statement. Name it **PACKT_VIEW_1** and use the **CREATE VIEW {view name} AS** syntax and execute it:

```
USE      PACKT_ONLINE_SHOP;
CREATE VIEW PACKT_VIEW_1
AS
SELECT   customers.CustomerID, orders.OrderDate,
         products.ProductID, products.ProductName,
         orderitems.Quantity * orderitems.UnitPrice AS
         'PerProductSpending'
FROM     customers INNER JOIN orders ON
             customers.CustomerID = orders.CustomerID
         INNER JOIN orderitems ON
             orders.OrderID = orderitems.OrderID
         INNER JOIN products ON
             orderitems.ProductID = products.ProductID;
```

3. Test the **PACKT_VIEW_1** view, as follows:

```
USE      PACKT_ONLINE_SHOP;

SELECT   CustomerID, OrderDate, ProductID, ProductName,
         PerProductSpending
FROM     PACKT_VIEW_1
WHERE    PerProductSpending > 14.99;
```

The output is as follows:

CustomerID	OrderDate	ProductID	ProductName	PerProductSpending
2	2017-03-02 00:00:00	1	Calculatre	49.98
2	2017-03-02 00:00:00	2	Penwrite	79.99
2	2017-03-02 00:00:00	3	Vortex Generator	4999.98
4	1930-04-19 00:00:00	11	power cell	191.56
4	1930-04-19 00:00:00	10	keyboard wrench	2799999.65
7	2930-04-19 00:00:00	2	Penwrite	159.98
3	2317-03-18 00:00:00	10	keyboard wrench	799999.90

Figure 7.9: PACKT_VIEW_1 view

Activity 7.03: Building a View

Consider you have been asked to generate an invoice for the *Packt Online Shop*.

To do this, you need to build a view that returns an **order ID**, **product ID**, item quantity, unit price, subtotal (as *item quantity * unit price*) for each item, and the subtotal category columns for the customers who have a last name of **Atreides**. Consider the following rules for the subtotal category:

- If **Subtotal** is less than **$25.00**, **Subtotal Category** is **Small**.

- If **Subtotal** is less than or equal to **$79.99**, **Subtotal Category** is **Medium**.

- If **Subtotal** exceeds **$79.99**, **Subtotal Category** is **Large**.

> **Note**
>
> The solution for this activity can be found on page 254.

Summary

In this chapter, we saw that subqueries, **CASE** statements, and views offer ways for us to build powerful queries that expand and extend the techniques we looked at in earlier chapters. Subqueries offer a way for us to relate multiple tables in one query, in addition to the join technique. Queries can use **CASE** statements to behave differently, based on defined data conditions, in a clean, structured way. Views offer a way to summarize, encapsulate, and gather data from different tables in a flexible, efficient, and secure way. These concepts will become important as we proceed with the next chapter and the remainder of this book.

In the next chapter, we will look at some advanced SQL concepts and see how we can effectively program and automate queries.

8

SQL Programming

Overview

In this chapter, we'll see how we can build programs and software that reliably automate database operations, thus returning huge savings of time, effort, and money.

By the end of this chapter, you'll be able to build and execute stored procedures that automate database operations. You will be able to build and execute functions that encapsulate repeated statements in defined, structured units. Moreover, you will be equipped to build and execute triggers that automatically execute database operations when predefined events occur.

Introduction

In the previous chapter, we explored SQL subqueries, CASE statements, and views. These features offer great flexibility when we work with database resources. To use these features, and all the other SQL product query features we have seen so far, we type a SQL command into the development environment, run it, and look for the results somewhere within that environment. This approach certainly works well enough, and we relied on it as we learned about MySQL. However, it won't work for applications that rely on SQL database products as data resources. We need a product feature that can somehow automate the queries we want to run and reliably handle all the required management and overhead. Fortunately, modern SQL products, including MySQL, offer the following features to solve this problem:

- Stored procedures

- Functions

- Triggers

These features involve actual programming, and in this chapter, we'll explore the basic programming concepts. We'll be working on the PACKT_ONLINE_SHOP database to understand these SQL programming features.

Programming for SQL Products – The Basics

MySQL programming, like all programming and software development, relies on a small set of core ideas. Variables are an important part of that idea set, and we'll see how they work as we begin to work with MySQL.

When we build programs in MySQL or in any other software development language, we use variables as *buckets* to hold information, or values, that the programs need. A variable has a name, and in most software products—including MySQL—it has an information type. In a structured, predictable way, the program can change the value of a variable based on the behavior of the program, information that comes into the program from outside of the program, or both. A variable will reliably hold the last value assigned to it. Before we look at SQL stored procedures and functions, we'll see how variables operate in MySQL.

Launch MySQL and place the following statements in the editor or the query window:

```
SET @var1 = NULL;          -- 1. Declare variable @var1
SELECT @var1;              -- 2. Output the value of @var1
SET @var1 = 3;             -- 3. Set @var1 to 3
SELECT @var1;              -- 4. Output the value of @var1
SET @var1 = @var1 - 7;     -- 5. Subtract 7 from @var1
SELECT @var1;              -- 6. Output the value of @var1
SET @var1 = @var1 + 5;     -- 7. Add 5 to @var1
SELECT @var1;              -- 8. Output the value of @var1
```

In each line, the text after the two consecutive hyphen characters, --, will not execute as they are comments. We can place the two consecutive hyphen characters anywhere, as shown here. These characters work the same way in a stored procedure. Therefore, we have to be careful with them because, in the middle of a stored procedure statement, they could lead to an error because SQL will ignore these characters and everything after them.

We can use this feature to write comments in the programs we build. Comments help explain how programs work. Although this example has short, simple comments, all the software we build should include detailed, descriptive comments to explain its development history, important engineering ideas, and so on to help later programmers—including you—understand how it works. Let's look at what each line states:

- Line 1 shows the first use of the **@var1** variable in this set of MySQL statements. MySQL does not require special statements, data types, or code to initially declare a variable; the first use of a variable is enough. To assign a value to a variable, MySQL expects the **SET** keyword, then the variable name, an equals sign, and then the actual value itself. Always prefix the variable name with the **@** symbol, every time you use that variable. When we place a variable name with **SET** on the left of an equal sign, as seen in lines 1, 3, 5, and 7, MySQL expects that statement to assign a value, even **NULL**, to that variable. For example, line 1 assigns **NULL** to **@var1**.

- Line 2 uses the **SELECT** keyword, which we saw earlier in this course, to output the latest value of **@var1**.

- Line 3 assigns a non-null value to **@var1**.

- Line 4 outputs that value.

- Line 5 subtracts 7 from **@var1**, changing its value in a predictable way.

- Line 6 once again outputs the latest value of **@var1**.

- Line 7 adds 5 to **@var1**.

- Line 8 outputs the latest **@var1** value.

MySQL requires a semicolon at the end of every statement of a stored procedure, a function, and a trigger. To see how these statement looks like In MYSQL, refer *Figure 8.1*:

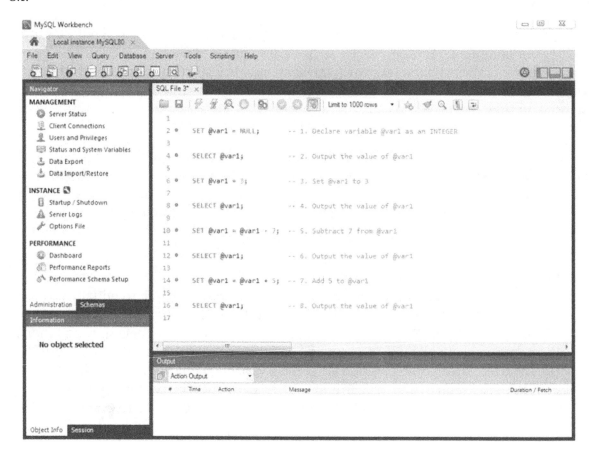

Figure 8.1: MySQL statements

To run all the statements at once, click the yellow lightning bolt at the top of the code pane, located near the top. MySQL now looks like this:

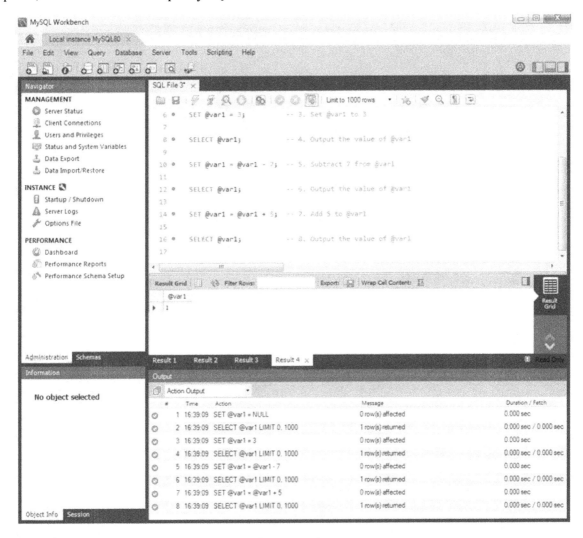

Figure 8.2: Result of running the MySQL statements

To run all the statements at once, click the yellow lightning bolt at the top of the code pane, located near the top. MySQL now looks like this:

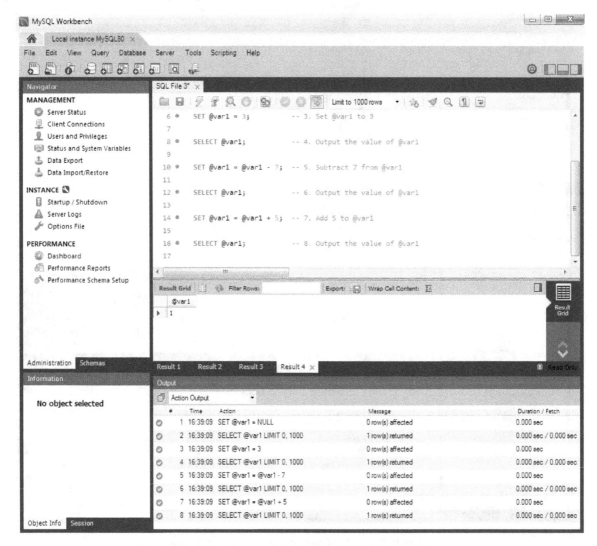

Figure 8.3: Example execution of SQL variable statements

MySQL shows diagnostics about each executed statement in the **Output** window. The **Result Grid** tabs show the actual output of each MySQL statement. As we can see from the preceding screenshot, there are several tabs that show the result. Here, we highlighted the **Result 4** tab. Clicking the **Result 1** tab will show the following output in **Result Grid**:

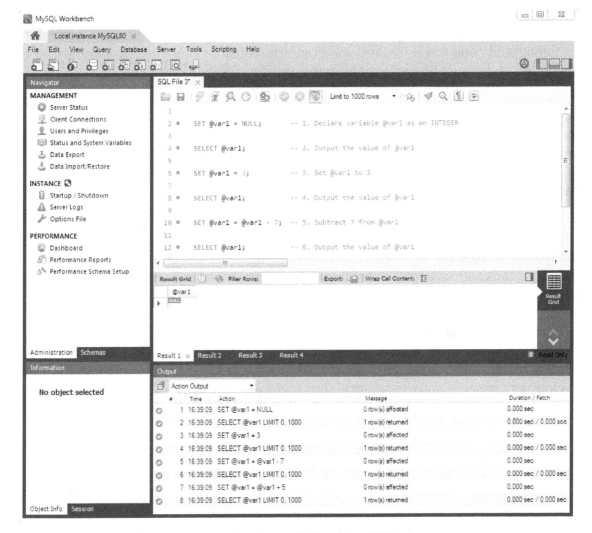

Figure 8.4: @var1: a variable with a NULL value

Everything makes sense, except for the output of the first **SELECT** statement. The **SELECT** **@var1** variable returns **NULL**.

When we declared the **@var1** variable, we assigned a **NULL** value to it. MySQL does not necessarily see this as wrong, at least in this example. However, keep in mind that it can cause problems as you build SQL programs. This happens because MySQL, a program that depends on the data MySQL returns, or both, may expect a non-null value at certain points.

MySQL allows us to highlight, or *paint*, specific lines in the programs we build for fine-grained control of the lines we execute. Depending on the specific situation, sometimes the highlighted code will work, and sometimes it won't. To execute this correctly, all the highlighted code must be correct because it must all work in one *batch*.

We should use this *painting* technique with caution, especially on a live, or production, database. We can easily run statements by mistake, which could damage live data. In *Chapter 11, Advanced SQL*, we'll learn about **transactions**, a technique that offers greater control and reversibility when we execute SQL statements.

Stored Procedures

MySQL defines a group of one or more SQL statements as a stored procedure, and this definition extends to other database products. A stored procedure has features that are similar to those of other programming languages and technologies. A stored procedure can easily accept input values from other stored procedures and even other programs. A university database system, for example, may rely on a stored procedure–probably many inter-related stored procedures–to efficiently and reliably calculate the current tuition balances at any time for one, some, or all of its students. The overall calculation will probably become complex, in part because it will pull data from many different tables. If the developers use stored procedures to build the solution, both the development process and the solution they build will become much more efficient, reliable, maintainable, and secure.

Stored procedures offer huge benefits. A stored procedure can gather complex SQL statements and queries into one package that returns consistent results and behaves in consistent ways each time we execute or call it. With proper configuration, external programs and applications can execute stored procedures in a clean, reliable way, and stored procedures can return result sets to the programs that call them in a structured, dependable way. Stored procedures have great flexibility because they use key concepts of programming and software development, as we'll see. A stored procedure can return, update, and delete table data. A stored procedure can call other stored procedures. In addition, SQL products compile stored procedure code, which optimizes its performance and scalability, even for solutions with heavy traffic volumes. This aspect of stored procedures enhances security because compilation converts the stored procedure code into machine code, which is difficult to read. A university administration department, for example, may use stored procedures in its database system because stored procedures offer an ideal way to translate complex business rules into clean, efficient, maintainable programs.

When we use MySQL to work with a specific database, the MySQL installation will see other databases. The MySQL installation process creates some of those databases for MySQL to use, and although we can see them ourselves, we need to leave them alone for now. In our case, we'll have at least the **PACKT_ONLINE_SHOP** database. Other MySQL resources, in other organizations, may have additional databases in their data resources. A specific database owns every SQL stored procedure within it, just like a specific database owns every SQL table within it. To build a stored procedure, we must first choose its database. In MySQL, choose the **PACKT_ONLINE_SHOP** database from the dropdown, as shown here:

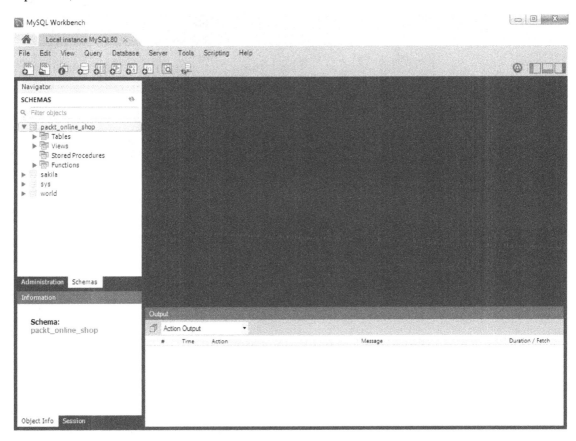

Figure 8.5: Choosing the specific database for the stored procedure

Next, drill down to **Stored Procedures** in the upper-left **SCHEMAS** directory, right-click, and then click **Create Stored Procedure...**, as shown here:

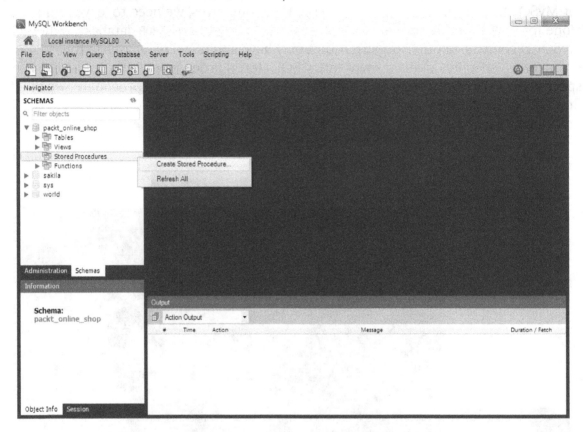

Figure 8.6: Creating a stored procedure

The stored procedure creation tool will open, as shown here:

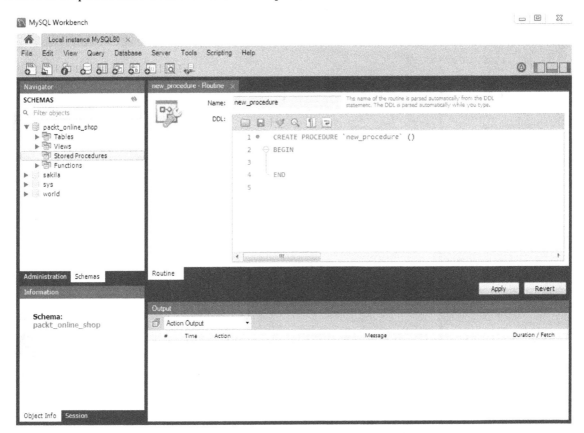

Figure 8.7: The CREATE PROCEDURE tool

Now, we can build a stored procedure for the **PACKT_ONLINE_SHOP** database. This code categorizes the products, depending on the product's price:

```
USE packt_online_shop;

SELECT     ProductName, WholesalePrice, NetRetailPrice,
           CASE
               WHEN     NetRetailPrice <= 24.99 THEN 'Cheap'
               WHEN     NetRetailPrice > 24.99 AND
                        NetRetailPrice <= 79.99 THEN 'Mid-price'
               WHEN     NetRetailPrice > 79.99 AND
                        NetRetailPrice <= 2499.99 THEN 'Expensive'
               ELSE     'Very Expensive'
           END AS 'Price Point',
           UnitKGWeight
FROM       products
ORDER BY   ProductName;
```

The output for this will be as follows:

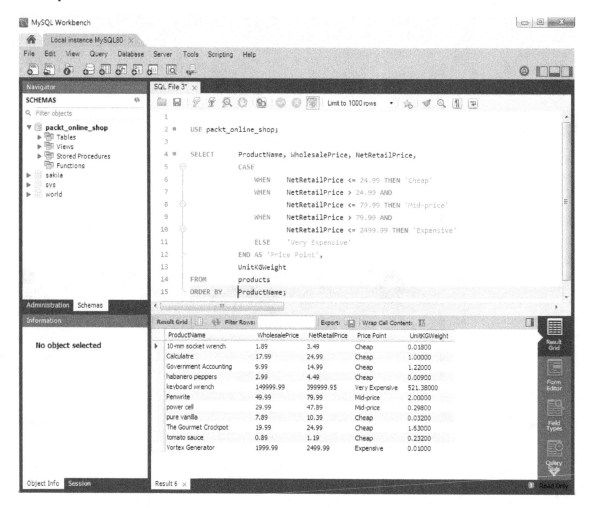

Figure 8.8: A MySQL query

This works well enough, but suppose the company's management now wants a new web page, but only for the products with a net retail price below a specific dollar price level. The following is a mockup of the web page:

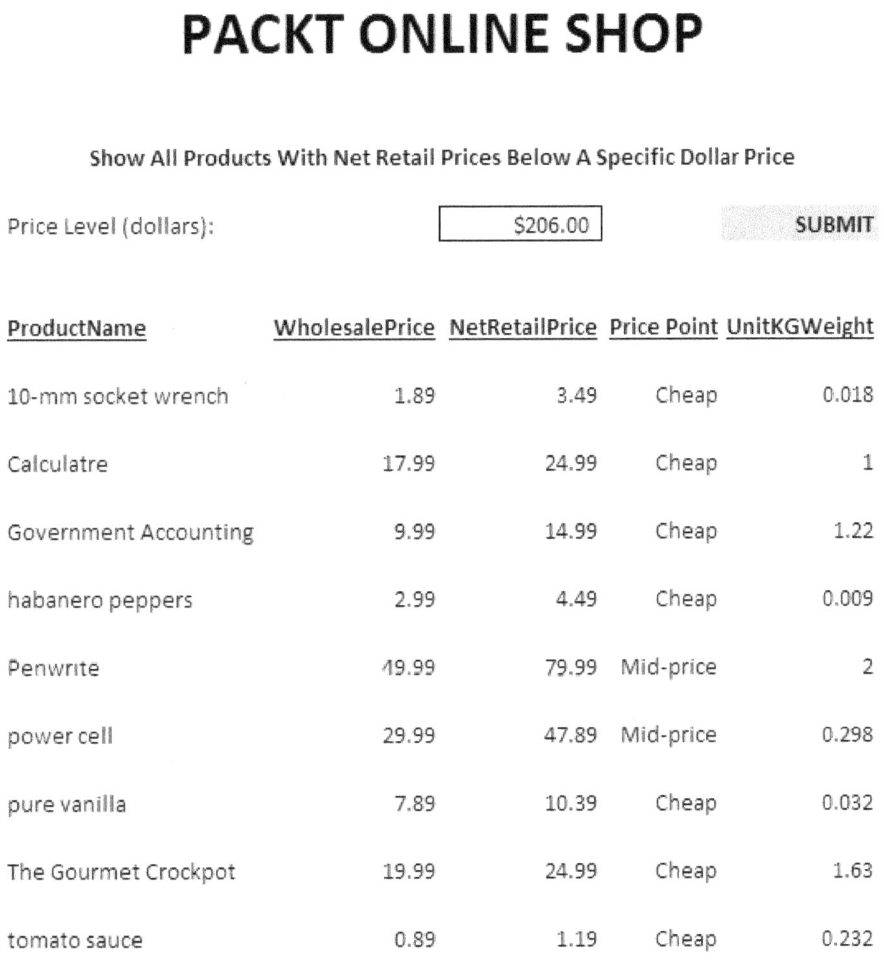

PACKT ONLINE SHOP

Show All Products With Net Retail Prices Below A Specific Dollar Price

Price Level (dollars): $206.00   SUBMIT

ProductName	WholesalePrice	NetRetailPrice	Price Point	UnitKGWeight
10-mm socket wrench	1.89	3.49	Cheap	0.018
Calculatre	17.99	24.99	Cheap	1
Government Accounting	9.99	14.99	Cheap	1.22
habanero peppers	2.99	4.49	Cheap	0.009
Penwrite	49.99	79.99	Mid-price	2
power cell	29.99	47.89	Mid-price	0.298
pure vanilla	7.89	10.39	Cheap	0.032
The Gourmet Crockpot	19.99	24.99	Cheap	1.63
tomato sauce	0.89	1.19	Cheap	0.232

Figure 8.9: A mockup of the web page

This shows the information that management wants. We need a flexible way to somehow filter the rows by net retail price and then pass those filtered rows to the company web server. A stored procedure will solve this problem. When a web page user clicks **Submit** on that page, the web server can send the request to the database server, and the database server will return the requested data as expected. Starting with the **SELECT** statement, just above it, place the following code:

```
CREATE PROCEDURE 'spFilterProductsByNRP' (IN priceLevel FLOAT)
BEGIN

# to test:      USE packt_online_shop;
#               CALL spFilterProductsByNRP(10.50);

SELECT     ProductName, WholesalePrice, NetRetailPrice,
           CASE
               WHEN NetRetailPrice <= 24.99 THEN 'Cheap'

               WHEN NetRetailPrice > 24.99 AND
                   NetRetailPrice <= 79.99 THEN 'Mid-price'

               WHEN NetRetailPrice > 79.99 AND
                   NetRetailPrice <= 2499.99 THEN 'Expensive'

               ELSE 'Very Expensive'
           END AS 'Price Point',
           UnitKGWeight
FROM       products
WHERE      NetRetailPrice <= priceLevel
ORDER BY   ProductName;

END
```

It will look like the following in MySQL Workbench:

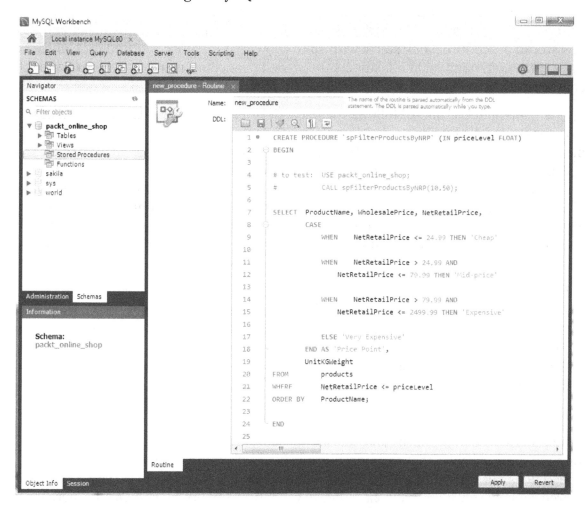

Figure 8.10: Building a stored procedure in a MySQL query window

This code looks a lot like the original **SELECT** statement we used earlier, with extra lines. Line 1 has the **CREATE PROCEDURE** keywords, with the name of the stored procedure. Different software development shops have different naming requirements, of course; this stored procedure name starts with **sp** to show that it names a stored procedure. The **CREATE** command on line 1 expects the stored procedure name to be in backtick ' characters.

At line 1, an input parameter follows the back-ticked stored procedure name. An input parameter works a lot like a variable, and we declare it like a variable. When another program calls a stored procedure, the input parameters will take information in a specific format from that other program and pass that information into the stored procedure to use. We call a value that moves from the calling program to the receiving program an *argument*. When that value arrives at the receiving program, we call it a *parameter*. A parameter declaration starts with a name, and we use **@** as the first character of the name. The input parameter type follows. In this case, **@priceLevel** has a float data type. A float data type works like a decimal value.

For the input parameter, the command expects the keyword **IN**, the parameter name, and the data type of that parameter. The parameter name does not start with a **@** character. If necessary, separate multiple parameters, each with this format, by commas. The comments at lines 4 and 5 are not required, but we'll see shortly that they will help us when we test the stored procedure. These comments start with a **#**, another valid MySQL commenting character. Notice the following **WHERE** clause on line 21:

```
WHERE      NetRetailPrice <= @priceLevel
```

When this stored procedure runs, this **WHERE** clause uses the **@priceLevel** parameter value to filter the rows that the stored procedure will return. The input parameter on line 21 does not start with a **@** character. Remember that in a real-world situation, a stored procedure will probably have heavy validation and error checking, to increase its reliability.

Although we can see the stored procedure code in the stored procedure window, we must compile, or build it, to make it an actual **PACKT_ONLINE_SHOP** database component. To do so, click the **Apply** button located in the bottom-right corner of the window.

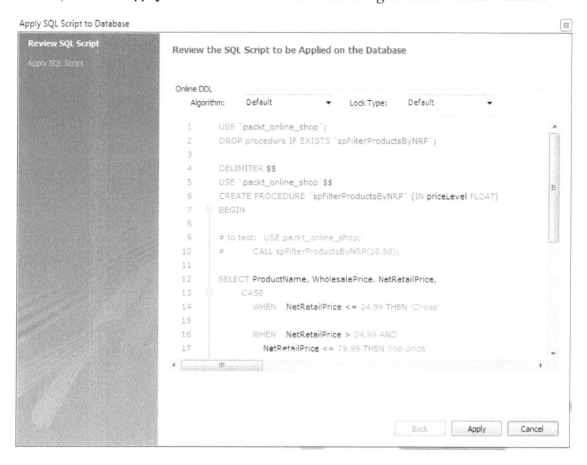

Figure 8.11: Building a new MySQL stored procedure

Click **Finish** in the window to return to the MySQL Workbench, as seen here:

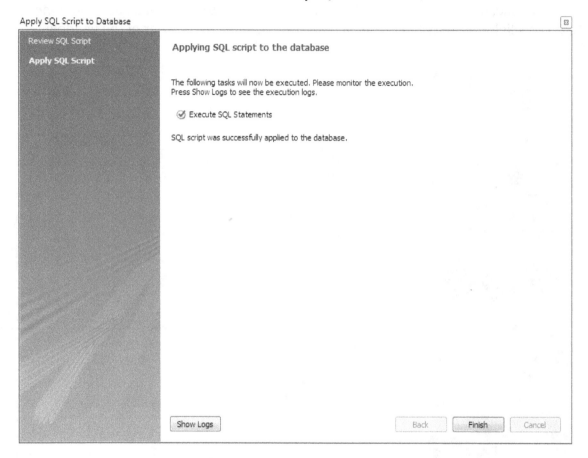

Figure 8.12: Building a new MySQL stored procedure – last step

To test the new stored procedure in the Workbench, drill down to **File** | **New Query** tab to open a new window.

The following MySQL command will run the stored procedure:

```
USE packt_online_shop;
CALL spFilterProductsByNRP(10.50);
```

It starts with the keyword **CALL**, then the stored procedure name, then open/close parentheses, and the argument of value **10.50** inside the parentheses. The line ends with a semicolon. Place multiple argument values in the parentheses, separating those values with commas. Run the program by clicking the execute button:

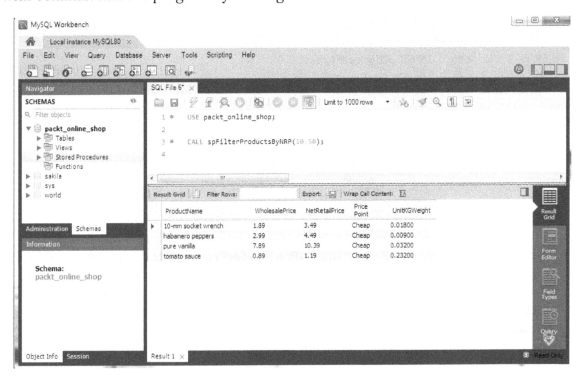

Figure 8.13: Testing a MySQL stored procedure

The result set should appear below the editor window.

Exercise 8.01: Building a MySQL Stored Procedure That Returns a List of Packt Online Shop Order Details

The *Packt Online Shop* managers need a report that shows the customer names, order numbers, and order dates. They may run this report at any time, and whenever they run it, they will need the latest, most up-to-date information possible. A stored procedure will generate the required information and solve the problem in an efficient way. Build a MySQL stored procedure to return the customer names, order numbers, and order dates from the **PACKT_ONLINE_SHOP** database. Only return the orders with order dates on or before a given order date parameter. Display the name in one column, in the following format, and name that column **Customer Name**. Remember the space between **FirstName** and **LastName**. Sort the result set by **Customer Name**.

1. Type the following query to build a stored procedure:

```
use packt_online_shop;
CREATE PROCEDURE 'spCustomerOrders' (IN orderDate datetime)

SELECT     CONCAT(C.FirstName, ' ', C.LastName) as 'Customer Name',
        O.OrderNumber, O.OrderDate
FROM     orders O INNER JOIN customers C ON
        C.CustomerID = O.CustomerID
WHERE     O.OrderDate <= orderDate

ORDER BY     'Customer Name';
```

2. Run the query. This results in the following output:

3 08:36:07 CREATE PROCEDURE 'spCustomerOrders' (IN orderDate datetime) SELECT CONCAT(C.FirstName, '', C.LastName) as 'Customer Name', O.OrderNumb...   0 row(s) affected   0.266 sec

Figure 8.14: A MySQL stored procedure

Eventually, we might need to change the **spFilterProductsByNRP** stored procedure. Suppose that the Packt company management likes how the web page supported by this stored procedure works, but now wants it to show the available quantity column from the products table. The web page will need some changes, of course, but as the data source, the **spFilterProductsByNRP** stored procedure will also need some changes. We can easily do this in MySQL.

Right-click the stored procedure name in the **Navigator** window and click **Alter Stored Procedure**, add an additional column as shown in the following screenshot, and add the **Apply** and **Finish** buttons:

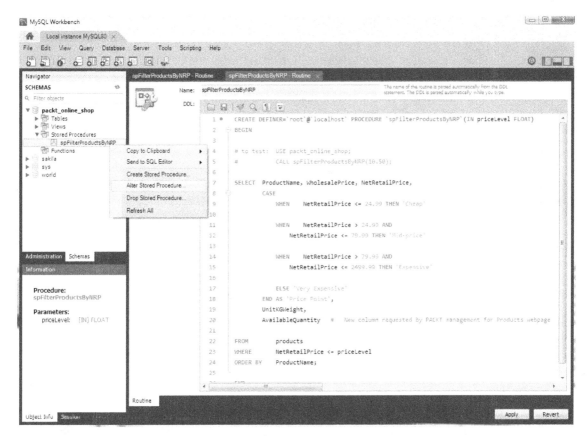

Figure 8.15: Edit an existing MySQL stored procedure

Drill down to **New Query Editor** window. The stored procedure will open in a new window, as shown here:

```
USE [PACKT_ONLINE_SHOP]
GO


SET ANSI_NULLS ON
GO


SET QUOTED_IDENTIFIER ON
GO


ALTER PROCEDURE [dbo].[spFilterProductsByNRP]

    @priceLevel float


AS
```

```
        -- to test: spFilterProductsByNRP 206.00

SELECT    ProductName, WholesalePrice, NetRetailPrice,
          CASE
              WHEN NetRetailPrice <= 24.99 THEN 'Cheap'
              WHEN NetRetailPrice > 24.99 AND
                   NetRetailPrice <= 79.99 THEN 'Mid-price'
              WHEN  NetRetailPrice > 79.99 AND
                   NetRetailPrice <= 2499.99 THEN 'Expensive'
              ELSE  'Very Expensive'
          END AS 'Price Point',
          UnitKGWeight,
          AvailableQuantity    --    New column requested by
          PACKT management for Product Price Report
          UnitKGWeight
FROM      products
WHERE     NetRetailPrice <= @priceLevel
ORDER BY  ProductName;
GO
```

This results in the following output:

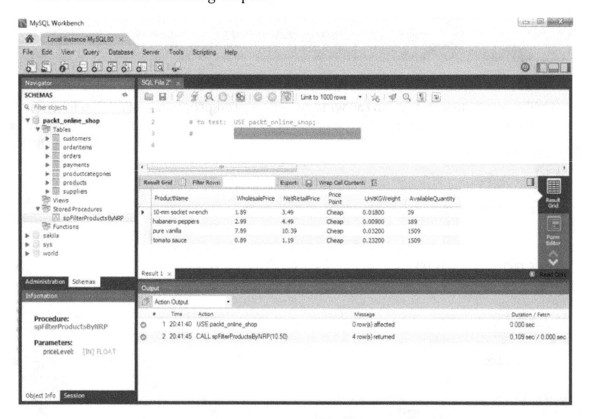

Figure 8.16: Editing an existing MySQL stored procedure

MySQL added lines 1 to 9, and line 38. We can ignore these added lines. The **ALTER** command on line 12 will save the changes that we make to this stored procedure, specifically the new column we added at line 33. When we **ALTER** a stored procedure, MySQL will ignore all the comments in the code, including those on lines 18 and 33. Click the blue cross to verify the SQL syntax, and then click **Execute**. Paint and run the test statement on line 18, as shown here:

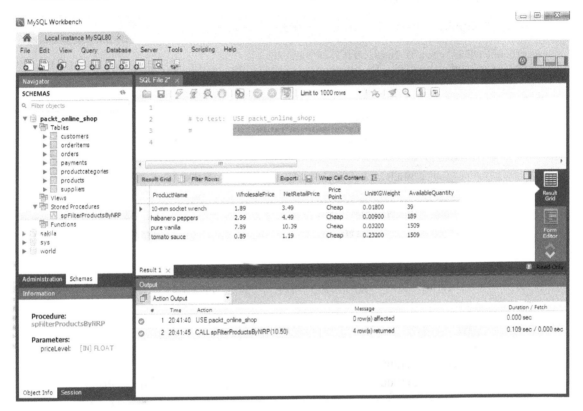

Figure 8.17: Testing an existing MySQL stored procedure

Now, let's **ALTER** a MySQL stored procedure to understand how to edit a stored procedure.

Exercise 8.02: Altering a MySQL Stored Procedure

The Packt managers now need an extra filter for the **spFilterProductsByNRP** MySQL stored procedure reports in order to filter by product weight. Add an additional parameter to the MySQL **spFilterProductsByNRP** stored procedure to filter by **UnitKGWeight**. The stored procedures should return rows with product weight values less than or equal to an additional specified weight parameter value.

1. Enter the following query to alter the stored procedure:

```
CREATE DEFINER='root'@'localhost' PROCEDURE
  `spFilterProductsByNRP`(IN priceLevel FLOAT, IN unitWeight FLOAT)


BEGIN


SELECT          ProductName, WholesalePrice, NetRetailPrice,
                CASE
                    WHEN    NetRetailPrice <= 24.99 THEN 'Cheap'

                    WHEN    NetRetailPrice > 24.99 AND
                            NetRetailPrice <= 79.99 THEN 'Mid-price'

                    WHEN    NetRetailPrice > 79.99 AND
                            NetRetailPrice <= 2499.99 THEN 'Expensive'

                          ELSE 'Very Expensive'
                    END AS 'Price Point',
                UnitKGWeight,
                AvailableQuantity     #      New column requested by PACKT
                                  #      management for Products webpage
FROM            products
WHERE           NetRetailPrice          <= priceLevel AND
                UnitKGWeight   <= unitWeight # Filter with unitWeight parameter value
ORDER BY        ProductName;


END
```

2. Run the query to test the stored procedure:

```
USE packt_online_shop;
filterProductsByNRP(10.50, 0.2);
```

You should get the following output:

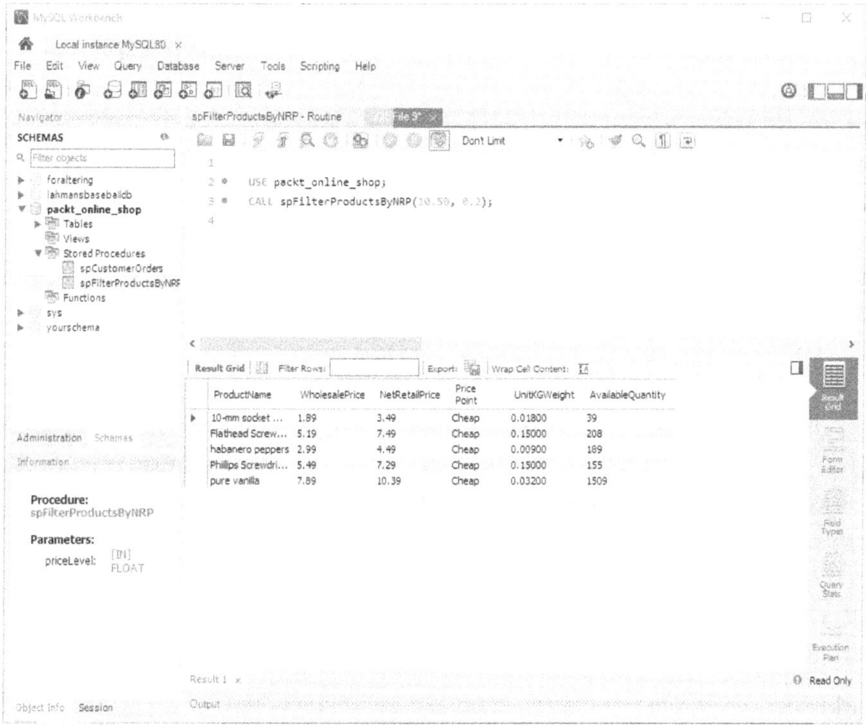

Figure 8.18: Altered stored procedures

Activity 8.01: Building a Stored Procedure

The *Packt Online Shop* management needs to know which orders have order item quantities that fall below the given value limits. These value limits could change, depending on specific management reporting needs. Build a stored procedure that returns all the orders with total order item quantity values that fall at or below an integer filter value. The stored procedure will have an integer input parameter that will become the filter value. These steps will help you to complete this activity:

1. First, build a basic SQL query. The query will add specific values in a specific column, so use the **SUM** function in the **SELECT** clause. The **SUM** function will need a **GROUP BY** clause in the **SELECT** query. Sort the result set by **OrderID**.

2. Build a stored procedure around the query and include the filter value in the **SELECT** query's **HAVING** clause.

> **Note**
>
> The solution for this activity can be found on page 256.

Functions

The complexity of the software we build expands as we build it. In part, this becomes unavoidable because the mass of the software itself also expands. However, we can definitely avoid the complexity of repeating blocks of code. Modern software development products give us a way to place one copy of a repeating block of code in one defined location. Then, in the software, we can replace all repeated instances of that code block with a call to that one defined copy of the code. We call this one defined block of software a function. Think of a function as a box that takes in zero or more values and returns one or more values in a structured way. A function simplifies software, and it makes the software we build much easier to maintain, repair, and enhance. If a program has the same identical code block repeated one hundred times, the same required change to all of those blocks would require the same work and testing—one hundred times. If we replace those blocks with one hundred calls to a single function, and in some way call the function when and where we need it, we can change and test the function code in one location. This would instantly give us an incredibly huge saving in time, effort, and expense. MySQL offers built-in functions that we can directly call in the Workbench query windows and in the stored procedures we build. MySQL and SQL products generally, include built-in functions that include the following categories:

- Date and time

- Datatype conversion

- Mathematical

- Statistical

- String

Even better, MySQL offers us a way to build our own custom functions. We'll see both types of MySQL functions. For example, we could easily build MySQL functions that calculate the number of hours between the time of function execution and the first second of January 1 of that year. These functions could have major value for finance, insurance, and inventory management applications. SQL functions offer many of the advantages of SQL stored procedures as described earlier, but a function does not offer the exact same advantages and flexibility. Functions can't update or delete table data. Functions can't call stored procedures. Additionally, external programs and applications can't call a SQL function as easily.

Launch MySQL and type these statements in the query window:

```
SET @var1 = NULL, @var2 = 'A test string';    # 1.       Declare variables and
                              #              assign a value to a variable

SET @var1 = 3;          # 2. Set @var1 to 3

SELECT LOG(@var1);         # 3. Select the natural log of @var1

SELECT @var1;        # 4. @var1 did not change

SELECT EXP(LOG(@var1));    # 5. Nested function calls: natural log, then exponential

SELECT LOG(EXP(@var1));    # 6. Nested function calls: exponential, then natural log

SELECT @var1;        # 7. @var1 did not change

SET @var1 = @var1 * 5;    # 8. @var1 has a new value

SELECT @var1;        # 9. Select @var1

SELECT @var2;        # 10. Set @var2 = natural log of @var1

SELECT UPPER(@var2);    # 11. Select UPPER CASE @var2
```

This screenshot shows the code in MySQL Workbench:

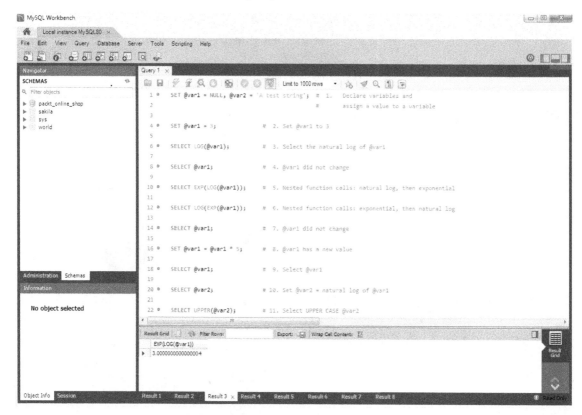

Figure 8.19: Example MySQL function code

The statement 1 variable declarations use the MySQL format, and each statement ends with a semicolon. Instead of an integer, statement 5 might produce a long decimal number. This happens because of rounding issues within MySQL functions and shows that we need to test the software that we build as we build it. Issues like this could cause problems when we ship software to customers. However, we can rely on the built-in functions with high confidence.

Although SQL products offer many built-in functions, we might need a new function to handle a new, unique requirement. Suppose a Packt Online Shop manager just emailed us a list of new reports that she needs, based on data from the PACKT_ONLINE_SHOP database. For a given customer, these reports will need total sales revenue, minus a discount. In other words, given a specific customer (for example, CustomerID = 3) we need to total all sales revenue across all orders that the customer has made. We'll use this calculation:

```
(Quantity of Product Ordered) X (Product Unit Price - Discount)
```

In MySQL, these statements calculate the value we need:

```
USE      packt_online_shop;
SET         @custID = 3;


SELECT          SUM((OI.Quantity * (OI.UnitPrice - OI.Discount)))
FROM          OrderItems OI INNER JOIN Orders O ON
       OI.OrderID = O.OrderID
WHERE          O.CustomerID = @custID;
```

However, many reports will use this exact same calculation, and therefore, these changes, combined with their enhancement, maintenance, and testing, will become complicated, difficult, and expensive. We need to build a function around these SQL statements and then call that function whenever we want. Starting with the preceding SQL statement, this function will solve the problem for us:

```
CREATE FUNCTION 'fnTotalSalesRvnByCust' (CustomerID Integer)
RETURNS FLOAT
DETERMINISTIC
BEGIN

    /*

       To test:

       SELECT packt_online_shop.fnTotalSalesRvnByCust (12);
       SELECT packt_online_shop.fnTotalSalesRvnByCust (3);


    */

    DECLARE      retVal FLOAT;

    SET          retVal = (
                 SELECT      SUM(OI.Quantity * (OI.UnitPrice -
OI.Discount))
                    FROM          OrderItems OI INNER JOIN Orders O ON
                       OI.OrderID = O.OrderID
                    WHERE          O.CustomerID = CustomerID
                 );

    IF (retVal IS NULL) THEN          -- If a customer has not placed an order, (s)he
                    -- has a total revenue value of null. We'll
```

```
                    -- have an easier time dealing with a 0.00
                    -- return value in that case.
        SET retVal = 0.00;
    END IF;

    RETURN (retVal);
END
```

To open a new function window, first drill down to **Create Function...** in the MySQL navigator, as shown here:

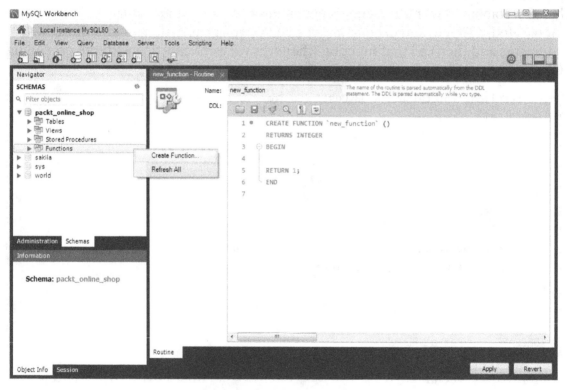

Figure 8.20: The MySQL function editor

We'll use this code for the function:

```
CREATE FUNCTION 'fnTotalSalesRvnByCust' (CustomerID Integer)
RETURNS FLOAT
DETERMINISTIC
BEGIN

    /*
        To test:

        USE packt_online_shop;

        SELECT packt_online_shop.fnTotalSalesRvnByCust (12);
        SELECT packt_online_shop.fnTotalSalesRvnByCust (3);

    */

    DECLARE     retVal FLOAT;

    SET         retVal = (
                    SELECT          SUM(OI.Quantity * (OI.UnitPrice -
OI.Discount))
                        FROM        OrderItems OI INNER JOIN Orders O ON
                    OI.OrderID = O.OrderID
                        WHERE       O.CustomerID = CustomerID
                );

IF (retVal IS NULL) THEN        -- If a customer has not placed an order, (s)he
-- has a total revenue value of null. We'll
-- have an easier time dealing with a 0.00
-- return value in that case.
        SET retVal = 0.00;
    END IF;

    RETURN (retVal);
END
```

We'll place it in the Workbench function editor:

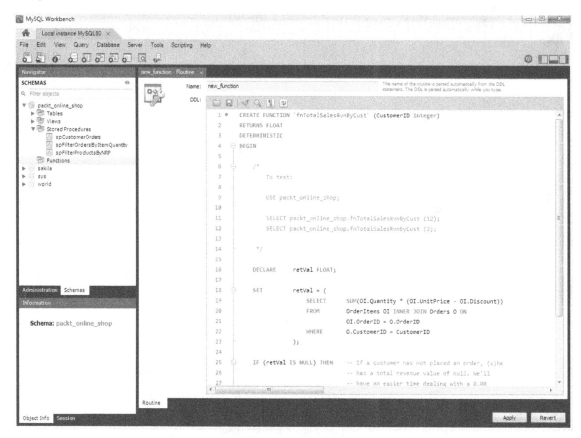

Figure 8.21: Building a new MySQL function

On line 1, start with **CREATE FUNCTION**. Then, type **fnTotalSalesRvnByCust** as the name of the function, using **fn** as the first two characters. This way, we will clearly state that this is a function. Place the function name in backtick characters. Place zero or more parameters inside the required parentheses, separated by commas. MySQL parameter names do not have a leading **@** character. Line 2 shows the data type of the return value. This function returns a decimal data type value, so we'll use float here. Line 3 has the word **DETERMINISTIC**, which MySQL requires for functions that consistently return the same results for the same input parameters. In a MySQL function, statements between **BEGIN** and **END** all end with a semicolon. Line 4 has the **BEGIN** statement, and line 33 (not seen in *Figure 8.21*) has **END** as the last statement. Lines 7 through 12 have commented lines as a block. We can use these commented statements to test the function. In addition to the **--** and **#** comment techniques we saw earlier, MySQL sees anything between and including **/*** and ***/** as a comment.

This commenting technique can become easier and more effective for large, multi-line comments. A SQL function returns a value, and line 16 declares **@retVal**, the variable that will hold this value. Its data type matches the return value of the function defined on line 1. For all the software that we build, formal variable declarations at the top of that software will make everyone's life easier because they give other people at other times a clearer picture of the situation. MySQL function and stored procedure variables declared with the **DECLARE** keyword do not require a leading **@** character. Line 18 assigns the value of the core **SELECT** statement to variable **retVal**, placing that **SELECT** statement in parentheses. *Line 22* uses the function input parameter **CustomerID** as a filter in the **WHERE** clause.

For some customers, the **SELECT** query will return a **NULL** value because they have not bought anything. A MySQL function can legally return a **NULL** value, but that could cause problems for other software that calls this function. If the function could return 0 for these cases, it would become easier to use elsewhere. The **IF** block of lines 25 through 30 will handle these situations. Line 25 checks the calculated value of **retVal** for **NULL**. If **retVal** has a **NULL** value, the MySQL **IF** block of lines 25 through 30 sets **retVal** to 0. If **retVal** does not have a **NULL** value, SQL will not execute that **IF** block.

Line 32 returns the calculated **retVal** value, and line 33 ends the function. To test the function, first open a new query window, as shown here:

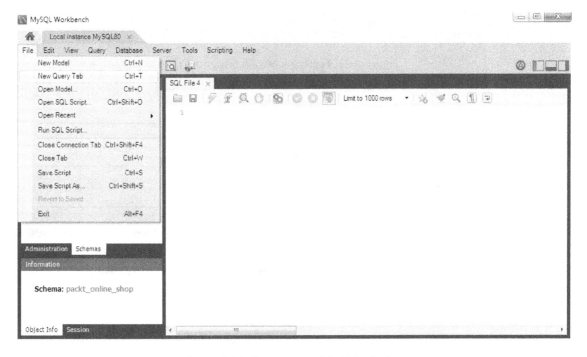

Figure 8.22: Open a new MySQL window

Place the test code from lines 9 to 12 in the window, and click the lightning icon to run the code:

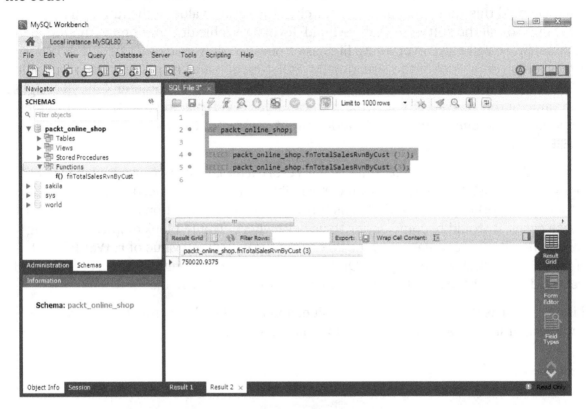

Figure 8.23: Testing a MySQL function

The function calls have the database name **packt_online_shop** before the function name, as shown here:

```
SELECT packt_online_shop.fnTotalSalesRvnByCust (12);
SELECT packt_online_shop.fnTotalSalesRvnByCust (3);
```

Although MySQL does not require this, it is good practice to do this with code that calls the functions that we build.

In *Figure 8.23*, the second result shows a value with four decimal places. We may need this exact numeric precision, or we might need a different level of numeric precision. This proves once again that we need to test the software that we build, as we build it, before we use it in production. If the software does not behave as we expect, we must investigate and find a solution.

A few weeks later, another Packt manager wants us to remove the discount from the **fnTotalSalesRvnByCust** calculations. We need to edit, or **ALTER**, the function. In the MySQL Navigator, highlight the function and drill down to **Alter Function...**, as shown here:

Figure 8.24: Alter a MySQL function

Edit line 18, as shown here:

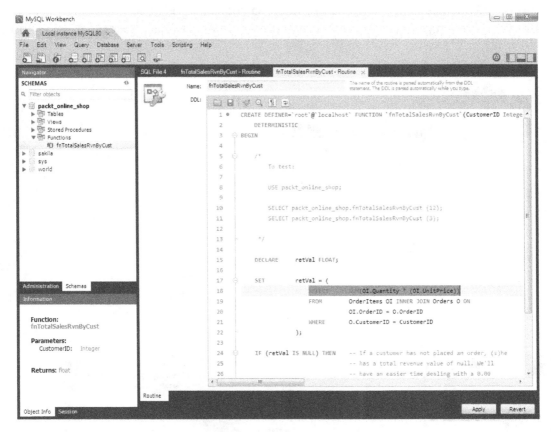

Figure 8.25: The edited MySQL function

As described earlier, click **Apply** | **Apply** | **Finish** in the windows that appear. Be sure to test the function changes as explained earlier.

Exercise 8.03: Build a MySQL Function

Build a MySQL function called **fnCountCustomerOrders** that will return the number of orders a specific customer has placed. The **COUNT** function might help; however, note that the **COUNT** function will not return a **NULL** value.

1. Write the following query:

```
CREATE DEFINER=`root`@`localhost` FUNCTION `fnCountCustomerOrders`(CustomerID
Integer) RETURNS int
    DETERMINISTIC
BEGIN
 DECLARE retVal INTEGER;
 SET retVal = (
  SELECT COUNT(O.OrderID)
```

```
    FROM Orders O
    WHERE O.CustomerID = CustomerID
  );
  RETURN (retVal);
END
```

2. Run the MySQL code. Once it is completed successfully, write the following query:

```
USE packt_online_shop;


SELECT packt_online_shop.fnCountCustomerOrders (12);
SELECT packt_online_shop.fnCountCustomerOrders (3);
```

3. Execute this query. You should get the following output:

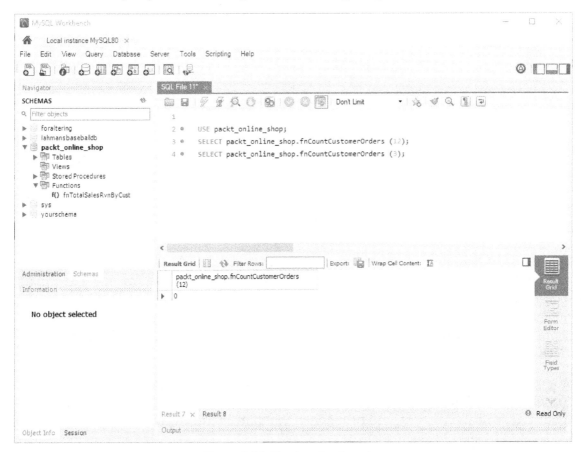

Figure 8.26: Testing the function

In this exercise, we built a complete MySQL function that returns the number of orders a specific customer has placed, proceeding from start to finish.

Activity 8.02: Working with MySQL Functions

In this activity, we'll build MySQL functions with more sophisticated business rules and logic. The Packt Online Shop management needs to know which orders have order item quantities that fall below given value limits. These value limits could change depending on specific management reporting needs. The Packt Online Shop management needs to know the total order quantity of specific, individual products. Build a function that will return this information. The function will have an integer input value that will become the filter value. If a specific product has no order items, its total order quantity will have a **NULL** value. In this case, return 0 (zero).

1. First, build a basic SQL query. Use a **CASE** statement in the **SELECT** clause to check for and handle a **NULL** value.

2. Set a variable to the calculated value.

3. Build the function around the query.

> **Note**
>
> The solution for this activity can be found on page 256.

Triggers

As users insert, update, and delete rows and columns in the database, we might want some type of action in the database to happen automatically. For a row insertion in a specific table, we might want to automatically update a row in another table based on a business rule. As an example, an e-commerce database system might automatically update its specific product inventory counts when customers place specific products into their carts and complete their purchase transactions.

For a row update event in a specific table, we might want to automatically update another table and insert a row in a third table. SQL triggers can handle this. A SQL trigger is a special type of stored procedure that automatically executes in response to a defined triggering event that the database detects. Triggers fire automatically—we can't call a trigger in a query window, a stored procedure, or a function. MySQL has one trigger type. To learn how triggers work, we'll first focus on a simple trigger. Next, we'll see a more substantial example.

Specific MySQL tables own their triggers, placed in designated subdirectories in the **Navigator**. MySQL does not have a dedicated create trigger tool, as shown here:

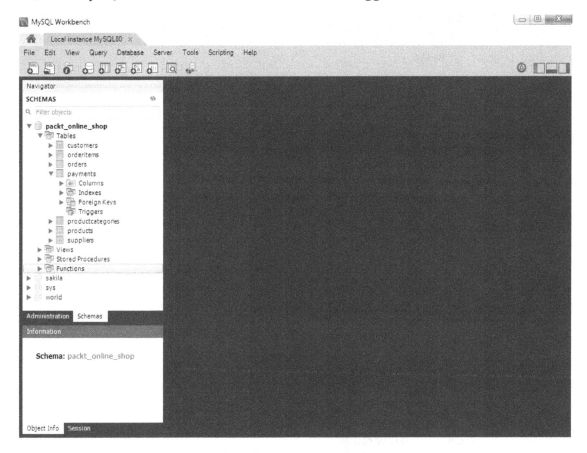

Figure 8.27: MySQL does not offer a dedicated trigger creation tool

Instead, all **CREATE** and **DROP** trigger operations happen in a query window. Additionally, MySQL does not support **ALTER** triggers. To edit a trigger, delete it and then create it with updated code.

To create a trigger, remember to include the delimiter code. We saw this earlier, when we created the MySQL **spFilterProductsByNRP** stored procedure in a query window. To learn how MySQL triggers work, we'll first focus on a simple trigger. Then we'll see a more substantial example.

To create a new trigger called **tr_Basic** for the MySQL **Payments** table, place this code in a new query window:

```
USE packt_online_shop;


#    drop trigger tr_Basic;


/*
    To test:    USE packt_online_shop;

            INSERT INTO Payments(OrderID, PaymentDate, PaymentType, PaymentRef, Amount,
              Notes, BalanceNotes)
            VALUES (1, '20140303', 'credit card', 'W26UA4',
                7.10, 'payment received', NULL);


            SELECT * FROM CUSTOMERS;
 */

DELIMITER $$
CREATE TRIGGER tr_Basic AFTER INSERT ON Payments
    FOR EACH ROW
    BEGIN

DECLARE    customerID INT;

    SET customerID = (
            SELECT O.CustomerID
            FROM    Orders O
            WHERE    O.OrderID = NEW.OrderID
        );

    UPDATE        Customers
    SET        Customers.BalanceNotes = CONCAT('Customer ',
            CAST(customerID AS CHAR), ' just got updated again')
    WHERE        Customers.CustomerID = customerID;

    END$$
DELIMITER ;
```

Then, click the lightning bolt icon at the top:

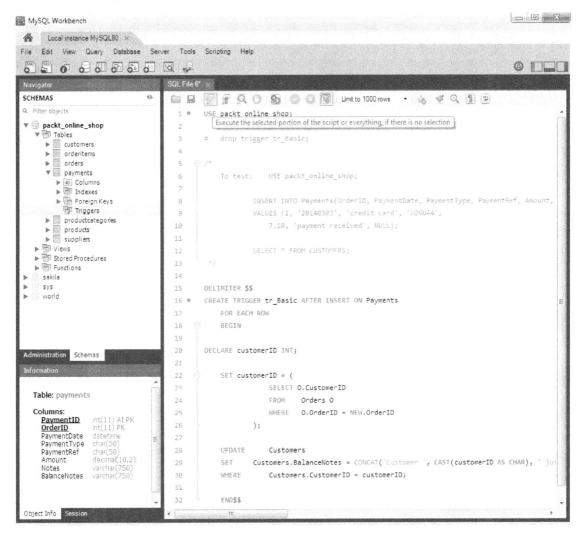

Figure 8.28: Create a MySQL trigger

This screenshot shows the trigger code in MySQL Workbench:

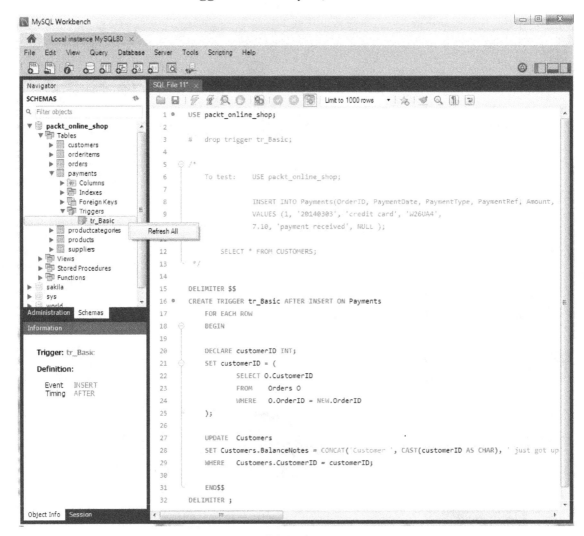

Figure 8.29: Create a MySQL trigger

In the **Navigator**, refresh the **Payments** table and the **Payments** table **Triggers** directory if necessary. The **Payments** table owns the **tr_Basic** trigger, and a **Payments** table insert event fires it. This trigger updates the **Customers.BalanceNotes** column with a string showing the **customerID** that made the payment.

The **tr_Basic** trigger shows all the important features of a MySQL trigger. On line 1, the **USE** statement tells the stored procedure to connect to the **packt_online_shop** database. The **Navigator** has no way to drop a trigger, so the commented line 3 code will **DROP** the **tr_Basic** trigger when specifically painted and executed. To test the trigger, lines 6 through 12 insert a line into the **Payments** table and then return all **Customers** table rows. Line 15 changes the trigger delimiter to **$$**, and line 32 restores the delimiter to its original value of **;**. On line 16, the required keywords create the trigger named **tr_Basic**, as shown in this code:

```
CREATE TRIGGER tr_Basic AFTER INSERT ON Payments
```

Although it's not required, prefix trigger names with **tr_** as a naming standard. The keywords specify that the trigger fires after a **Payments** table insert event:

```
AFTER INSERT ON Payments
```

A trigger can map to only one table—in this case, the **Payments** table. A MySQL trigger can fire **BEFORE** or **AFTER** an insert/update/delete table event. The required keywords on line 17 specify that the trigger will cover all inserted **Payments** table rows:

```
FOR EACH ROW
```

The begin/end block from lines 18 to 31 has the actual executed trigger code.

For MySQL insert, update, and delete triggers, the **OLD** and **NEW** tables clone the rows whose event(s) fired the triggers. The **OLD** table receives all the data and data types of the triggering row before the triggering event fired, and the **NEW** table receives all the data and data types of the triggering row after the triggering event fired. Trigger code queries can use the **OLD** and **NEW** tables in **SELECT** statements, **WHERE** clauses, and so on, but they can't **UPDATE** or **DELETE** rows in the **OLD** or **NEW** tables.

A MySQL trigger can't return a result set. Therefore, we can't place a simple **SELECT** statement in a MySQL trigger because a **SELECT** statement returns a result set. As a workaround, we can assign a **SELECT** statement result set to a variable in a MySQL trigger. Lines 20 and 21 show the technique. Line 20 declares the **customerID** variable. The **SELECT** query from lines 22 to 24 queries the **Orders** table for **CustomerID**, filtering on the **OrderID** in the NEW table. Then, line 21 assigns this value to the **customerID** variable with a **SET** statement. Lines 27 through 29 **UPDATE** the **Customers.BalanceNotes** column. Line 31 tells MySQL Workbench that the trigger has ended, and line 32 resets the delimiter.

We can build a similar trigger to update the **Customers.BalanceNotes** column for every **OrderItems** table row insertion. We can also build a similar trigger to update the **Customers.BalanceNotes** column for every **Payments** table insertion. A new order in the MySQL **PACKT_ONLINE_SHOP** database will insert a new row in the **Orders** table, and at least one row in the **OrderItems** table. This makes sense because every order has at least one ordered item. Also, an order will map to one customer. In a similar way, a payment in that database will insert a new row in the **Payments** table. The payment will map to a specific order because every payment has an **OrderID** value. Since every **OrderID** value maps to a specific customer, a payment will indirectly map to a customer. This diagram shows the table relationships:

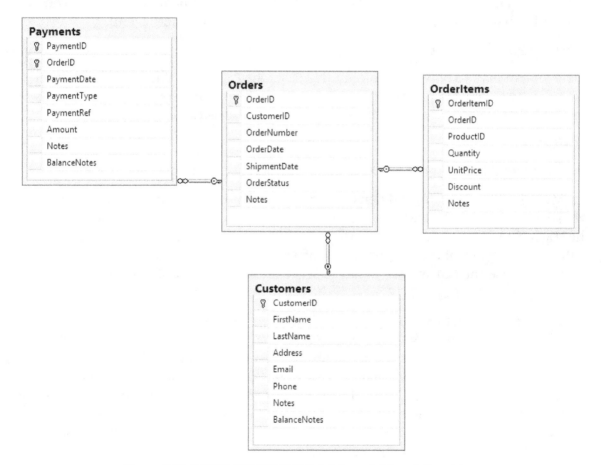

Figure 8.30: PACKT_ONLINE_SHOP database table relationships

Because of these relationships, when a customer orders at least one item, or makes at least one payment on an order, we can calculate a running balance for that customer. The running balance covers all payments and all order item charges. Insert triggers on both the **Payments** and **OrderItems** tables can calculate the customer running balances. Because a trigger resembles a stored procedure, a trigger on one **PACKT_ONLINE_SHOP** database table can see all the tables in the database, including the **Payments** and **OrderItems** tables. This way, a **PACKT_ONLINE_SHOP** trigger can see all the information it would need to calculate the customer running balances. We need a trigger on the **OrderItems** table that will calculate a customer's running balance every time the customer adds an order item in the **OrderItems** table. That trigger should automatically update the **Customers.BalanceNotes** column with the running balance calculation result for that customer. The **Payments** table needs a similar trigger that fires every time the customer makes a payment with a new row in the **Payments** table.

This code builds the **tr_OrderItems_OnInsert** trigger:

tr_OrderItems_OnInsert

```
1   USE packt_online_shop;
2
3   #    drop trigger tr_OrderItems_OnInsert
4
5   DELIMITER $$
6
7   CREATE TRIGGER tr_OrderItems_OnInsert AFTER INSERT ON OrderItems
8       FOR EACH ROW
9       BEGIN
10
11          DECLARE balanceNotesText VARCHAR(1000);
12          DECLARE customerID INT;
13          DECLARE orderBalance DECIMAL(10, 2);
14          DECLARE orderIDVal INT;
15          DECLARE paymentBalance DECIMAL(10, 2);
16          DECLARE runningTotal VARCHAR(50);
17
18      #    The "NEW" table has the CustomerID and OrderID values
19      #    from the new inserted row that we'll need.
20
21          SET    orderIDVal = (
22              SELECT NEW.orderID
23          );
```

The full code can be found at: https://packt.live/2EYAkig

In MySQL Workbench, these figures show the **tr_OrderItems_OnInsert** trigger:

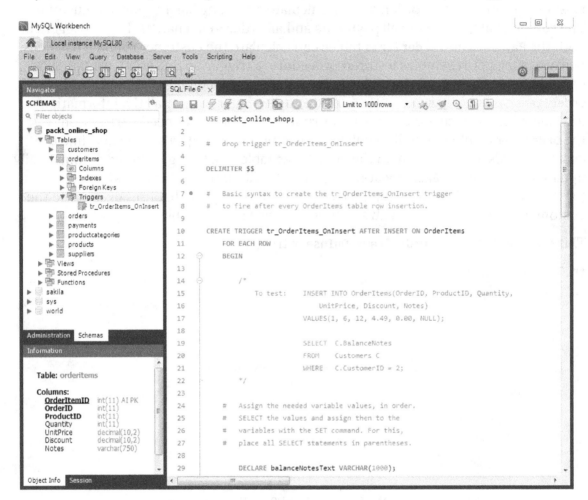

Figure 8.31: #1 – The tr_OrderItems_OnInsert trigger

MySQL query window showing line numbers 29 to 57:

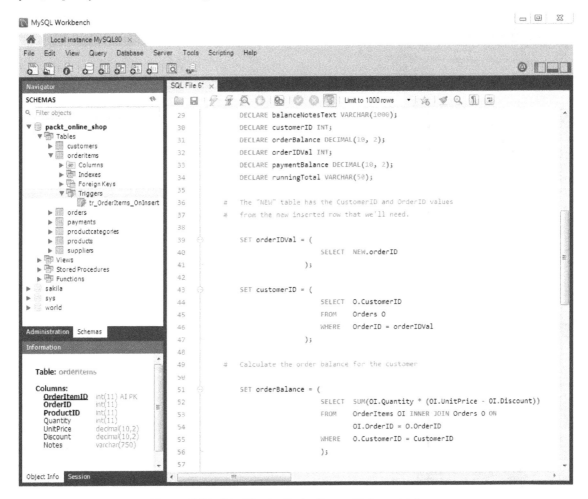

Figure 8.32: #2 – The tr_OrderItems_OnInsert trigger

MySQL query window showing line numbers 58 to 85:

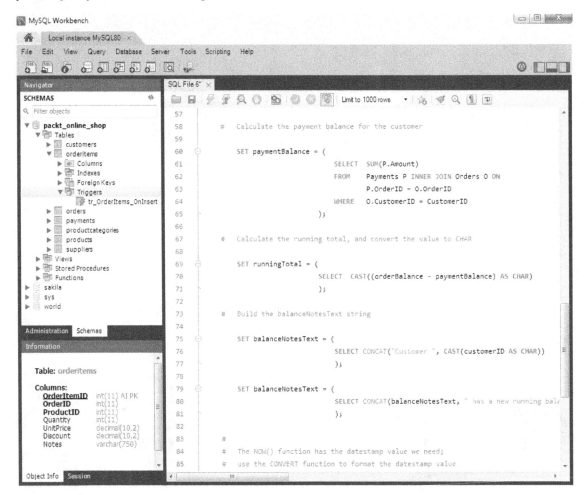

Figure 8.33: #3 – The tr_OrderItems_OnInsert trigger

MySQL query window showing line numbers 86 to 104:

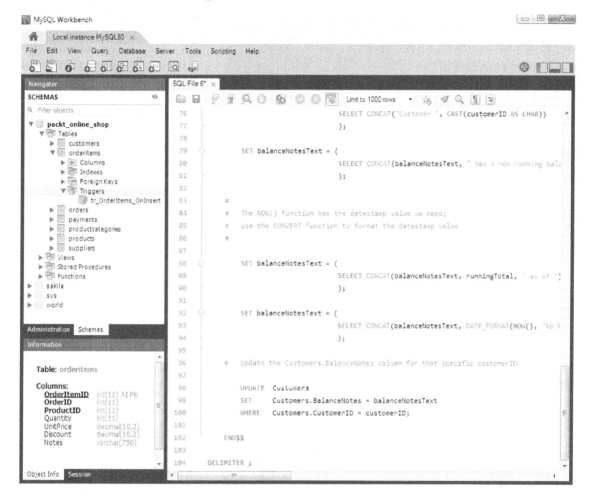

Figure 8.34: #4 – The tr_OrderItems_OnInsert trigger

Test it a few times with the code of lines 15 to 21:

```
INSERT INTO   OrderItems(OrderID, ProductID, Quantity, UnitPrice, Discount, Notes)
VALUES(1, 6, 12, 4.49, 0.00, NULL);


SELECT    C.BalanceNotes
FROM      Customers C
WHERE     C.CustomerID = 2;
```

Notice that the **Customers.BalanceNotes** value increases by $53.88 for each payment. This makes sense because each test code order item row has a quantity of twelve. In this example test code, each item costs $4.49 with no discount, so each inserted **OrderItems** table row here has a total of $53.88. Therefore, the running balance amount for **CustomerID = 2** will increase by $53.88 each time we run the **INSERT** statement. Now, we'll take a closer look at the code itself.

As explained earlier, a trigger is a special type of stored procedure, and the **tr_ OrderItems_OnInsert** trigger clearly shows this. In this code, the comment block between lines 7 and 15 explains how to test the trigger shown in these screenshots:

Lines 29 through 34 declare the variables that the trigger code needs. The line 39 **SELECT** statement retrieves the **OrderID** value from the **INSERTED** table and then assigns that value to the **orderIDVal** variable. This technique uses a feature of MySQL triggers. When MySQL inserts a row into a table, another table called **NEW** receives an exact copy of that inserted row. This copy clones all the data of the original inserted row, and that cloned data has data types that match the original data. The **NEW** table supports only **SELECT** queries, and only **INSERT** and **UPDATE** triggers can access the **NEW** table. A **DELETE** trigger has a similar **OLD** table, which holds an exact copy of the **DELETED** row, with similar matching data types and visibility restrictions—only **DELETE** triggers can access the **OLD** table. A MySQL **UPDATE** trigger does not have a dedicated **UPDATED** table. Instead, an **UPDATE** trigger can look for data changes in the **NEW** and **OLD** tables to see which row columns changed, and how they changed.

The line 39 **SET** statement finds the **orderID** value mapped to the new order and sets the **orderIDVal** variable to that **orderID** value. In a similar way, line 43 finds the **customerID** value mapped to the order and sets the **customerID** variable to that **customerID** value. Line 51 calculates the current order balance value for the customer, assigning the value to the **orderBalance** variable. Line 60 calculates the current payment balance value for the customer, assigning the value to the **paymentBalance** variable. Line 69 adds these values for the **runningTotal** variable. Later string operations in this trigger will need this balance total value in a string format, so line 34 declared the **runningTotal** variable with a **VARCHAR** data type.

Lines 75 through 94 build a string that shows the latest running total for the customer. The **CONCAT** string function assembles the data into a finished string. We'll see more about string functions later. On line 93, the **DATE_FORMAT** function converts the **NOW()** datestamp function value to a "Jan 1, 2006" format. Finally, the **UPDATE** statement on line 98 updates the **Customers.BalanceNotes** column with the finished **balanceNotesText** value for the specific **customerID** value.

Although this trigger might look somewhat complicated, it only has logical queries and operations that solve the problem in a step-by-step way. Understanding how SQL works, knowledge of the **PACKT_ONLINE_SHOP** database structure, all combined with well-defined business rules, led to this solution.

We can also build a similar **tr_Payments_OnInsert** trigger. This second MySQL trigger operates exactly like **tr_OrderItems_OnInsert**, except it updates **Customers.BalanceNotes** for every **OrderItems** table row insertion. This code almost clones the earlier MySQL **tr_OrderItems_OnInsert** trigger code as well:

tr_OrderItems_OnInsert.sql

```
1 CREATE TRIGGER tr_Payments_OnInsert AFTER INSERT ON payments
2     FOR EACH ROW
3     BEGIN
4
5         DECLARE balanceNotesText VARCHAR(1000);
6       DECLARE customerID INT;
7       DECLARE orderBalance DECIMAL(10, 2);
8       DECLARE orderIDVal INT;
9       DECLARE paymentBalance DECIMAL(10, 2);
10        DECLARE runningTotal DECIMAL(10, 2);
11
12  #    The "NEW" table has the CustomerID and OrderID values
13  #    from the new inserted row that we'll need.
14
15     SET    orderIDVal = (
16                   SELECT NEW.orderID
17               );
18
19     SET    customerID = (
20                   SELECT    O.CustomerID
21                   FROM    Orders O
22                   WHERE    OrderID = orderIDVal
23               );
```

The full code can be found at: https://packt.live/2EYAkig

It differs only in the **CREATE TRIGGER** signature and the commented test block code, both at the top. With both triggers in place, we can see the latest, most current customer balance information in the **Customers.BalanceNotes** column, updated with each inserted **OrderItems** table and **Payments** table row.

Exercise 8.04: Build a MySQL Trigger

Build a MySQL trigger called **tr_Products_OnInsert**. The **Products** table has a **SupplierID** column. For a **Products** table insert event, this trigger will calculate the total number of products that Packt offers that map to the **SupplierID** value in the inserted row. The trigger will update the **Suppliers**. Notes column with a string showing this product count. Include the **SupplierID** and a formatted date stamp in the string. This supplier (supplier 4) has three products available here at Packt as of Jun 08, 2019:

1. Build the **tr_Products_OnInsert** trigger:

tr_Products_OnInsert

```
USE packt_online_shop;

# drop trigger tr_Products_OnInsert

DELIMITER $$

# Basic syntax to create the tr_Products_OnInsert trigger
# to fire after every OrderItems table row insertion.

CREATE TRIGGER tr_Products_OnInsert AFTER INSERT ON Products
FOR EACH ROW
BEGIN

 /*
  To test: INSERT INTO Products(ProductCategoryID, SupplierID,
      ProductName, ProductImage, NetRetailPrice,
      AvailableQuantity, WholesalePrice,
      UnitKGWeight, Notes)

     VALUES(3, 3, 'peanut butter', NULL, 3.79, 1000, 2.69,
       0.75, 'caution: high calorie');

     SELECT P.*
     FROM Products P
     WHERE P.SupplierID = 3;
 */

  DECLARE supplierID INT;
  DECLARE supplierProductCount INT;
  DECLARE supplierCountText VARCHAR(1000);

# The "NEW" table has the SupplierID
# value we'll need

  SET supplierID = (
   SELECT NEW.supplierID
  );

# Calculate the supplier product count,
# and convert the value to TEXT

  SET supplierProductCount = (
   SELECT COUNT(P.ProductID)
   FROM Products P INNER JOIN Suppliers S ON
    P.SupplierID = S.SupplierID
   WHERE S.SupplierID = supplierID
  );
```

```
  SET supplierCountText = (
   SELECT CONCAT("This supplier (Supplier ", CAST(supplierID AS CHAR), ")")
  );

  SET supplierCountText = (
   SELECT CONCAT(supplierCountText, " has ", CAST(supplierProductCount AS CHAR))
  );

  SET supplierCountText = (
   SELECT CONCAT(supplierCountText, " products available here at Packt as of ")
  );

  SET supplierCountText = (
   SELECT CONCAT(supplierCountText, DATE_FORMAT(NOW(), "%b %d, %Y"))
  );

# Update the Customers.BalanceNotes column
# for that specific customerID

  UPDATE Suppliers
  SET Suppliers.Notes = supplierCountText
  WHERE Suppliers.SupplierID = supplierID;

END$$

DELIMITER ;
```

The full code can be found at: https://packt.live/2Mzocsh

2. Test the trigger using the following code:

```
INSERT INTO Products(ProductCategoryID, SupplierID,
ProductName, ProductImage, NetRetailPrice,
AvailableQuantity, WholesalePrice,
UnitKGWeight, Notes)
VALUES(3, 3, 'peanut butter', NULL, 3.79, 1000, 2.69,
0.75, 'caution: high calorie');

SELECT S.*
FROM Suppliers S
WHERE S.SupplierID = 3;
```

3. Execute the query. You should get the following output:

Figure 8.35: Testing the tr_Products_OnInsert trigger

In this exercise, we built a MySQL trigger, and we saw how triggers can further automate the management of large database resources.

Activity 8.03: Building a Trigger

If an insert into the **OrderItems** table would bring the **Products** table's **AvailableQuantity** column below five for that product, update the **Products** table's **Notes** column with a warning message. As a result of the **OrderItems** table insert, the warning message should explain that the available quantity for that product will drop below five.

> **Note**
>
> The solution for this activity can be found on page 257.

Summary

In this chapter, we saw that we can build powerful, structured software with SQL stored procedures, SQL functions, and SQL triggers. These tools integrate core programming concepts with SQL machinery to build reliable, flexible solutions to complex programming problems. With these tools, we can leverage the power and potential of SQL database products. In the next chapter, we will cover the best practices for securing database resources from common potential threats.

9

Security

Overview

By the end of this chapter, you will be able to understand the need for access control. We will learn how to create users and user roles in MySQL. We will also learn how to grant and revoke permissions to user roles.

Introduction

In the previous chapter, we learned about SQL programming. We saw that SQL stored procedures, functions, and triggers help us automate database queries and integrate web and desktop applications with SQL database resources. We can now approach database tasks, problems, and questions with confidence. However, we have only worked in sandboxes, or safe, isolated environments. We haven't had to worry about security threats and hazards. Unfortunately, real-world scenarios potentially involve major security threats and hazards, which can lead to the theft of and damage to valuable data.

Database resources are valuable, and bad actors have plenty of motivation to steal, damage, and/or destroy data. Databases that house data involving national security information, financial information, medical histories, and personal employment histories are subject to malicious attacks from hostile actors. Hackers have successfully attacked government and corporate databases from the outside for many years. Sometimes, trusted employees can simply walk out the front door with the data. For example, the 2017 Equifax data breach impacted 148 million people, and the settlement and penalties for it cost Equifax at least $700 million.

> **Note**
>
> You can read more about the Equifax data breach at https://packt.live/3527R6j.

The 2015 Anthem Inc. medical data breach impacted almost 79 million people, who must now deal with potential identity theft.

> **Note**
>
> You can read more about the Anthem Inc. medical data breach at https://packt.live/2Kd5Zj0.

These attacks will continue for a long time. Although data security has become a profession, we must proactively think through and try to prevent problems before they occur. This chapter will address potential threats that can endanger database resources, and how we can neutralize those threats. In this chapter, we'll look at various best practices to secure the `PACKT_ONLINE_SHOP` database, along with techniques that extend to cover MySQL databases generally.

Access Control (Authorization)

So far, we've had full rights and control over our database resources because we created them as **operating system (OS)** account administrators. We could make any changes we wanted. Therefore, for modern databases, security focuses on who can do what to specific database resources in a granular way.

First, the database needs to identify or authenticate every user who wishes to access the database resources. A user will typically see a prompt to supply a login string (username) and a password string, to enter the system. MySQL has tools that define users with those login and password strings. Next, the database needs to authorize, or allow, each user one or more specific actions on one or more database components.

For a modern database, a user must supply a login string and a password string to gain entry to the system. Then, we can use those tools to give users permission to view, create, delete, and/or update all the database resources within the server. We'll see how this works in the next exercise.

Exercise 9.01: Creating New MySQL users

In this exercise, we'll first create a new MySQL user account. MySQL uses host-based authentication for local environment logins. However, we can also create a new MySQL user through MySQL itself. Launch MySQL with host authentication to get "root authentication."

1. In the Navigator, click the **Administration** tab, and then click **Users and Privileges** as shown in the following screenshot:

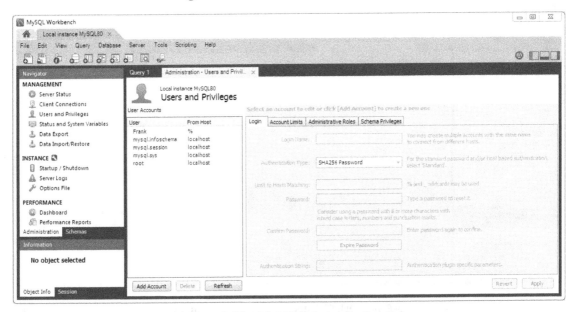

Figure 9.1: The MySQL Administration Tab

2. To create a new user account for **TEMP_ACCOUNT_1** with the password string **abcdabcd**, click **Add Account** at the bottom to build a new user account.

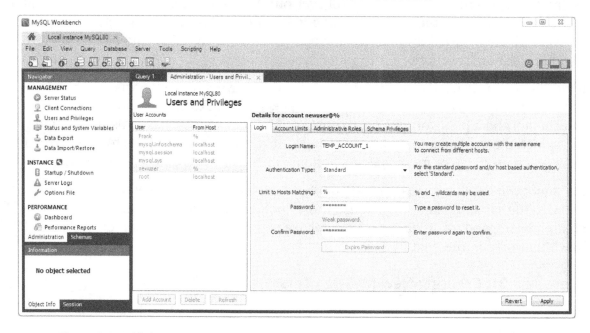

Figure 9.2: Add the New TEMP_ACCOUNT_1 account in the MySQL Administration Tab

3. Click **Apply** at the bottom-right corner and the new user will appear in the **User Accounts** list, as seen here:

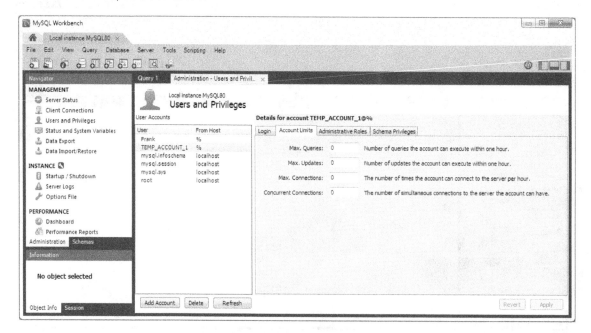

Figure 9.3: The TEMP_ACCOUNT_1 account in the MySQL Administration tab

In this exercise, we created a new Windows user called **TEMP_ACCOUNT_1**, and then we created a new MySQL user account based on that new Windows user.

Exercise 9.02: Granting EXECUTE permission in MySQL

In MySQL, we will grant **EXECUTE** permission on the **Orders** table for **TEMP_ACCOUNT_1**. While MySQL has roles, they do not offer the granular configuration and control of MySQL roles. However, we can easily grant specific permissions on specific database objects to specific users or sets of users.

1. The **GRANT EXECUTE** statement has the flexibility we need. The statements shown here grant the execution privilege on the stored procedure to the **TEMP_ACCOUNT_1** user. We **GRANT** a specific privilege—in this case, **EXECUTE**—on the stored procedure, to the **TEMP_ACCOUNT_1** user:

    ```
    USE packt_online_shop;


    GRANT EXECUTE ON PROCEDURE
      packt_online_shop.spFilterProductsByNRP TO 'TEMP_ACCOUNT_1';
    ```

    In the MySQL Workbench, it will look like this:

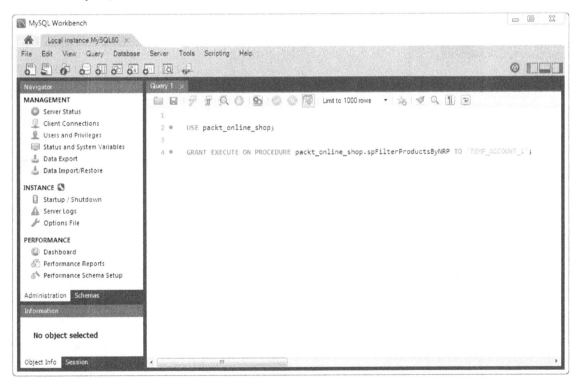

Figure 9.4: Assign a permission in the MySQL Workbench

2. If needed, we can extend this to multiple users in a comma-delimited list. Although the stored procedure name does not require the database name, it's good practice to add it in front:

```
packt_online_shop.spFilterProductsByNRP
```

3. Use the **SHOW GRANTS** command to see the permission granted to **TEMP_ACCOUNT_1**. It has this syntax:

```
SHOW GRANTS FOR user name;
```

The output should be as follows:

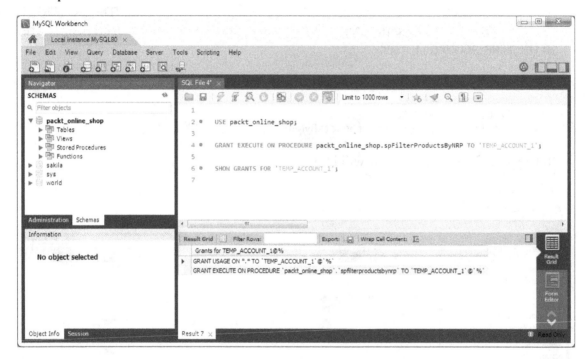

Figure 9.5: Grant and Show Permissions in MySQL

In this exercise, we granted a defined permission to a specific account for a specific MySQL resource. We also saw the permission granted to that account.

Similar to the **EXECUTE** permission, there are other permissions that can be provided to a user:

- **CREATE**: Provides the user with the permission to create schemas

- **DROP**: Provides the user with the permission to drop databases and tables

- **INSERT**: Provides the user with the permission to insert rows into specific MySQL table

- **DELETE**: Provides the user with the permission to delete rows from specific MySQL table

- **SELECT**: Provides the user with the permission to read the database

- **UPDATE**: Provides the user with the permission to update table rows

- **ALL PRIVILEGES**: Provides the user with all privileges

The syntax for these permissions remain the same. Replacing **EXECUTE**, with other permissions would provide the required permissions.

Activity 9.01: Grant UPDATE permission on a table in MySQL

For this activity, first, create a new Windows user named **TEMP_ACCOUNT_2**. In MySQL, grant **UPDATE** permission on the **PACKT_ONLINE_SHOP.PRODUCTS** table to the user named **TEMP_ACCOUNT_2**.

> **Note**
>
> The solution to this activity can be found on page 260.

Summary

In this chapter, we saw that MySQL offers flexible tools that allow the fine-grained security configuration of virtually all database resources. We have a responsibility to research the security needs of organization stakeholders, age lever these security tools to protect the database resources entrusted to us and defend the organizations that rely on those resources.

In the next chapter, we'll return back to programming and see some of the methods that will be used to provide statistical data from the database.

10

Aggregate Functions

Overview

In this chapter, we'll use SQL aggregate functions and solve problems with them. By the end of this chapter, you'll be able to use SQL aggregate functions and the **GROUP BY** clause, implement the SQL **HAVING** clause, explain the differences between the **HAVING** and **WHERE** clauses, use the SQL **OVER** and **PARTITION BY** clauses, and implement the **RANK** and **DENSE_RANK** functions.

Introduction

In the previous chapters, we saw that the WHERE clause can be used to filter SQL query result sets in an efficient, almost intuitive way. For example, say we want to identify the total number of executives in a department, or we want the total number of dependents who are covered by a medical claim. In such cases, more than the details, we are looking for a single calculated value. For such cases, where we need calculated results based on database rows, we use SQL aggregate functions. They can also be used to calculate values across subsets of query result rows. We will also look at advanced clauses, such as the GROUP BY and the HAVING clauses, and see how they can help us to fine-tune our results.

Aggregate Functions (SUM, COUNT, AVG, MIN, and MAX) and the GROUP BY Clause

MySQL provides functions that return single calculated values based on defined sets of values. We'll first look at the general way to use these functions in a SQL query, and then we'll examine each function individually:

- SUM: Adds, or *sums*, relevant values

- COUNT: Returns a count of the relevant values

- AVG (average): Calculates the average of a set of relevant values

- MIN (minimum value): Returns the lowest value of a set of values

- MAX (maximum value): Returns the highest value of a set of values

Say that a store manager wants the average weight of the products in each PACKT_ONLINE_SHOP product category. In the PACKT_ONLINE_SHOP database, each ProductCategory table row maps to one or more products in the Products table. We can start with this query:

```
USE      packt_online_shop;

SELECT   PC.ProductCategoryID, PC.ProductCategoryName, P.UnitKGWeight
         AS 'PRODUCT KG WEIGHT'
FROM     ProductCategories PC INNER JOIN
         Products P ON PC.ProductCategoryID = P.ProductCategoryID;
```

This is what we get:

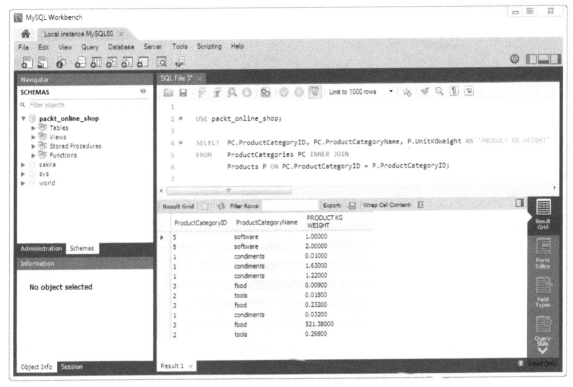

Figure 10.1: MySQL query

This query returned a row for every product in each product category, and every row shows the **UnitKGWeight** value for each individual product. This clearly won't solve the problem. We need a way to gather, or *aggregate*, the average weights of all the products in each category. The SQL **AVG**, or average, function will solve the problem. Like all aggregate functions, **AVG** needs **GROUP BY** in the queries that use containing the **AVG** function. **GROUP BY** will organize the rows of results for an aggregate function, and the next query has a **GROUP BY** clause at the end. The SQL **GROUP BY** clause separates the results of a **SELECT** query into one or more row groups based on a specific separation criterion. With the defined row groups, the query can execute one or more aggregate functions. If we add the **AVG** function and the **GROUP BY** clause to the query, as seen here, your result will be modified:

```
USE         packt_online_shop;

SELECT      PC.ProductCategoryID, PC.ProductCategoryName,
            AVG(P.UnitKGWeight) AS 'AVERAGE PRODUCT KG WEIGHT'
FROM        ProductCategories PC INNER JOIN

            Products P ON PC.ProductCategoryID = P.ProductCategoryID
GROUP BY    PC.ProductCategoryName, PC.ProductCategoryID;
```

Here's the output:

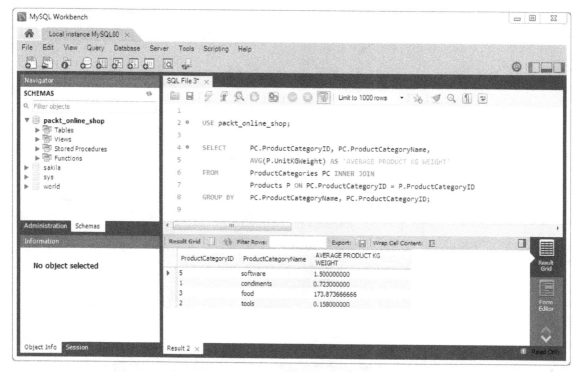

Figure 10.2: A MySQL query with the AVG aggregate function

In MySQL, we'll solve the problem. In the query, the **AVG** function on line 5 calculates the average of the **UnitKGWeight** column in the **Products** table. This makes sense. However, we need to somehow collect the **Products** table rows into individual product category groups for the aggregate function to work. The query has the required data to do this because every child **Product** table row has a parent in the **ProductCategories** table. The **GROUP BY** clause on line 8 will solve this problem.

As seen here, that **GROUP BY** clause literally groups the **Products** table rows by category. Then, the **AVG** function in the **SELECT** clause can calculate the average **UnitKGWeight** for all the products in each separate group of products. For aggregate functions, this idea is important. This example shows a general rule that will help us. *Place every* **SELECT** *clause column that is not an aggregate function in the* **GROUP BY** *clause.*

The **GROUP BY** clause will group by every unique value of the combination of **ProductCategoryName** and **ProductCategoryID**. That is, if two products have the same category name and the same category ID, they will be placed in the same group.

Look at this query:

```
USE        packt_online_shop;

SELECT     PC.ProductCategoryID, PC.ProductCategoryName,
           AVG(P.UnitKGWeight) AS 'AVERAGE PRODUCT KG WEIGHT',
           MIN(P.NetRetailPrice) AS 'MINIMUM NET RETAIL PRICE'
FROM       ProductCategories PC INNER JOIN
           Products P ON PC.ProductCategoryID = P.ProductCategoryID
GROUP BY   PC.ProductCategoryName, PC.ProductCategoryID;
```

Here's the output:

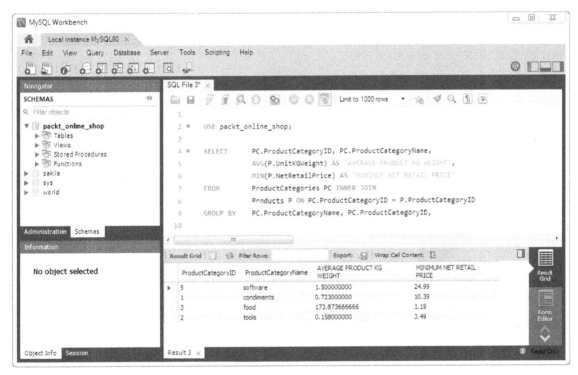

Figure 10.3: Multiple aggregate functions in a MySQL query

We included the **MIN** aggregate function on line 6. As an aggregate function, **MIN** returns the smallest value of a column for all the rows in each separate group. In this query, the **MIN** function finds the minimum **NetRetailPrice** value in each product category group.

We can use the **ORDER BY** clause in a MySQL query with an aggregate function, and we can order an aggregate function column. We have some flexibility for this. Say that we need to sort the preceding query by the **AVERAGE PRODUCT KG WEIGHT** column. This MySQL query has an **ORDER BY** clause that uses the column alias name of the third column:

```
USE        packt_online_shop;

SELECT     PC.ProductCategoryID, PC.ProductCategoryName,
           AVG(P.UnitKGWeight) AS 'AVERAGE PRODUCT KG WEIGHT',
           MIN(P.NetRetailPrice) AS 'MINIMUM NET RETAIL PRICE'
FROM       ProductCategories PC INNER JOIN
           Products P ON PC.ProductCategoryID = P.ProductCategoryID
GROUP BY   PC.ProductCategoryName, PC.ProductCategoryID
ORDER BY   'AVERAGE PRODUCT KG WEIGHT';
```

Here's the output:

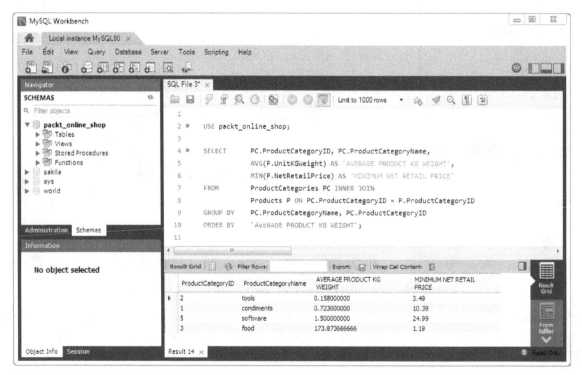

Figure 10.4: A MySQL aggregate function query with an ORDER BY clause

An **ORDER BY** clause will accept a column alias name, or the actual aggregate function itself (in this case, **AVG(P.UnitKGWeight)**), as seen in this query:

```
USE         packt_online_shop;

SELECT      PC.ProductCategoryID, PC.ProductCategoryName,
            AVG(P.UnitKGWeight) AS 'AVERAGE PRODUCT KG WEIGHT',
            MIN(P.NetRetailPrice) AS 'MINIMUM NET RETAIL PRICE'
FROM        ProductCategories PC INNER JOIN

            Products P ON PC.ProductCategoryID = P.ProductCategoryID
GROUP BY    PC.ProductCategoryName, PC.ProductCategoryID
ORDER BY    AVG(P.UnitKGWeight);
```

On execution, your output should be as follows:

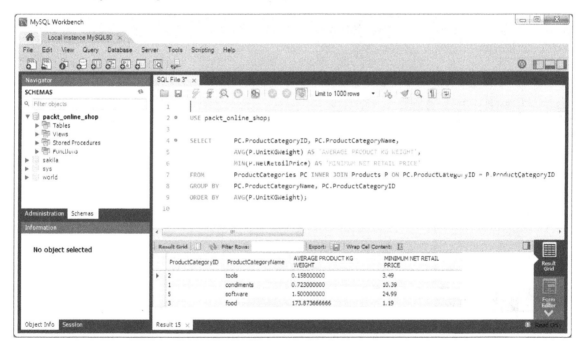

Figure 10.5: A MySQL aggregate function query with an ORDER BY clause

We took a close look at the **AVG** and **MIN** aggregate functions to build a basic understanding of SQL aggregate functions. This SQL query in MySQL shows the five SQL aggregate functions:

```
USE         packt_online_shop;

SELECT      PC.ProductCategoryID, PC.ProductCategoryName,
            AVG(P.UnitKGWeight) AS 'AVERAGE PRODUCT KG WEIGHT',
            MIN(P.NetRetailPrice) AS 'MINIMUM NET RETAIL PRICE',
            MAX(P.WholesalePrice) AS 'MAX WHOLESALE PRICE',
            COUNT(P.AvailableQuantity) AS 'COUNT AVAILABLE QUANTITY',
            SUM(P.AvailableQuantity) AS 'SUM AVAILABLE QUANTITY'
FROM        ProductCategories PC INNER JOIN

            Products P ON PC.ProductCategoryID = P.ProductCategoryID
GROUP BY    PC.ProductCategoryName, PC.ProductCategoryID;
```

The result of executing the preceding query is as follows:

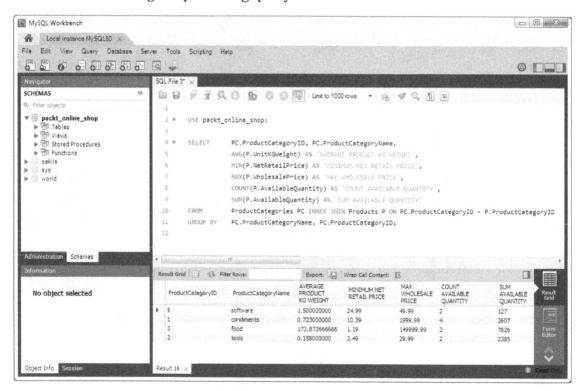

Figure 10.6: The five SQL aggregate functions in MySQL

The remaining three functions, as described here, operate just like the **AVG** and **MIN** functions we saw earlier:

- The **MAX** function returns the largest value in a column for all the rows in each separate row group

- The **COUNT** function counts all the rows in each separate row group

- The **SUM** function returns the **SUM** of all values of a column for all the rows in each separate row group

Exercise 10.01: Implementing Aggregate Functions

For every customer order in the *Packt Online Shop*, use SQL aggregate functions to find the price of the highest and lowest-priced products. We'll build a query with these columns to make the result set clear: **OrderID**, **LastName**, **PRICE OF LOWEST PRICED**, and **PRICE OF HIGHEST PRICED**:

1. Build a basic query that joins the tables we need:

```
SELECT  O.OrderID, C.LastName
FROM    Customers C INNER JOIN Orders O ON
        C.CustomerID = O.CustomerID
        INNER JOIN OrderItems OI ON
        O.OrderID = OI.OrderID;
```

2. Add columns for the aggregate functions:

```
SELECT  O.OrderID, C.LastName,
        MIN(OI.UnitPrice) AS 'PRICE OF LOWEST PRICED PRODUCT
        OF THE ORDER',
        MAX(OI.UnitPrice) AS 'PRICE OF HIGHEST PRICED PRODUCT
        OF THE ORDER'
FROM    Customers C INNER JOIN Orders O ON
        C.CustomerID = O.CustomerID
        INNER JOIN OrderItems OI ON
        O.OrderID = OI.OrderID;
```

3. Remember the **GROUP BY** clause:

```
SELECT    O.OrderID, C.LastName,
          MIN(OI.UnitPrice) AS 'PRICE OF LOWEST PRICED PRODUCT OF
          THE ORDER',
          MAX(OI.UnitPrice) AS 'PRICE OF HIGHEST PRICED PRODUCT
          OF THE ORDER'
FROM      Customers C INNER JOIN Orders O ON
          C.CustomerID = O.CustomerID
          INNER JOIN OrderItems OI ON
          O.OrderID = OI.OrderID
GROUP BY  C.LastName, O.OrderID;
```

The result will be as follows:

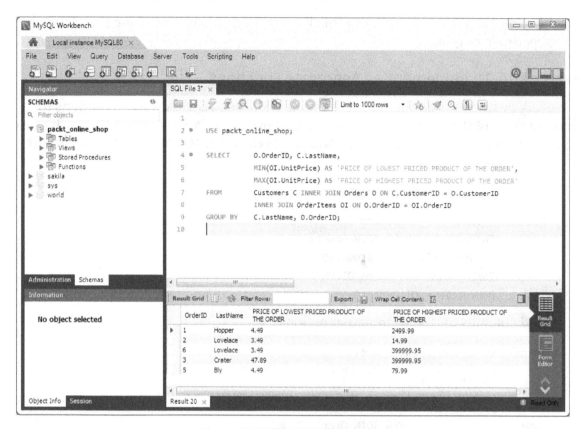

Figure 10.7: The GROUP BY clause

The HAVING Clause

As we saw, the aggregate functions will solve many problems for us. Eventually, however, we'll want to filter the aggregate function value of a query result set. We have learned how to build SQL queries that calculate aggregate function values. If we want to filter the query results on those aggregate function values, the **WHERE** clause won't work. For example, we might want to see the query results of a SQL **MAX** function that land below a specific value. We might need the query results of a SQL **AVG** function that match a specific value. The **HAVING** clause will help. Starting with this query, suppose we want only those rows with **MINIMUM NET RETAIL PRICE** values greater than **5.00** in the result set:

```
USE         packt_online_shop;

SELECT      PC.ProductCategoryID, PC.ProductCategoryName,
            AVG(P.UnitKGWeight) AS 'AVERAGE PRODUCT KG WEIGHT',
            MIN(P.NetRetailPrice) AS 'MINIMUM NET RETAIL PRICE'
FROM        ProductCategories PC INNER JOIN
```

```
                  Products P ON PC.ProductCategoryID = P.ProductCategoryID
GROUP BY    PC.ProductCategoryName, PC.ProductCategoryID;
```

In this query, we tried a **WHERE** clause for the filter:

```
USE         packt_online_shop;

SELECT      PC.ProductCategoryID, PC.ProductCategoryName,
            AVG(P.UnitKGWeight) AS 'AVERAGE PRODUCT KG WEIGHT',
            MIN(P.NetRetailPrice) AS 'MINIMUM NET RETAIL PRICE'
FROM        ProductCategories PC INNER JOIN
            Products P ON PC.ProductCategoryID = P.ProductCategoryID
WHERE       MIN(P.NetRetailPrice) > 5.00
GROUP BY    PC.ProductCategoryName, PC.ProductCategoryID;
```

When you run the query, this won't work:

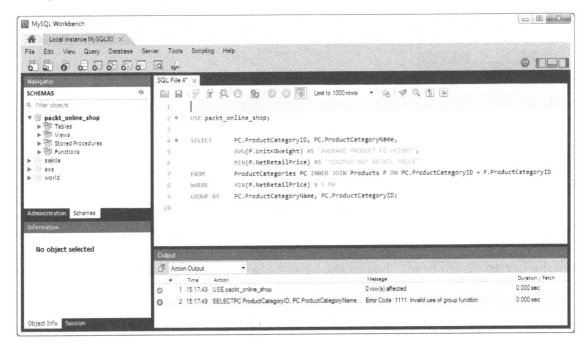

Figure 10.8: Error – filtering an aggregate function column with a WHERE clause

The **WHERE** clause only filters on the rows that its **SELECT** query sees. By design, the **WHERE** clause can't operate on row groups or row aggregates. The **HAVING** clause will solve the problem. Place it below the **GROUP BY** clause in this query:

```
USE         packt_online_shop;

SELECT      PC.ProductCategoryID, PC.ProductCategoryName,
            AVG(P.UnitKGWeight) AS 'AVERAGE PRODUCT KG WEIGHT',
            MIN(P.NetRetailPrice) AS 'MINIMUM NET RETAIL PRICE'
```

```
FROM        ProductCategories PC INNER JOIN
            Products P ON PC.ProductCategoryID = P.ProductCategoryID
GROUP BY  PC.ProductCategoryName, PC.ProductCategoryID
HAVING      MIN(P.NetRetailPrice) > 5.00;
```

You can see the **HAVING** clause on line 10:

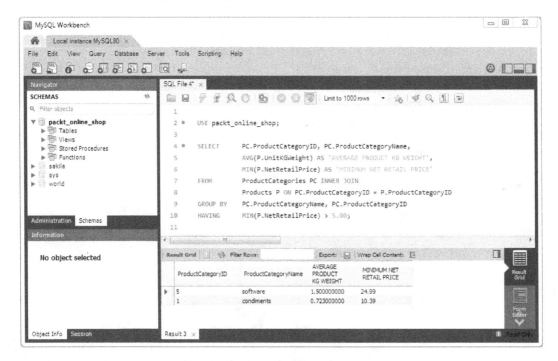

Figure 10.9: Filtering an aggregate function result set with a HAVING clause

The **HAVING** clause filters the results as we expect. Note that the line 6 column alias, **'MINIMUM NET RETAIL PRICE'**, won't work in the **HAVING** clause on line 10 because SQL runs the **HAVING** clause before it sees the **SELECT** clause. This means that it does not know about the column alias, seen here on line 6.

Exercise 10.02: Implementing the HAVING Clause

In the **PACKT_ONLINE_SHOP** database, every row in the **ProductCategories** table has at least one child row in the **Products** table. In the **Products** table, the **AvailableQuantity** column shows the available quantity for each product. Use the SQL **HAVING** clause to build a list of product categories with more than 250 total available product items, covering all products in each category:

1. We'll build a query with these:

```
SELECT    PC.ProductCategoryName,
          SUM(P.AvailableQuantity) AS 'TOTAL COUNT OF ALL
          PRODUCTS IN PRODUCT CATEGORY'
```

```
FROM      Products P INNER JOIN ProductCategories PC ON
          P.ProductCategoryID = PC.ProductCategoryID;
```

2. Add the **GROUP BY** clause and sort the results by **ProductCategoryName**:

```
SELECT    PC.ProductCategoryName,
          SUM(P.AvailableQuantity) AS 'TOTAL COUNT OF ALL
          PRODUCTS IN PRODUCT CATEGORY'
FROM      Products P INNER JOIN ProductCategories PC ON
          P.ProductCategoryID = PC.ProductCategoryID
GROUP BY  PC.ProductCategoryName
ORDER BY  ProductCategoryName;
```

3. Add the **HAVING** clause:

```
SELECT    PC.ProductCategoryName,
          SUM(P.AvailableQuantity) AS 'TOTAL COUNT OF ALL
          PRODUCTS IN PRODUCT CATEGORY'
FROM      Products P INNER JOIN ProductCategories PC ON
          P.ProductCategoryID = PC.ProductCategoryID
GROUP BY  PC.ProductCategoryName
HAVING    SUM(P.AvailableQuantity) > 250
ORDER BY  ProductCategoryName;
```

The result will be as follows:

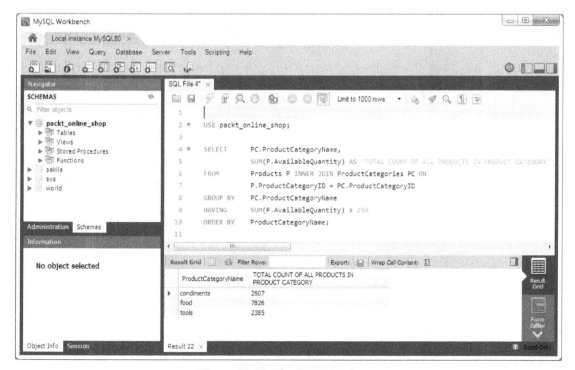

Figure 10.10: The HAVING clause

The Differences between the SQL HAVING and WHERE Clauses

We saw earlier that a **WHERE** clause filter won't work with an aggregate function column. However, the **HAVING** clause will filter a *regular*, or non-aggregate column. To do this, we must include the **GROUP BY** clause. Have a look at this query:

```
USE         packt_online_shop;

SELECT      PC.ProductCategoryID, PC.ProductCategoryName,
            AVG(P.UnitKGWeight) AS 'AVERAGE PRODUCT KG WEIGHT',
            MIN(P.NetRetailPrice) AS 'MINIMUM NET RETAIL PRICE'
FROM        ProductCategories PC INNER JOIN
            Products P ON PC.ProductCategoryID = P.ProductCategoryID
HAVING      PC.ProductCategoryID = 2;
```

Here's the output:

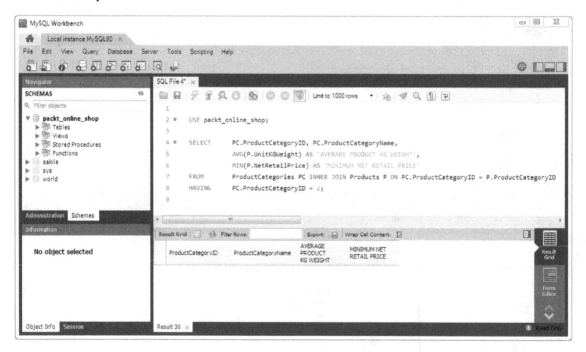

Figure 10.11: Trying to filter a table column with a HAVING clause

It did not work because we forgot the **GROUP BY** clause. If we add the **GROUP BY** clause, it will work:

```
USE         packt_online_shop;

SELECT      PC.ProductCategoryID, PC.ProductCategoryName,
            AVG(P.UnitKGWeight) AS 'AVERAGE PRODUCT KG WEIGHT',
            MIN(P.NetRetailPrice) AS 'MINIMUM NET RETAIL PRICE'
FROM        ProductCategories PC INNER JOIN
```

```
           Products P ON PC.ProductCategoryID = P.ProductCategoryID
GROUP BY   PC.ProductCategoryID, PC.ProductCategoryName
HAVING     PC.ProductCategoryID = 2;
```

Here's the output:

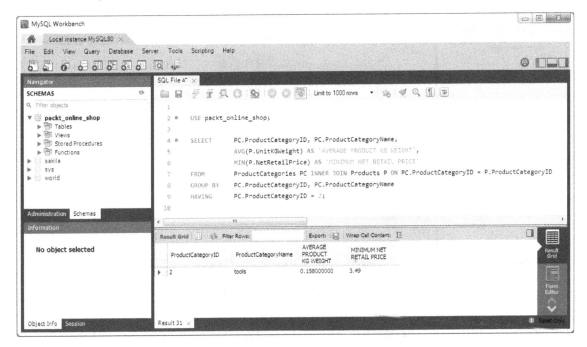

Figure 10.12: Correctly filtering a table column with a HAVING clause

As we can see, the query worked.

If we set up the **GROUP BY** clause correctly, as explained previously, we can use both **WHERE** and **HAVING** clauses in the same query. This query combines **WHERE** and **HAVING** clauses in one query:

```
USE        packt_online_shop;

SELECT     OI.OrderID, P.ProductName,
           SUM((OI.UnitPrice - OI.Discount) * OI.Quantity) AS
           'TOTAL REVENUE PER PRODUCT PER ORDER'
FROM       OrderItems OI INNER JOIN
           Products P ON OI.ProductID = P.ProductID
WHERE      OI.OrderID = 5
GROUP BY   OI.OrderID, P.ProductName
HAVING     SUM((OI.UnitPrice - OI.Discount) * OI.Quantity) > 4.50
ORDER BY   'TOTAL REVENUE PER PRODUCT PER ORDER' ASC;
```

This is what it looks like in MySQL:

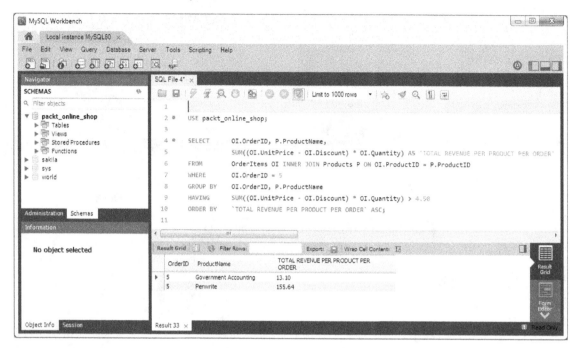

Figure 10.13: Combining WHERE and HAVING clauses in one query

The line 5 **SUM** aggregate function requires the line 8 **GROUP BY** clause, and the line 9 **HAVING** clause filters on the **SUM** function values. The line 7 **WHERE** clause filters the **OrderItems.OrderID** values. As explained earlier, we could have placed all the filters in the **HAVING** clause, combining them with the **AND** keyword:

```
USE        packt_online_shop;

SELECT     OI.OrderID, P.ProductName,
           SUM((OI.UnitPrice - OI.Discount) * OI.Quantity) AS
           'TOTAL REVENUE PER PRODUCT PER ORDER'
FROM       OrderItems OI INNER JOIN
           Products P ON OI.ProductID = P.ProductID
WHERE      OI.OrderID = 5
GROUP BY   OI.OrderID, P.ProductName
HAVING     (SUM((OI.UnitPrice - OI.Discount) * OI.Quantity) > 4.50)
           AND (OI.OrderID = 5)
ORDER BY   'TOTAL REVENUE PER PRODUCT PER ORDER' DESC
```

Look at the **HAVING** clause on line 9:

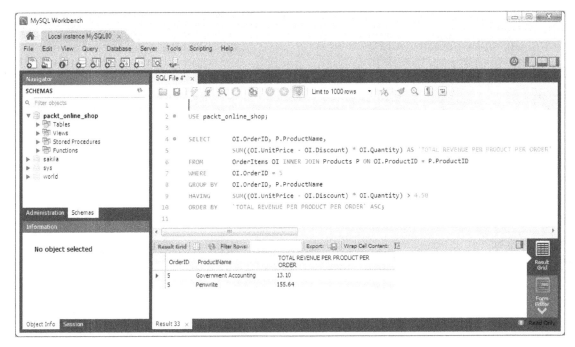

Figure 10.14: HAVING clause filters instead of WHERE clause filters

However, we want as much filtering as possible to happen in the **WHERE** clause and as little as possible in the **HAVING** clause. As MySQL runs a query, it evaluates the **WHERE** clause early on. This eliminates as many rows as possible as early as possible. MySQL then runs the **GROUP BY** clause if it sees one, and then runs the **HAVING** clause if it sees one. If a query eliminates as many rows as possible with the **WHERE** clause, MySQL can avoid operations on fewer rows. That way, it will use fewer resources and the query will have better performance.

SQL OVER and PARTITION BY

So far, we have seen the SQL aggregate calculations operate on an entire query result set. This works well and is a powerful tool. We have also seen that the **GROUP BY** clause will divide a SQL query result set into separate sets of rows based on specified criteria. We might want to use a **GROUP BY** clause in a SQL query, and then we might want to run an aggregate function to the query results, applying the function to each separate group of rows. **OVER** and **PARTITION BY** will help with this.

The Packt management likes the query results shown in *Figure* 10.14, but now they want every row to show both the total sales per order and the number of items per order. They want this for all orders and all order items. If a web page or report will use these results, this information could be useful for custom calculations. As a first step, we can modify the query from *Figure* 10.14 to this new query:

```
INSERT INTO Products(ProductCategoryID, SupplierID,
ProductName, ProductImage, NetRetailPrice,
AvailableQuantity, WholesalePrice,
UnitKGWeight, Notes)
VALUES(3, 3, 'peanut butter', NULL, 3.79, 1000, 2.69,
0.75, 'caution: high calorie');


SELECT S.*
FROM Suppliers S
WHERE S.SupplierID = 3;
```

This is what it looks like in MySQL:

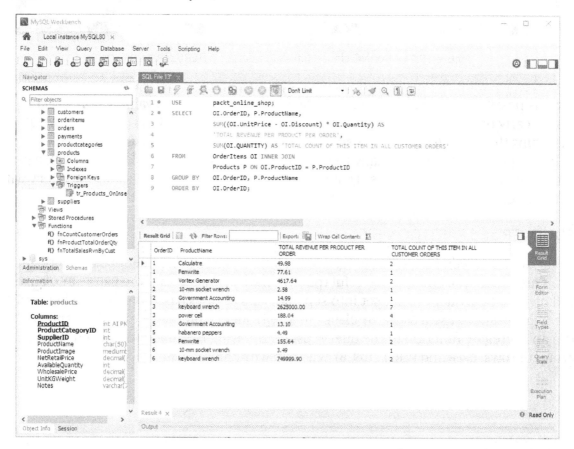

Figure 10.15: Output displaying total sales and the number of items per order

We can add the MySQL **OVER** and **PARTITION BY** clauses after the **SUM** and **COUNT** aggregate functions:

```
USE packt_online_shop;

SELECT  OI.OrderID, P.ProductName,
        SUM((OI.UnitPrice - OI.Discount) * OI.Quantity) AS
        'TOTAL REVENUE PER PRODUCT PER ORDER',
        SUM(SUM((OI.UnitPrice - OI.Discount) * OI.Quantity))
        OVER(PARTITION BY OI.OrderID)
AS 'TOTAL_SALES_PER_ORDER',
COUNT(OI.OrderItemID) OVER(PARTITION BY OI.OrderID)
AS 'NUMBER OF ITEMS IN CUSTOMER''S ORDER'
FROM    OrderItems OI INNER JOIN
Products P ON OI.ProductID = P.ProductID
GROUP BY    OI.OrderID, P.ProductName
ORDER BY    OI.OrderID;
```

This is what it looks like in MySQL:

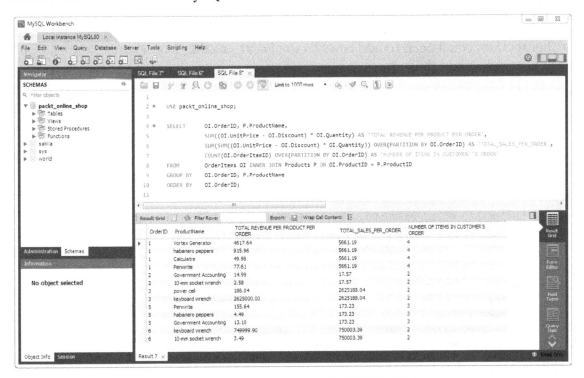

Figure 10.16: Using the OVER and PARTITION BY clauses

Placed after the aggregate functions on those lines, the **OVER(PARTITION BY OI.OrderID)** clause applies the aggregate functions on those lines against subsets of rows, each row subset grouped by the **OI.OrderID** column. With the **OVER(PARTITION BY OI.OrderID)**, the line 6 **SUM** function calculates the **TOTAL_SALES_PER_ORDER** value for each different **OrderID**. The line 7 **COUNT** function makes a similar calculation, counting the number of ordered items in each customer order. Line 7 wrapped, or "nested," the original **SUM** aggregate function inside another **SUM()**:

```
SUM(SUM((OI.UnitPrice - OI.Discount) * OI.Quantity)) OVER(PARTITION
  BY OI.OrderID)
```

Although these nested functions might look a little strange, it's perfectly legal syntax. It tells MySQL to apply the function calculation on every row set, as defined by each individual OrderID value. Note that in the PARTITION BY clause, we can use other columns to build the row subsets, depending on the solutions we need.

The RANK and DENSE_RANK Functions

The **RANK** and **DENSE_RANK** functions can be used to assign a rank to each row in the ordered partition.

For this section, you'll need to add rows to the **PACKT_ONLINE_SHOP.Products** table. Run this SQL script to add those rows:

```
USE PACKT_ONLINE_SHOP;

INSERT INTO Products ( ProductCategoryID, SupplierID,
  ProductName, ProductImage, NetRetailPrice, AvailableQuantity,
  WholesalePrice, UnitKGWeight, Notes )

VALUES
(4, 1, 'Helios 5', NULL, 24999.99, 22, 17999.99, 15,
  'helium airship'),
(4, 1, 'Arctan Pi', NULL, 84999.99, 3, 77999.99, 2,
  'high-lift freight dirigible'),
(4, 1, 'Fermat Radian', NULL, 199999.95, 18, 185999.99,
  17.4, 'passenger airship'),
(2, 4, 'Hammer', NULL, 39.95, 19, 33.49, 0.5,
  'basic hammer'),
(2, 4, 'Dishwasher Airgap', NULL, 14.95, 34, 10.89, 0.45,
  'countertop airgap'),
(2, 4, 'Flathead Screwdriver', NULL, 7.49, 208, 5.19, 0.15,
  'regular screwdriver'),
(2, 4, 'Phillips Screwdriver', NULL, 7.29, 155, 5.49, 0.15,
  'phillips-head screwdriver'),
```

```
(2, 4, 'Pliers', NULL, 19.95, 44, 15.23, 0.45, 'pliers'),
(6, 4, 'Wealth of Nations', NULL, 24.95, 144, 19.49, 0.65,
  'Great economics book');
```

> **Note**
>
> The preceding code can also be found at: https://packt.live/2Ss9KWy

This query counts all of the products in each product category:

```
USE         packt_online_shop;

SELECT      PC.ProductCategoryID, PC.ProductCategoryName,
            COUNT(P.ProductID) AS 'PRODUCT COUNT IN CATEGORY'
FROM        ProductCategories PC INNER JOIN
            Products P ON PC.ProductCategoryID = P.ProductCategoryID
GROUP BY    PC.ProductCategoryID, PC.ProductCategoryName;
```

This is what it looks like in MySQL, along with the output:

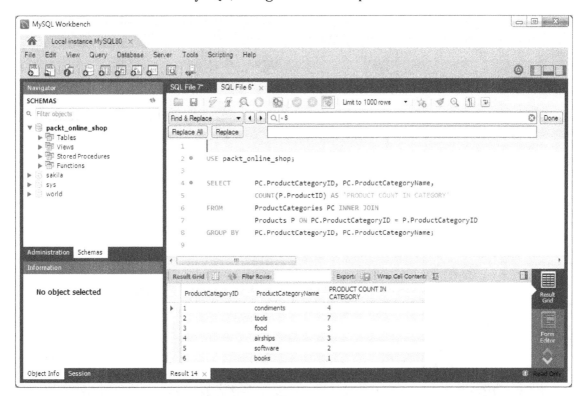

Figure 10.17: A query to count all the products in each product category

However, the Packt management wants a ranked list of these categories. In other words, they want to know which category has the highest number of products, which has the next highest number, and so on, down to the category with the lowest number of products. In our solution, the category with the highest number of products should have a ranking value of 1, the category with the next highest number of products should have a ranking value of 2, and so on. If we include the **RANK** function in the *Figure 10.17* query, we'll see the ranking values we want:

```
SELECT     PC.ProductCategoryID, PC.ProductCategoryName,
           COUNT(P.ProductID) AS 'PRODUCT COUNT IN CATEGORY',
           RANK () OVER (
                ORDER BY COUNT(P.ProductID) DESC
           ) AS 'PRODUCT COUNT RANK'
FROM       ProductCategories PC INNER JOIN
           Products P ON PC.ProductCategoryID = P.ProductCategoryID
GROUP BY   PC.ProductCategoryID, PC.ProductCategoryName;
```

Here's the code and output in MySQL:

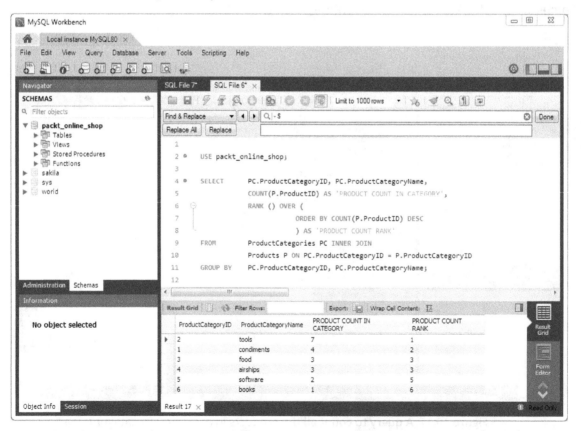

Figure 10.18: A SQL query with the RANK function

On line 6, the **RANK** function places the row ranking values in the **PRODUCT COUNT RANK** column. The required **ORDER BY** clause on line 7 sorts the rows in descending order. In the query results, note that rows 3 and 4 have the same **PRODUCT COUNT RANK** value, as we would expect. However, note the row 5 **PRODUCT COUNT RANK** value. If the **RANK** function sees a tie, it will skip the value for the next rank value it calculates. The **DENSE_RANK** function will return ranking values without skips. This query replaces the line 6 **RANK** function as seen in *Figure 10.18* with the **DENSE_RANK** function:

```
SELECT    PC.ProductCategoryID, PC.ProductCategoryName,
          COUNT(P.ProductID) AS 'PRODUCT COUNT IN CATEGORY',
          DENSE_RANK () OVER (
              ORDER BY COUNT(P.ProductID) DESC
          ) AS 'PRODUCT COUNT DENSE_RANK'
FROM      ProductCategories PC INNER JOIN
          Products P ON PC.ProductCategoryID = P.ProductCategoryID
GROUP BY  PC.ProductCategoryID, PC.ProductCategoryName;
```

Here's how the query looks like in MySQL, along with the output:

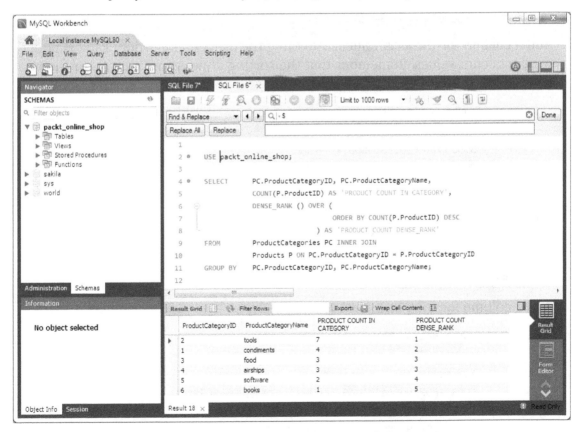

Figure 10.19: A SQL query with the DENSE_RANK function

On line 5 in the results pane, the **DENSE_RANK** function did not skip a number in the **PRODUCT COUNT DENSE_RANK** column.

Exercise 10.03: Implementing RANK

Build a list of **PACKT_ONLINE_SHOP** suppliers, the product counts of each supplier, and the **RANK** and **DENSE_RANK** function of each supplier based on its product count. Sort the list by supplier product count in descending order. The list should have these columns: **SupplierID**, **SupplierName**, **PRODUCT COUNT OF SUPPLIER**, **SUPPLIER RANK**, **SUPPLIER DENSE_RANK**.

1. First, build a query for the supplier and product count data:

```
USE          packt_online_shop;

SELECT       S.SupplierID, S.SupplierName,
             COUNT(P.ProductID) AS 'PRODUCT COUNT OF SUPPLIER'
FROM         Suppliers S INNER JOIN
             Products P ON S.SupplierID = P.SupplierID
GROUP BY     S.SupplierID, S.SupplierName;
```

2. Add a column for the **RANK** values, reflecting the descending order of the supplier product count values. Remember that the sorting does not happen at the query level:

```
USE          packt_online_shop;

SELECT       S.SupplierID, S.SupplierName,
             COUNT(P.ProductID) AS 'PRODUCT COUNT OF SUPPLIER',
             RANK () OVER (
                 ORDER BY COUNT(P.ProductID) DESC
             ) AS 'SUPPLIER RANK'
FROM         Suppliers S INNER JOIN
             Products P ON S.SupplierID = P.SupplierID
GROUP BY     S.SupplierID, S.SupplierName;
```

3. Add a column for the **DENSE_RANK** values:

```
USE          packt_online_shop;

SELECT       S.SupplierID, S.SupplierName,
             COUNT(P.ProductID) AS 'PRODUCT COUNT OF SUPPLIER',
             RANK () OVER (
                 ORDER BY COUNT(P.ProductID) DESC
             ) AS 'SUPPLIER RANK',
```

```
            DENSE_RANK () OVER (
                ORDER BY COUNT(P.ProductID) DESC
            ) AS 'SUPPLIER DENSE_RANK'
FROM        Suppliers S INNER JOIN
            Products P ON S.SupplierID = P.SupplierID
GROUP BY    S.SupplierID, S.SupplierName;
```

The result will be as follows:

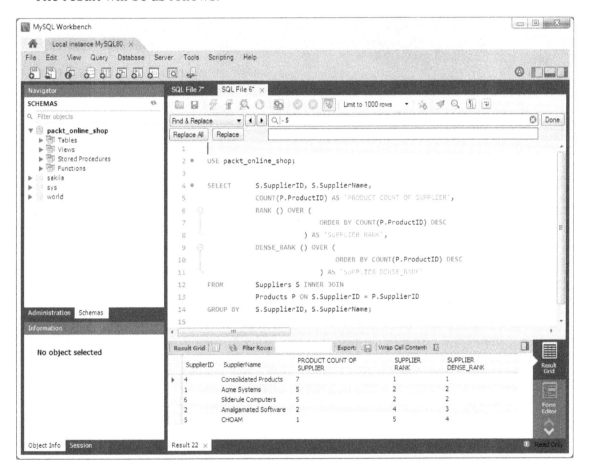

Figure 10.20: A MySQL query with the RANK and DENSE_RANK functions

Activity 10.01: Working with Aggregates

Using data in the **PACKT_ONLINE_SHOP** database, build a report showing the following:

- Order ID

- Product name

- The count of each separate product in the order

- The total count of all products in the order

- The count of the product with the highest count in the order

> **Note**
>
> The solution for this activity can be found on page 261.

Summary

In this chapter, we learned that SQL aggregate functions provide an efficient, flexible way to calculate summary values in SQL query result sets. We discovered that the **GROUP BY** clause will separate the results of a **SELECT** query into one or more row groups to support the design and execution of queries with aggregate functions. We saw that the **HAVING** clause provides a pinpoint way to filter aggregate function calculations. Although they're similar, we learned about the differences between **WHERE** and **HAVING** clauses. Finally, we saw that when we use **OVER** and **PARTITION BY** in creative ways, MySQL will efficiently expand the range of problems it can solve for us. We can also order the items with a group using the **RANK** and **DENSE RANK** functions. In the next chapter, we will look at some advanced features of SQL programming.

11

Advanced SQL

Overview

By the end of this chapter, you will be able to implement **STRING** functions and manipulate string data. You will be able to use the **COALESCE** function to return the first non-zero values from a list and will learn how to identify and deal with duplicate values in a table.

Introduction

Now that we have covered the core topics of SQL database design and development, we can focus on more complex problems that reach past the material we looked at in earlier chapters. Building on what we've learned, we'll look at more SQL topics and tools and how to expand our existing skills to cover new situations. SQL database products offer huge feature spaces to developers—much bigger than what we have seen so far. Developers can lever these features to efficiently add value and solve problems. In this chapter, we'll explore a small sample of these feature spaces to get a sense of the potential of SQL database products and how to approach them as new tools to solve new problems.

String Functions

In the previous chapters, we saw that text or string data is an important part of real-world database resources. SQL database products offer dedicated functions to handle and manipulate string data. As we'll see, this makes them useful in a **SELECT** clause. In addition, although the **LIKE** operator is not a string function, it searches for string patterns in other strings. This makes it incredibly useful in a **WHERE** clause. We'll see this as well. Since we can use string functions in **SELECT** statements and **WHERE** clauses, we can also use them in stored procedures, user-defined functions, and triggers. One example of a string function is the UPPER function. This function converts a string value into all uppercase characters. Consider the following query:

```
USE packt_online_shop;
SELECT ProductID, ProductName, UPPER(ProductName) AS 'UPPER CASE PRODUCT NAME'
FROM    Products;
```

Running the preceding code in the SQL query window yields the following output:

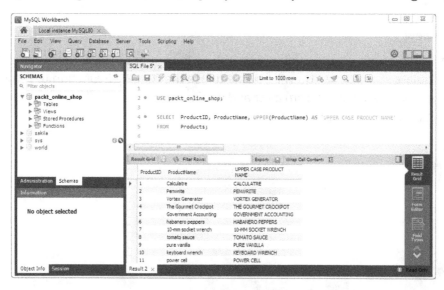

Figure 11.1: The MySQL UPPER string function

In the **SELECT** clause, the **UPPER** function converted all the **ProductName** column characters in all the rows into uppercase.

In MySQL, you can convert a numeric value into a textual representation of it by using **CAST** function:

```
CAST( numeric_float_value AS CHAR|VARCHAR)
```

Depending on the values it receives, it can round and even truncate its return values.

Expression	Description
BINARY	Expression to BINARY (binary string)
CHAR	Expression to CHAR (fixed-length string)
DATE	Expression to DATE (format: 'YYYY-MM-DD')
DATETIME	Expression to DATETIME (format: 'YYYY-MM-DD HH:MM:SS')
SIGNED	Expression to SIGNED (signed 64-bit integer)
TIME	Expression to TIME (format: 'HH:MM:SS')
UNSIGNED	Expression to UNSIGNED (unsigned 64-bit integer)

Figure 11.2: A table demonstrating expressions and their descriptions

Now, consider another example query:

```
USE packt_online_shop;
SELECT OrderItemID, Quantity, UnitPrice,
   CAST((Quantity * UnitPrice) AS CHAR) AS 'Quantity * UnitPrice'
FROM    OrderItems;
```

The preceding query will now give the following output:

OrderItemID	Quantity	UnitPrice	Quantity * UnitPrice
1	2	24.99	49.98
2	1	79.99	79.99
3	2	2499.99	4999.98
4	1	14.99	14.99
5	1	3.49	3.49
6	4	47.89	191.56
7	7	399999.95	2799999.65
8	2	79.99	159.98
9	1	4.49	4.49
10	1	14.99	14.99
11	2	399999.95	799999.90
12	1	3.49	3.49

Figure 11.3: The MySQL STR string function

The second **STR** function parameter sets the return value's total length to 10, while the third parameter sets the number of decimal places to the right of the decimal point to two. The query returned the calculated values we need, but most of those values have a lot of blank spaces because the **STR** function added extra spaces to fill the string length to 10. For example, in row five, the last column has six extra spaces in front of the value. The MySQL **LTRIM** function removes or trims leading spaces from a string, while the **RTRIM** function removes or trims trailing spaces from a string. We can nest these functions to remove all leading and trailing spaces.

> **Note**
>
> SQL Server 2017 offers a **TRIM** function that clones these nested functions and puts them in one function.

Here is the code we can use to remove all leading and trailing spaces:

```
USE packt_online_shop;
SELECT   OrderItemID, Quantity, UnitPrice,
   LTRIM(RTRIM(CAST((Quantity * UnitPrice) AS CHAR)))
   AS 'Quantity * UnitPrice'
FROM  OrderItems;
```

Running this query yields the following output:

OrderItemID	Quantity	UnitPrice	Quantity * UnitPrice
1	2	24.99	49.98
2	1	79.99	79.99
3	2	2499.99	4999.98
4	1	14.99	14.99
5	1	3.49	3.49
6	4	47.89	191.56
7	7	399999.95	2799999.65
8	2	79.99	159.98
9	1	4.49	4.49
10	1	14.99	14.99
11	2	399999.95	799999.90
12	1	3.49	3.49

Figure 11.4: The output of LTRIM and RTRIM string functions

As you can see, the values in the fourth column no longer have leading or trailing spaces. Now that we have a solid grounding of SQL string functions, we'll use them in an exercise to see them in action.

Exercise 11.01: Building a MySQL Query that Returns the OrderID, Quantity, and Notes Columns

Suppose the Packt management team needs a report showing the columns of the `OrderItems` table, in the following format:

OrderID	ITEM_QUANTITY_ORDERED_AND_NOTES
1	2: Ordered: HANDLE WITH CARE

Figure 11.5: Format of the output

Here are the steps to complete this exercise:

1. Open a new query window and type in the following query:

```
USE packt_online_shop;


SELECT    OrderID, LTRIM(RTRIM(CONCAT(CAST(Quantity AS CHAR),
              ' Ordered: ', UPPER(Notes))))
          AS 'ITEM_QUANTITY_ORDERED_AND_NOTES'


FROM OrderItems;
```

Here, we used the **UPPER** function to convert the notes into uppercase. Then, we used the **CONCAT** string to append concatenate values from all three different columns into a single column.

2. Execute the query by pressing F5. You should get the following output:

OrderID	ITEM_QUANTITY_ORDERED_AND_NOTES
1	2 Ordered: HANDLE WITH CARE
1	1 Ordered: KEEP AWAY FROM MAGNETIC FIELDS
1	2 Ordered: AVOID EXPOSURE TO LIGHT
2	1 Ordered: OPEN SOURCE SOFTWARE
2	1 Ordered: EXCEEDINGLY RARE
3	4 Ordered: HIGH-DEMAND PRODUCT
3	7 Ordered: HIGH GRAVITY
5	2 Ordered: CUSTOMER TRANSITIONING FROM ...
5	1 Ordered: HEAVY SCOVILLE UNITS
5	1 Ordered: FINANCIAL PLANNING
6	2 Ordered: AIRCRAFT CONSTRUCTION
6	1 Ordered: TEST FOR MAGNETISM BEFORE USE

Figure 11.6: Using string functions to get output in a particular format

Previously, we learned that we can filter a result set with the SQL **WHERE** clause. For numeric values, we have seen examples where the queries return more than one row. We have also seen how the **LIKE** operator can be used to generate multiple entries. However, the **LIKE** operator can also be used in stored procedures. The following exercise illustrates this.

Exercise 11.02: Using LIKE in a Stored Procedure

The store manager wants to get details of the customers who come from an educational institution at the end of every month. To identify whether the customer is from an educational background, check whether their email IDs end with *.edu*. Since we want to perform this operation every month, we want to write this in a stored procedure. Perform the following steps:

1. Create a stored procedure called **spFilterCustomers** to filter out email IDs with **.edu**:

```
CREATE PROCEDURE spFilterCustomers
(emailString    VARCHAR(100))
--  to test: CALL spFilterCustomers('.edu')
SELECT    C.CustomerID, C.FirstName, C.LastName, C.Address,
          C.Email, C.Phone, C.Notes, C.BalanceNotes
FROM      Customers C
WHERE     C.email LIKE CONCAT('%', emailString, '%');
```

2. Execute the query. To test run the following command:

```
CALL spFilterCustomers('.edu')
```

3. Your output should be as follows:

CustomerID	FirstName	LastName	Address	Email	Phone	Notes	BalanceNotes
8	Yuri	Gagarin	1 Ad Astra	yuri@rheysdagf.edu	(310) 555-5462	First human to space	NULL
9	NULL	Jones	126 Bonhomme Richard Ave.	jpjones@bonhommerichard.edu	(216) 555-6232	Admiral	NULL
10	NULL	Smith	1818 Eratosthenes Blvd.	alsmith@dytsdrg.edu	(345) 555-5434	Writer	NULL
11	NULL	Pythagoras	32 Hypotenuse Way	pythagoras@sdrg.edu	(260) 555-3461	Mathematician	NULL
13	Aristotle	NULL	32 Parthenon Way	aristotle@ertyasdf.edu	(310) 555-9182	Scholar	NULL
14	Cicero	NULL	25 Appian Way	Cicero@ghyu45y.edu	(310) 555-0822	Orator	NULL
15	Srinivasa	Ramanujan	123 Bernoulli Number Drive	srinivasa@imaginarynumber.edu	(211) 555-1111	Sharp Mathematician	NULL
16	Orville	Wright	80 Bicycle Lane	owright@sdg98.edu	(211) 555-4444	First pilot	NULL

Figure 11.7: A output of stored procedure with the LIKE operator

In this stored procedure, the **LIKE** filter surrounds the **emailString** parameter with single-quoted percent signs. Often, we'll need to build a query with a **WHERE** clause that filters in a flexible way. Specifically, we'll want to search for a specific string, as a substring, anywhere in a text data value. The **LIKE** operator will help solve this problem, as we'll see next in the following activity.

Activity 11.01: Implementing the LIKE Operator

All feedback from the customers are stored in the Notes column. You are asked to check whether there is any customer-related feedback on all shipments after 1 May 1995. You will need to query the data to:

- Check whether **ShipmentDate** is greater than **May 1, 1995**.

- Check whether **Notes** contains the **CUST** substring.

To do this you can use the LIKE operator to match the string in the notes section and use the greater than operator to check the ShipmentDate.

> **Note**
>
> The solution for this activity can be found on page 262.

Dealing with NULL and COALESCE

If a SQL operation combines multiple values, that operation will return **NULL** if at least one of the combining values has a **NULL** value of its own.

In MySQL, the queries shown here would yield **NULL** result sets:

```
SELECT CONCAT('A', '^', NULL, 'asdf') AS "A + '^' + NULL + 'asdf'";


SELECT 3 * 12.356 * NULL AS "3 * 12.356 * NULL";


SET @val1 = 1;   -- TRUE
SET @val2 = 0;   -- FALSE


SELECT @val1 & NULL & @val2 AS "TRUE + NULL + FALSE";
```

This can be seen in the following output:

Figure 11.8: NULL values in MySQL SELECT statements

Consider the following MySQL statements:

```
SET @val1 = 1;  -- TRUE
SET @val2 = 0;  -- FALSE


SELECT @val1 & NULL & @val2 AS "TRUE + NULL + FALSE";
```

In the preceding code, the **BIT** data type variables, **@val1** and **@val2**, operate as Booleans, the final query essentially *adds* these Boolean values with the **&** operator.

Now, have a look at the following query:

```
USE PACKT_ONLINE_SHOP;


SELECT    FirstName, MiddleName, LastName,
   CONCAT(FirstName, ' ', MiddleName, ' ', LastName) as 'CombinedName'
FROM    Customers;
```

It provides the following output:

FirstName	MiddleName	LastName	CombinedName
Joe	Greg	Smith	Joe Greg Smith
Grace	Murray	Hopper	Grace Murray Hopper
Ada	NULL	Lovelace	NULL
Joseph	Force	Crater	Joseph Force Crater
Jacqueline	Jackie	Cochran	Jacqueline Jackie Cochran
William	NULL	Shakespeare	NULL
Nellie	NULL	Bly	NULL
Yuri	Alekseyevich	Gagarin	Yuri Alekseyevich Gagarin
NULL	Paul	Jones	NULL
NULL	Al	Smith	NULL
NULL	NULL	Pythagoras	NULL
NULL	NULL	Bleriot	NULL
Aristotle	NULL	NULL	NULL
Cicero	NULL	NULL	NULL
Srinivasa	NULL	Ramanujan	NULL
Orville	NULL	Wright	NULL

Figure 11.9: NULL values in a MySQL SELECT statement

The **CombinedName** column has a **NULL** value if the value of either **FirstName**, **MiddleName**, or **LastName** is **NULL**:

```
CONCAT(FirstName, ' ', MiddleName, ' ', LastName) LastName as 'CombinedName'
```

In a **SELECT** statement, columns and expressions of all data types will return **NULL** if the column expression, or at least one component of the expression, has a **NULL** value. We want to avoid a **NULL** value in a **SELECT** statement result set because it could cause problems for applications that receive that result set. The **ISNULL** function we saw earlier can help, but it could involve some fairly complicated code. Instead, SQL products offer **COALESCE** as a cleaner, more efficient solution.

The COALESCE Function

The **COALESCE** function can be used to obtain the first not null parameter it finds, starting from left to right. The syntax for it is as follows:

```
COALESCE ( param_1, param_2, param_3 . . . param_n )
```

If it finds only **NULL** values, it returns **NULL**. Let's see how this works using the following query:

```
USE PACKT_ONLINE_SHOP;


SELECT    COALESCE(FirstName, ' ') AS 'FirstName',
          COALESCE(MiddleName, 'SUBSTITUTE MIDDLE NAME') AS 'MiddleName',
          COALESCE(LastName, ' ') AS 'LastName'


FROM      Customers;
```

The output should be as follows:

FirstName	MiddleName	LastName
Joe	Greg	Smith
Grace	Murray	Hopper
Ada	SUBSTITUTE MIDDLE NAME	Lovelace
Joseph	Force	Crater
Jacqueline	Jackie	Cochran
William	SUBSTITUTE MIDDLE NAME	Shakespeare
Nellie	SUBSTITUTE MIDDLE NAME	Bly
Yuri	Alekseyevich	Gagarin
	Paul	Jones
	Al	Smith
	SUBSTITUTE MIDDLE NAME	Pythagoras
	SUBSTITUTE MIDDLE NAME	Bleriot
Aristotle	SUBSTITUTE MIDDLE NAME	
Cicero	SUBSTITUTE MIDDLE NAME	
Srinivasa	SUBSTITUTE MIDDLE NAME	Ramanujan
Orville	SUBSTITUTE MIDDLE NAME	Wright

Figure 11.10: The output of MySQL COALESCE function

Notice the modifications that were made to the original result set column values with the **COALESCE** function. We substitute a ' ' value for every **NULL** value in the **customers. FirstName** column **customers.LastName** column. We also substitute '**SUBSTITUTE MIDDLE NAME**' for the **NULL** values. Note that an empty string value will work in the **COALESCE** function parameter list, but we should avoid this because, like **NULL**, it could cause problems with other software system components.

COALESCE works with other data types as well, including Boolean, integer, float, and so on. In this MySQL example, we have the following:

```
SET     @intVal1 = NULL;

SELECT COALESCE(@intVal1, -5) + 4 AS 'COALESCE(@intVal1, -5) + 4';
```

The **@intVal1** variable is declared with a **NULL** value. The **COALESCE** function changes the variable to **-5** for the result set calculation:

Figure 11.11: The output of MySQL COALESCE function with a non-string data type value

As a result of the **COALESCE** function is **-5**, the addition is performed on **-5**. The result of -5 + 4 is **-1**, which is displayed. Even a simple query can return a result set with **NULL** values. In the next exercise, we'll use the **COALESCE** function to handle the **NULL** values in a **PACKT_ONLINE_SHOP** query.

Exercise 11.03: Using the COALESCE Function to Handle a NULL Value in a Combined Set of Values

In this exercise, we will build a query that returns the **FirstName**, **MiddleName**, and **LastName** columns values of the **Customers** table and combines those values in a column named **CombinedName**. Replace the **NULL** values of **FirstName** and **LastName** with single space ' ' values. We'll replace the **NULL** values of **MiddleName** with **SUBSTITUTE MIDDLE NAME** values and then separate all name values with single spaces. To do this, perform the following steps:

1. Open a new query window and enter the following query:

```
USE PACKT_ONLINE_SHOP;

SELECT    CONCAT(COALESCE(FirstName, ' '), ' ',
          COALESCE(MiddleName, 'SUBSTITUTE MIDDLE NAME'), ' ',
          COALESCE(LastName, ' ')) as 'CombinedName'

FROM      customers;
```

2. Execute the query. You should get the following output:

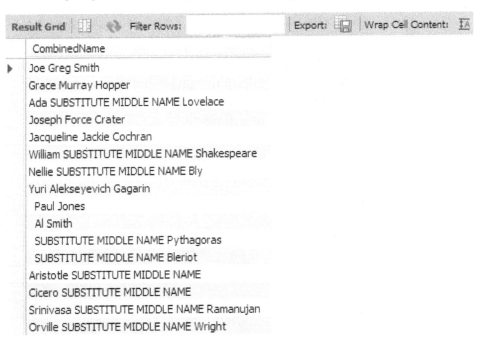

Figure 11.12: Exercise 11.03 solution

Notice how all the **NULL** values in the first and the last name have been replaced with space and that the **NULL** values in the middle name have been replaced with a string called **SUBSTITUTE MIDDLE NAME**.

Finding Duplicate Table Rows

As database resources evolve and expand, duplicate rows may end up in the tables. This could happen because of stored procedure or function bugs, problems with a frontend application, issues with a high-volume data import, and so on. We want to avoid this in a relational database. To remove duplicate table rows, first, we need to find them. To illustrate this, run the following queries:

```
INSERT Products (ProductCategoryID, SupplierID, ProductName,
    ProductImage, NetRetailPrice, AvailableQuantity,
    WholesalePrice, UnitKGWeight, Notes)

VALUES (3, 2, 'portable camera', NULL, 89.95, 6128, 119.99,
        521.38, 'handle with care'),
       (3, 2, 'portable camera', NULL, 89.95, 6128, 119.99,
        521.38, 'handle with care'),
       (3, 2, 'portable camera', NULL, 89.95, 6128, 119.99,
        521.38, 'handle with care'),
       (3, 2, 'portable camera', NULL, 89.95, 6128, 119.99,
        521.38, 'handle with care'),
       (3, 2, 'portable camera', NULL, 89.95, 6128, 119.99,
        521.38, 'handle with care');

SELECT ProductID, ProductCategoryID, SupplierID, ProductName, ProductImage,
        NetRetailPrice, AvailableQuantity, WholesalePrice, UnitKGWeight, Notes
FROM    Products;
```

MySQL statements **INSERT VALUES** have been used to insert five duplicate rows into **PACKT_ONLINE_SHOP** database's **Products** table. This statement does not include the **ProductID** column because we defined that column in this table as an identity column. The preceding **INSERT** statement inserts five duplicate rows, as shown here:

ProductID	ProductCategoryID	SupplierID	ProductName	ProductImage	NetRetailPrice	AvailableQuantity	WholesalePrice	UnitKGWeight	Notes
1	5	2	Calculatre	NULL	24.99	100	17.99	1.00000	calculation application
2	5	5	Penwrite	NULL	79.99	27	49.99	2.00000	word processing product
3	1	6	Vortex Generator	NULL	2499.99	1000	1999.99	0.01000	space engine component
4	1	6	The Gourmet Crockpot	NULL	24.99	72	19.99	1.63000	cookbook
5	1	6	Government Accounting	NULL	14.99	26	9.99	1.22000	government accounting book
6	3	6	habanero peppers	NULL	4.49	189	2.99	0.00900	hot peppers
7	2	1	10-mm socket wrench	NULL	3.49	39	1.89	0.01800	important tool
8	3	4	tomato sauce	NULL	1.19	1509	0.89	0.23200	bottled in glass
9	1	6	pure vanilla	NULL	10.39	1509	7.89	0.03200	high-quality vanilla
10	3	2	keyboard wrench	NULL	399999.95	6128	149999.99	521.38000	handle with care
11	2	1	power cell	NULL	47.89	2346	29.99	0.29800	ten amp-hours per cell
12	3	2	portable camera	NULL	89.95	6128	119.99	521.38000	handle with care
13	3	2	portable camera	NULL	89.95	6128	119.99	521.38000	handle with care
14	3	2	portable camera	NULL	89.95	6128	119.99	521.38000	handle with care
15	3	2	portable camera	NULL	89.95	6128	119.99	521.38000	handle with care
16	3	2	portable camera	NULL	89.95	6128	119.99	521.38000	handle with care
NULL	NULL	NULL	NULL	NULL	NULL	NULL	NULL	NULL	NULL

Figure 11.13 The products table with duplicate rows

If the highest **ProductID** value in the products table is **11** (eleven), this query will delete, at any time, the rows that the preceding statements inserted:

```
DELETE FROM Products WHERE ProductID > 11;
```

To find and delete the **Products** table's duplicate rows, we'll start with a Common Table Expression, group all the rows into duplicate sets, number the rows in each group, and delete the duplicates. Note that a single, non-duplicate row will become a one-row group. We will not delete any of the rows in these one-row groups.

A **Common Table Expression (CTE)** temporarily holds a result set that another SQL statement can use. Run the following query to see what the CTE looks like:

```
USE PACKT_ONLINE_SHOP;


WITH demoCTE AS
(
    SELECT      ProductID, ProductCategoryID, SupplierID, ProductName,
                NetRetailPrice, AvailableQuantity, WholesalePrice,
                UnitKGWeight, Notes
    FROM        Products
)

    SELECT      ProductID, ProductCategoryID, SupplierID, ProductName,
                NetRetailPrice, AvailableQuantity, WholesalePrice,
                UnitKGWeight, Notes
    FROM        demoCTE;
```

The output will be as follows:

ProductID	ProductCategoryID	SupplierID	ProductName	NetRetailPrice	AvailableQuantity	WholesalePrice	UnitKGWeight	Notes
1	5	2	Calculatre	24.99	100	17.99	1.00000	calculation application
2	5	5	Penwrite	79.99	27	49.99	2.00000	word processing product
3	1	6	Vortex Generator	2499.99	1000	1999.99	0.01000	space engine component
4	1	6	The Gourmet Crockpot	24.99	72	19.99	1.63000	cookbook
5	1	6	Government Accounting	14.99	26	9.99	1.22000	government accounting book
6	3	6	habanero peppers	4.49	189	2.99	0.00900	hot peppers
7	2	1	10-mm socket wrench	3.49	39	1.89	0.01800	important tool
8	3	4	tomato sauce	1.19	1509	0.89	0.23200	bottled in glass
9	1	6	pure vanilla	10.39	1509	7.89	0.03200	high-quality vanilla
10	3	2	keyboard wrench	399999.95	6128	149999.99	521.38000	handle with care
11	2	1	power cell	47.89	2346	29.99	0.29800	ten amp-hours per cell
12	3	2	portable camera	89.95	6128	119.99	521.38000	handle with care
13	3	2	portable camera	89.95	6128	119.99	521.38000	handle with care
14	3	2	portable camera	89.95	6128	119.99	521.38000	handle with care
15	3	2	portable camera	89.95	6128	119.99	521.38000	handle with care
16	3	2	portable camera	89.95	6128	119.99	521.38000	handle with care

Figure 11.14: The MySQL common table expression

In the preceding code, **WITH demoCTE AS** names the CTE as **demoCTE** using the required keywords; that is, **WITH** and **AS**. As shown in the code, we place the query that generates the CTE result set between the required parentheses. A SQL statement that uses the CTE must immediately follow that CTE. Don't place a semicolon, **;**, at the end of the CTE. The SQL statements return the expected result set.

Next, we need to group the duplicate rows together and then number the rows in each group—starting with 1 in each different group. Finally, we'll delete the rows in each group with row numbers greater than 1. This will ignore all the unique rows because those rows become one-row groups. To number the rows in each row group, we'll add the **ROW_NUMBER()** function to the **SELECT** statement of **demoCTE**, as shown here:

```
USE PACKT_ONLINE_SHOP;
WITH demoCTE AS
(
    SELECT      ProductID, ProductCategoryID, SupplierID, ProductName,
                NetRetailPrice, AvailableQuantity, WholesalePrice,
                UnitKGWeight, Notes,
                ROW_NUMBER() OVER (
                    PARTITION BY  ProductCategoryID, SupplierID,
                                  ProductName, NetRetailPrice,
                                  AvailableQuantity, WholesalePrice,
                                  UnitKGWeight, Notes
                    ORDER BY  ProductID
                ) AS RowNumber
    FROM Products
)
SELECT      ProductID, ProductCategoryID, SupplierID, ProductName,
            NetRetailPrice, AvailableQuantity, WholesalePrice,
            UnitKGWeight, Notes, RowNumber
FROM        demoCTE
ORDER BY  ProductID;
```

The preceding query yields the following output:

	ProductID	ProductCategoryID	SupplierID	ProductName	NetRetailPrice	AvailableQuantity	WholesalePrice	UnitKGWeight	Notes	RowNumber
▶	1	5	2	Calculatre	24.99	100	17.99	1.00000	calculation application	1
	2	5	5	Penwrite	79.99	27	49.99	2.00000	word processing product	1
	3	1	6	Vortex Generator	2499.99	1000	1999.99	0.01000	space engine component	1
	4	1	6	The Gourmet Crockpot	24.99	72	19.99	1.63000	cookbook	1
	5	1	6	Government Accounting	14.99	26	9.99	1.22000	government accounting book	1
	6	3	6	habanero peppers	4.49	189	2.99	0.00900	hot peppers	1
	7	2	1	10-mm socket wrench	3.49	39	1.89	0.01800	important tool	1
	8	3	4	tomato sauce	1.19	1509	0.89	0.23200	bottled in glass	1
	9	1	6	pure vanilla	10.39	1509	7.89	0.03200	high-quality vanilla	1
	10	3	2	keyboard wrench	399999.95	6128	149999.99	521.38000	handle with care	1
	11	2	1	power cell	47.89	2346	29.99	0.29800	ten amp-hours per cell	1
	12	3	2	portable camera	89.95	6128	119.99	521.38000	handle with care	1
	13	3	2	portable camera	89.95	6128	119.99	521.38000	handle with care	2
	14	3	2	portable camera	89.95	6128	119.99	521.38000	handle with care	3
	15	3	2	portable camera	89.95	6128	119.99	521.38000	handle with care	4
	16	3	2	portable camera	89.95	6128	119.99	521.38000	handle with care	5

Figure 11.15: Duplicate table rows identified with a common table expression

In the result set pane of the preceding screenshot, look at the **RowNumber** column, where the product name is **portable camera**. The **RowNumber** column flagged all the duplicate rows with integer values exceeding **1**.

The **ROW_NUMBER()** function divides the result set into subsets, or partitions, and then sequentially numbers the rows in each partition, starting with the numbers at **1** for each subset it sees. Here, the **ROW_NUMBER()** function defines the row subsets with all of the products table's columns, except the **ProductID** column.

This makes sense because the **ProductID** column serves as the table key column. If we include **ProductID** in the **PARTITION BY** columns, **PARTITION BY** would see all the rows as unique. If we leave out **ProductID** and include all the other columns in the **PARTITION BY** column list, we'll get the set(s) of duplicate rows that we want. The **ROW_NUMBER()** function requires the **ORDER BY** clause to know of the sequence of the rows in each row subset, before the rows receive their **ROW_NUMBER()** values. The **ORDER BY** clause requires at least one product table column, so we picked **ProductID**. The **SELECT** statement returns all product table rows, plus the **RowNumber** column.

Transactions

As part of database management, soon enough, we will probably make direct data changes through database management tools. In other words, we may use a MySQL query window to make a direct insert, update, and delete changes to live *production* data. We know how to make those changes with relevant SQL statements, but so far, we have not looked at a way to reverse these changes. Even one mistake could potentially destroy data resources worth billions. Fortunately, SQL products offer the **TRANSACTION** function as a way to execute SQL statements in a reversible way.

From the **PACKT_ONLINE_SHOP** database, from the **Products** table, let's query the product with the product ID **3**:

```
USE PACKT_ONLINE_SHOP;


SELECT     ProductID, Availablequantity
FROM       Products
WHERE      productid = 3;
```

This query will yield the following output:

ProductID	Availablequantity
3	1000
NULL	NULL

Figure 11.16: The output of the query before update

From the output, we can see that the product with product ID **3** has 1,000 available quantities. Now, let's say that a customer purchased 850 pieces—you'd have to update the database. To do this, perform the following query:

```
UPDATE     Products
SET        AvailableQuantity = 150
WHERE      ProductID = 3
```

This query changes the **AvailableQuantity** value for the row to **150**. However, we may want to reverse the change right after it happened if we made a mistake. To do this, we need to use a **TRANSACTION**. An SQL **transaction** involves one or more SQL statements that change data and that execute as a reversible unit. To make the same changes using a transaction, the query would be as follows:

```
USE PACKT_ONLINE_SHOP;


SELECT     ProductID, Availablequantity
FROM Products
WHERE Productid = 3;


START TRANSACTION;


UPDATE Products
SET AvailableQuantity = 150   --   Original value = 1000
WHERE ProductID = 3;


--   COMMIT;
ROLLBACK;
```

Before the transaction, the query would lead to the following output:

Figure 11.17: Usage of TRANSACTION

We want to execute, and then reverse, the **UPDATE** statement. **START TRANSACTION** is the statement that begins the transaction block. To close off the **TRANSACTION** block, we can use either the **COMMIT** statement to lock it in, or **ROLLBACK** the transaction to reverse it. All transactions will have the **START TRANSACTION** statement. The structure seen here uses transactions flexibility in a safe way, and we'll see why we commented out the **COMMIT** statement shortly. We can see the changes that were made to the data at any time with the **SELECT** statement.

To effectively use this transaction structure, highlight and run the statements one at a time. First, highlight and run the **START TRANSACTION** statement to begin the transaction. Then, highlight and run the **UPDATE** statement. Highlight and run **SELECT** query to see the data change. You will obtain the following output:

Figure 11.18: A transaction

To **ROLLBACK** that change, highlight and run the **ROLLBACK** query. The output is shown here:

Figure 11.19: Rolling back a transaction

The structure of the final two lines in the code makes it easy to reverse the change if the transaction is open. To **COMMIT** the transaction, highlight and run the **COMMIT** statement after the -- comment symbols, as shown here:

```
1 •   USE PACKT_ONLINE_SHOP;

2

3 •   SELECT   ProductID, Availablequantity

4     FROM Products

5     WHERE Productid = 3;

6

7 •   START TRANSACTION;

8

9 •   UPDATE Products

10    SET AvailableQuantity = 150   --   Original value = 1000

11    WHERE ProductID = 3;

12

13    -- COMMIT;

14 •  ROLLBACK;

15
```

Figure 11.20: Committing a MySQL transaction

Those symbols make it difficult to **COMMIT** the transaction, and the structure makes it easy to reverse the transaction with **ROLLBACK**. This structure forces us to think through and verify what we do as we make the changes. Make sure to balance every **BEGIN TRANSACTION** execution with either a **COMMIT** or a **ROLLBACK**. An unbalanced **BEGIN TRANSACTION** will cause problems with the MySQL instance itself. We can run **ROLLBACK TRANSACTION** as many times as we want, although it will return a message for each unbalanced **ROLLBACK TRANSACTION** statement, as shown here:

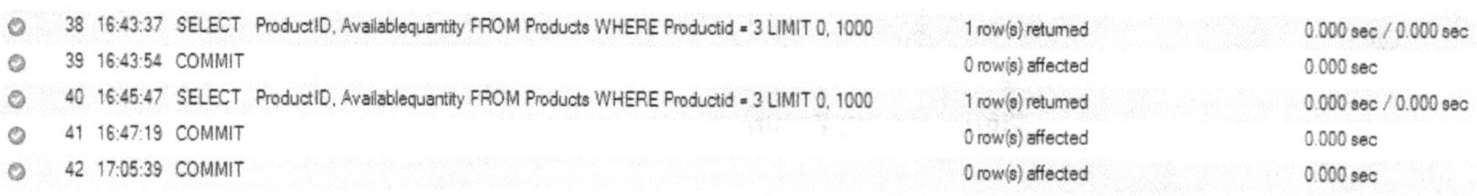

⊘	38 16:43:37	SELECT ProductID, Availablequantity FROM Products WHERE Productid = 3 LIMIT 0, 1000	1 row(s) returned	0.000 sec / 0.000 sec
⊘	39 16:43:54	COMMIT	0 row(s) affected	0.000 sec
⊘	40 16:45:47	SELECT ProductID, Availablequantity FROM Products WHERE Productid = 3 LIMIT 0, 1000	1 row(s) returned	0.000 sec / 0.000 sec
⊘	41 16:47:19	COMMIT	0 row(s) affected	0.000 sec
⊘	42 17:05:39	COMMIT	0 row(s) affected	0.000 sec

Figure 11.21: An unbalanced transaction rollback

You can run the **SELECT** query at any time to see the latest data state. As we learned in this topic, this chapter, and throughout this course, we must use extreme care when we work with data resources. Used wisely, transactions can help protect against mistakes and errors that can damage data on which businesses and lives depend.

Activity 11.02: Using Transactions

You are asked to delete all products with order ID 5, but you are also told that this may need to be reversed at a later date. Write a transaction to delete all products with the order ID as 5, then rollback the transaction to test that you can return to the previous state of the database.

> **Note**
>
> The solution for this activity can be found on page 262.

Summary

In this chapter, we explored the features and aspects of SQL database products that can expand our skill sets. These tools have great value and importance because we can solve better solutions and solve more complex problems. We now have a path forward to solve problems that we could not solve before, and we also reinforced our experience teaching ourselves with the new skills we may need to build the solutions we need. Let's take a moment to get some perspective. When you started this course, you had probably heard a lot about databases and database development, but you likely had little to no hands-on experience with those products. Maybe you did not know about high-quality SQL products that are available to everyone to download for free. Now, you definitely know about all of this, and much more. You built an impressive skillset that you can use to solve database problems and build database solutions. More importantly, with that skill set, you can teach yourself new material so that you can cover new situations and solve new problems. You have successfully joined a thriving community.

Appendix

About

This section is included to assist the students to perform the activities present in the book. It includes detailed steps that are to be performed by the students to complete and achieve the objectives of the book.

Chapter 1: SQL Basics

Activity 1.01: Inserting Values into the Products Table in the PACKT_ONLINE_ SHOP Database

Solution:

1. Create the **Products** table with the same column names that were provided in the Excel spreadsheet:

```
use packt_online_shop;
CREATE TABLE Products
(
    ProductID INT NOT NULL,
    ProductCategoryID INT NOT NULL,
    SupplierID INT NOT NULL,
    ProductName CHAR(50) NOT NULL,
    NetRetailPrice DECIMAL(10, 2) NULL,
    AvailableQuantity INT NOT NULL,
    WholesalePrice DECIMAL(10, 2) NOT NULL,
    UnitKGWeight DECIMAL(10, 5) NULL,
    Notes VARCHAR(750) NULL,
    PRIMARY KEY (ProductID)
);
```

2. Enter the values into the **Products** table:

```
INSERT INTO Products ( ProductID, ProductCategoryID, SupplierID, ProductName,
NetRetailPrice, AvailableQuantity, WholesalePrice, UnitKGWeight, Notes )
VALUES
(1, 5, 2, 'Calculatre', 24.99, 100, 17.99, 1, 'calculation application'),
(2, 5, 5, 'Penwrite', 79.99, 27, 49.99, 2, 'word processing product'),
(3, 1, 6, 'Vortex Generator', 2499.99, 1000, 1999.99, 0.01, 'space engine
component'),
(4, 1, 6, 'The Gourmet Crockpot', 24.99, 72, 19.99, 1.63, 'cookbook'),
(5, 1, 6, 'Account Books', 14.99, 26, 9.99, 1.22, 'government accounting book'),
(6, 3, 6, 'habanero peppers', 4.49, 189, 2.99, 0.009, 'hot peppers'),
(7, 2, 1, '10-mm socket wrench', 3.49, 39, 1.89, 0.018, 'important tool'),
(8, 3, 4, 'tomato sauce', 1.19, 1509, 0.89, 0.232, 'bottled in glass'),
(9, 1, 6, 'pure vanilla', 10.39, 1509, 7.89, 0.032, 'high-quality vanilla'),
(10, 3, 2, 'keyboard wrench', 399999.95, 6128, 149999.99, 521.38, 'handle with
care'),
(11, 2, 1, 'power cell', 47.89, 2346, 29.99, 0.298, 'ten amp-hours per cell');
```

When you check the contents of the file, it should look similar to this:

ProductID	ProductCategoryID	SupplierID	ProductName	NetRetailPrice	AvailableQuantity	WholesalePrice	UnitKGWeight	Notes
1	5	2	Calculatre	24.99	100	17.99	1.00000	calculation application
2	5	5	Penwrite	79.99	27	49.99	2.00000	word processing product
3	1	6	Vortex Generator	2499.99	1000	1999.99	0.01000	space engine component
4	1	6	The Gourmet Crockpot	24.99	72	19.99	1.63000	cookbook
5	1	6	Account Books	14.99	26	9.99	1.22000	government accounting book
6	3	6	habanero peppers	4.49	189	2.99	0.00900	hot peppers
7	2	1	10-mm socket wrench	3.49	39	1.89	0.01800	important tool
8	3	4	tomato sauce	1.19	1509	0.89	0.23200	bottled in glass
9	1	6	pure vanilla	10.39	1509	7.89	0.03200	high-quality vanilla
10	3	2	keyboard wrench	399999.95	6128	149999.99	521.38000	handle with care
11	2	1	power cell	47.89	2346	29.99	0.29800	ten amp-hours per cell
NULL	NULL	NULL	NULL	NULL	NULL	NULL	NULL	NULL

Figure 1.20: Populated Products table

You'll find all 11 entries in the **Products** table.

Chapter 2: Manipulating Data

Activity 2.01: Inserting Additional values to the Products Table

Solution:

1. Create the **FoodProducts** table with default values:

```
CREATE TABLE FoodProducts
(
ProductID INT NOT NULL AUTO_INCREMENT,
ProductCategoryID INT NOT NULL DEFAULT 1,
SupplierID INT NOT NULL DEFAULT 1,
ProductName CHAR(50) NOT NULL,
NetRetailPrice DECIMAL(10, 2) NULL DEFAULT 5.99,
AvailableQuantity INT NOT NULL,
WholesalePrice DECIMAL(10, 2) NOT NULL DEFAULT 3.99,
UnitKGWeight DECIMAL(10, 5) NULL,
Notes VARCHAR(750) NULL,
PRIMARY KEY (ProductID)
);
```

2. Insert multiple values:

```
insert into FoodProducts ( ProductName, AvailableQuantity, UnitKGWeight, Notes )
values ('Pancake batter', 50, 0.25, 'Contains eggs'),
('Breakfast cereal', 10, 0.25, 'Add milk'),
('Siracha sauce', 10, 0.25, 'Spicey');
```

3. Observe the result:

```
select * from foodProducts;
```

Your output should be as follows:

ProductID	ProductCategoryID	SupplierID	ProductName	NetRetailPrice	AvailableQuantity	WholesalePrice	UnitKGWeight	Notes
1	1	1	Pancake batter	5.99	50	3.99	0.25000	Contains eggs
2	1	1	Breakfast cereal	5.99	10	3.99	0.25000	Add milk
3	1	1	Siracha sauce	5.99	10	3.99	0.25000	Spicey
NULL	NULL	NULL	NULL	NULL	NULL	NULL	NULL	NULL

Figure 2.14: Populated Products table

Thus, we have created a new table and inserted values.

Chapter 3: Normalization

Activity 3.01: Building a Relationship between the Orders and the OrderItems table

Solution:

1. Create the **OrderItems** table:

```
Use packt_online_shop;
CREATE TABLE OrderItems
(
    OrderItemID INT NOT NULL AUTO_INCREMENT,
    OrderID INT NOT NULL,
    ProductID INT NOT NULL,
    Quantity INT NOT NULL,
    UnitPrice DECIMAL(10, 2) NOT NULL,
    Discount DECIMAL(10, 2) NULL,
    Notes VARCHAR(750) NULL,
    PRIMARY KEY (OrderItemID)
);
```

2. Create the **Orders** (child) table:

```
Create Table Orders(
    OrderID INT NOT NULL AUTO_INCREMENT,
    CustomerID INT NOT NULL,
    OrderNumber CHAR(50) NOT NULL,
    OrderDate DATETIME NOT NULL,
    ShipmentDate DATETIME NULL,
    OrderStatus CHAR(10) NULL,
    Notes VARCHAR(750) NULL,
    PRIMARY KEY (OrderID)
);
```

3. Provide foreign key reference:

```
ALTER TABLE OrderItems
ADD FOREIGN KEY (OrderID) REFERENCES Orders(OrderID);
```

You should now be able to see the two additional tables in the Schemas section of the Navigator pane.

Figure 3.23: Populated Products table

Chapter 4: The SELECT Statement

Activity 4.01: Displaying Particular Columns from the Table

Solution:

1. In the **New Query** window, switch to the **PACKT_ONLINE_SHOP** database:

```
USE PACKT_ONLINE_SHOP
```

2. Write the following query, to extract the required data, in the desired format:

```
SELECT FirstName as 'First Name', LastName as
  'Last Name', Phone as 'Phone Number'
FROM Customers
```

3. Run the query. Your output should be as follows:

First Name	Last Name	Phone Number
Joe	Smith	(310) 555-1212
Grace	Hopper	(818) 555-3678
Ada	Lovelace	(717) 555-3457
Joseph	Crater	(212) 555-5678
Jacqueline	Cochran	(717) 555-3457
William	Shakespeare	(213) 555-3421
Nellie	Bly	(213) 555-8523
Yuri	Gagarin	(310) 555-5462
NULL	Jones	(216) 555-6232
NULL	Smith	(345) 555-5434
NULL	Pythagoras	(260) 555-3461
NULL	Bleriot	(818) 555-3562
Aristotle	NULL	(310) 555-9182
Cicero	NULL	(310) 555-0822
Srinivasa	Ramanujan	(211) 555-1111
Orville	Wright	(211) 555-4444

Figure 4.21: Columns from the Customers table

The query will list all the rows of the **FirstName**, **LastName**, **Phone** columns renamed as **First Name**, **Last Name**, and **Phone Number**.

Activity 4.02: Extracting the Top Five Highest Paid Items

Solution:

1. Execute the following query:

```
SELECT
    Products.ProductName as 'Product Name',
    Products.NetRetailPrice as 'Product Retail Price',
    Products.AvailableQuantity as 'Available Quantity',
    Products.AvailableQuantity * Products.NetRetailPrice as 'Total Price of
Available QTY'
FROM Products


ORDER BY Products.NetRetailPrice Desc
LIMIT 5;
```

2. Execute the query, your output should be as follows:

Product Name	Product Retail Price	Available Quantity	Total Price of Available QTY
keyboard wrench	399999.95	6128	2451199693.60
Vortex Generator	2499.99	1000	2499990.00
Penwrite	79.99	27	2159.73
power cell	47.89	2346	112349.94
Calculatre	24.99	100	2499.00

Figure 4.22: Columns from the Customers table

Chapter 5: Shaping Data with the WHERE Clause

Activity 5.01: Combining Conditions to Extract Store Data

Solution:

1. First, enter the **SELECT** statement. This is used so as to display the results using the requested column names:

```
SELECT
    ProductName as 'Product Name',
    NetRetailPrice as 'Product Retail Price',
    AvailableQuantity as 'Available Quantity'
From Products
WHERE NetRetailPrice <= 24.99
    AND AvailableQuantity >=38
```

2. Execute the query, you should get the following output in the result grid:

Result Grid		Filter Rows:	Export:	Wrap Cell Content:

Product Name	Product Retail Price	Available Quantity
Calculatre	24.99	100
The Gourmet Crockpot	24.99	72
habanero peppers	4.49	189
10-mm socket wrench	3.49	39
tomato sauce	1.19	1509
pure vanilla	10.39	1509

Figure 5.19: Columns from the Customers table

Chapter 6: JOINS

Activity 6.01: Implementing JOINS

Solution:

1. Look at the tables involved in obtaining and identifying the common columns. If you look closely at the following diagram, you will notice that the data that's required is scattered across not just two tables but three, that is, **Orders**, **OrderItems**, and **Products**.

    In cases like these, we'll have to perform multiple joins, with the first join being between the **Orders** and **OrderItems** table to get price details, and the second join being between the **OrderItems** and **Products** table to get the product information.

2. In a new query window, implement this logic into the query:

```
SELECT Orders.OrderNumber,
OrderItems.UnitPrice,
OrderItems.Quantity,
Products.ProductName
FROM Orders JOIN OrderItems ON Orders.OrderID =
   OrderItems.OrderID
      JOIN Products ON OrderItems.ProductID = Products.ProductID
```

    In this query, we joined the **Orders** and **OrderItems** tables using the **OrderID** and joined the **Products** and **OrderItems** tables using the **ProductID** column.

3. Execute the query, you should get the following output:

OrderNumber	UnitPrice	Quantity	ProductName
ABC123	24.99	2	Calculatre
ABC123	79.99	1	Penwrite
ABC123	2499.99	2	Vortex Generator
BCQ857	14.99	1	Government Accounting
BCQ857	3.49	1	10-mm socket wrench
RST321	47.89	4	power cell
RST321	399999.95	7	keyboard wrench
DTR321	79.99	2	Penwrite
DTR321	4.49	1	habanero peppers
DTR321	14.99	1	Government Accounting
BCQ858	399999.95	2	keyboard wrench
BCQ858	3.49	1	10-mm socket wrench

Figure 6.12: Columns from the Customers table

By doing this, we've retrieved data from three different tables by mapping the common columns from the **OrderID** and **ProductID** tables.

Chapter 7: Subqueries, Cases, and Views

Activity 7.01: Finding the Product Category Name Using a Subquery

Solution:

1. Enter the following query:

```
USE packt_online_shop;


SELECT   PC.ProductCategoryName
FROM     ProductCategories PC
WHERE    ProductCategoryID IN


(SELECT ProductCategoryID FROM Products WHERE
    ProductName = 'habanero peppers');
```

2. Run the query. Your output will be as follows:

Figure 7.10: Category of the habanero peppers food item

Activity 7.02: Categorizing the Shipments Using CASE Statements

Solution:

1. Enter the following query:

```
USE packt_online_shop;
SELECT OrderNumber, ShipmentDate,
CASE
WHEN ShipmentDate < ' 2010-12-10' THEN 'Past Shipment Date'
WHEN ShipmentDate >= ' 2010-12-10' AND
ShipmentDate < ' 2019-12-18' THEN
'Recent Shipment Date'
ELSE 'Future Shipment Date'
END AS 'Shipment Date Category'
FROM Orders;
```

2. Execute the query. You should get the following output:

OrderNumber	ShipmentDate	Shipment Date Category
ABC123	2017-02-12 00:00:00	Recent Shipment Date
BCQ857	2317-03-08 00:00:00	Future Shipment Date
RST321	1933-05-22 00:00:00	Past Shipment Date
YQW672	2010-01-17 00:00:00	Past Shipment Date
DTR321	2933-05-22 00:00:00	Future Shipment Date
BCQ858	2317-03-29 00:00:00	Future Shipment Date

Figure 7.11: Displaying the shipment details

Activity 7.03: Building a View

Solution:

1. Create a view using the following query:

```
CREATE VIEW Hopper_Sales_View AS
SELECT OI.OrderID, OI.ProductID, OI.Quantity, OI.UnitPrice,
(OI.Quantity * OI.UnitPrice) AS 'subtotal',
CASE
WHEN (OI.Quantity * OI.UnitPrice) < 25.00 THEN 'Small'
WHEN (OI.Quantity * OI.UnitPrice) <= 79.99 THEN 'Medium'
ELSE 'Large'
END AS 'Subtotal Category'

FROM OrderItems OI INNER JOIN
Orders O ON OI.OrderID = O.OrderID

WHERE O.CustomerID IN

(SELECT CustomerID FROM Customers WHERE LastName = 'Hopper' );
```

2. Run a select statement to check the output:

```
select * from Hopper_Sales_View;
```

The output is as follows:

OrderID	ProductID	Quantity	UnitPrice	subtotal	Subtotal Category
1	1	2	24.99	49.98	Medium
1	2	1	79.99	79.99	Medium
1	3	2	2499.99	4999.98	Large

Figure 7.12: Building Hopper_Sales_View

Chapter 8: SQL Programming

Activity 8.01: Building a Stored Procedure

Solution:

1. Execute the following query:

```
CREATE DEFINER=`root`@`localhost` PROCEDURE `spFilterOrdersByItemQuantity`(IN
orderItemQuantityVal int)
BEGIN
  SELECT  OI.OrderID, SUM(OI.Quantity)
      AS 'Total Order Item Quantity'
  FROM  OrderItems OI
  GROUP BY OI.OrderID
  HAVING SUM(OI.Quantity) <= orderItemQuantityVal
  ORDER BY OI.OrderID;
END
```

2. Test the stored procedure using the following query:

```
USE packt_online_shop;
CALL spFilterOrdersByItemQuantity(25);
```

Activity 8.02: Working with MySQL Functions

Solution:

1. Write the following query:

```
CREATE DEFINER =`root`@`localhost` FUNCTION `fnProductTotalOrderQty`(ProductID INT)
RETURNS INT
DETERMINISTIC
BEGIN

DECLARE retVal INT;

SET retVal = (
SELECT
```

```
CASE
    WHEN      SUM(OI.quantity) IS NULL THEN 0
ELSE
    SUM(OI.quantity)
END AS 'quantity'

FROM     OrderItems OI
WHERE     OI.Productid = ProductID
);

RETURN retVal;
END
```

2. Write the code to test the query:

```
USE packt_online_shop;

    SELECT packt_online_shop.fnProductTotalOrderQty(12);
    SELECT packt_online_shop.fnProductTotalOrderQty(3);
```

Activity 8.03: Building a Trigger

Solution:

1. Build the trigger using the following code:

```
USE packt_online_shop;
# drop trigger tr_OrderItems_OnInsert
DELIMITER $$
CREATE TRIGGER tr_OrderItems_OnInsert AFTER INSERT ON OrderItems
FOR EACH ROW
BEGIN
 DECLARE availableQuantity INT;
 DECLARE orderQuantity INT;
 DECLARE productID INT;
 DECLARE productNameText VARCHAR(50);
 DECLARE productNotesText VARCHAR(1000);

 # The "INSERTED" table has the ProductID and OrderQuantity
 # values we'll need from the OrderItems table insert . . .
```

```
SET productID = (
 SELECT NEW.ProductID
);
SET orderQuantity = (
 SELECT NEW.Quantity
);

# Find the available quantity for that productID
# value from the Products table . . .

SET availableQuantity = (
 SELECT P.AvailableQuantity
 FROM Products P
 WHERE P.ProductID = productID
);
IF ((availableQuantity - orderQuantity) < 5) THEN
 SET productNameText = (
  SELECT Products.ProductName
  FROM Products
  WHERE Products.ProductID = productID
 );
 SET productNotesText = (
  SELECT CONCAT("The available quantity for product ID ",
    CAST(productID AS CHAR), ")")
 );
 SET productNotesText = (
  SELECT CONCAT(productNotesText, " (", productNameText, ") ",
  "will fall below five items")
 );

        UPDATE Products
        SET  Products.AvailableQuantity = (Products.AvailableQuantity -
            orderQuantity)
        WHERE Products.ProductID = productID;
```

```
    UPDATE Products
    SET   Products.Notes = productNotesText
    WHERE Products.ProductID = productID;
   END IF;
 END$$
 DELIMITER ;
```

2. Test the code using the following query:

```
      USE packt_online_shop;
      INSERT INTO    OrderItems(OrderID, ProductID, Quantity, UnitPrice,
                               Discount, Notes)
      VALUES         (1, 2, 23, 59.99, 0, 'Trigger Test Order');
      SELECT    P.Notes
      FROM      Products P
      WHERE     P.ProductID = 2;
```

3. Execute the query, you should get the following output:

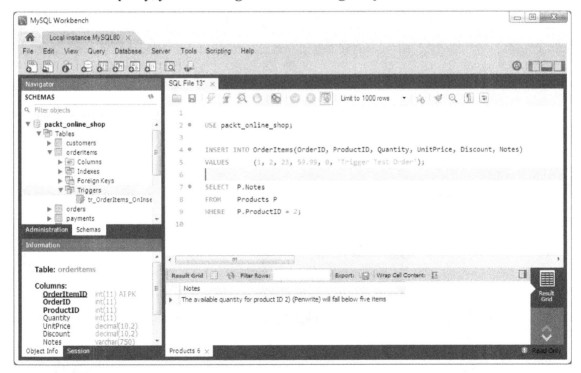

Figure 8.20: Testing the Trigger

Chapter 9: Security

Activity 9.01: Grant UPDATE permission on a table in MySQL

Solution:

1. Update the permission for **TEMP_ACCOUNT_2** using the following code:

```
USE packt_online_shop;

GRANT UPDATE ON TABLE packt_online_shop.products TO 'TEMP_ACCOUNT_2';
```

2. Write the following code to view the

```
SHOW GRANTS FOR 'TEMP_ACCOUNT_2';
```

3. Execute the query, you should get the result:

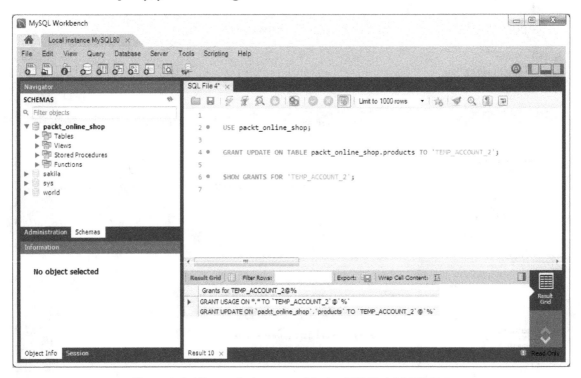

Figure 9.6: All permissions provided to TEMP_ACCOUNT_2

Chapter 10: Aggregate Functions

Activity 10.01: Working with Aggregates

1. Write the following code in a new query tab:

```
SELECT OI.OrderID, P.ProductName,
    SUM(OI.Quantity) AS
        'COUNT OF EACH SEPARATE PRODUCT IN THE ORDER',
            SUM(SUM(OI.Quantity)) OVER(PARTITION BY OI.OrderID)
            AS 'TOTAL COUNT OF PRODUCTS IN THE ORDER',
            MAX(MAX(OI.Quantity)) OVER(PARTITION BY OI.OrderID)
            AS 'COUNT OF THE PRODUCT WITH THE HIGHEST
            ORDER COUNT IN THE ORDER'
FROM        OrderItems OI INNER JOIN
            Products P ON OI.ProductID = P.ProductID
GROUP BY  OI.OrderID, P.ProductName
ORDER BY  OI.OrderID;
```

2. Execute the query, it should provide you the following result:

OrderID	ProductName	COUNT OF EACH SEPARATE PRODUCT IN THE ORDER	TOTAL COUNT OF PRODUCTS IN THE ORDER	COUNT OF THE PRODUCT WITH THE HIGHEST ORDER COUNT IN THE ORDER
1	Calculatre	2	5	2
1	Penwrite	1	5	2
1	Vortex Generator	2	5	2
2	Government Accounting	1	2	1
2	10-mm socket wrench	1	2	1
3	power cell	4	11	7
3	keyboard wrench	7	11	7
5	Penwrite	2	4	2
5	habanero peppers	1	4	2
5	Government Accounting	1	4	2
6	keyboard wrench	2	3	2
6	10-mm socket wrench	1	3	2

Figure 10.21: Aggregating Orders

Chapter 11: Advanced SQL

Activity 11.01: Implementing the LIKE Operator

Solution:

1. Enter the following query:

```
SELECT O.OrderID, O.CustomerID, O.OrderNumber, O.OrderDate,
       O.ShipmentDate, O.OrderStatus, O.Notes
FROM   Orders O
WHERE  O.Notes LIKE '%CUST%' AND O.ShipmentDate > '01051995'
```

We have set two filter conditions. Only when both are satisfied will the product be displayed.

2. On execution of the query, your result will look similar to the following:

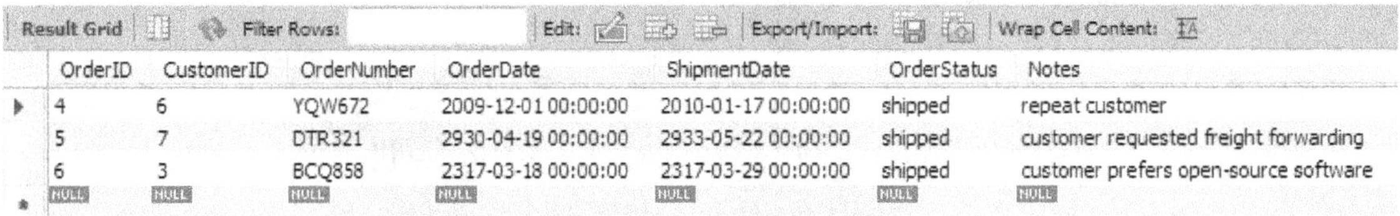

OrderID	CustomerID	OrderNumber	OrderDate	ShipmentDate	OrderStatus	Notes
4	6	YQW672	2009-12-01 00:00:00	2010-01-17 00:00:00	shipped	repeat customer
5	7	DTR321	2930-04-19 00:00:00	2933-05-22 00:00:00	shipped	customer requested freight forwarding
6	3	BCQ858	2317-03-18 00:00:00	2317-03-29 00:00:00	shipped	customer prefers open-source software
NULL	NULL	NULL	NULL	NULL	NULL	NULL

Figure 11.22: Customer notes post May 5, 1995

Notice that there are only three orders that have an order date post **May 1, 1995** and have **CUST** as part of the **Notes** section.

Activity 11.02: Using Transactions

Solution:

1. Execute the following code to verify the existence of the specific **OrderItems** rows:

```
USE PACKT_ONLINE_SHOP;


SELECT    OrderItemID, OrderID, ProductID, Quantity,
          UnitPrice, Discount, Notes
FROM      OrderItems
WHERE     OrderID = 5;
```

The output is as follows:

OrderItemID	OrderID	ProductID	Quantity	UnitPrice	Discount	Notes
8	5	2	2	79.99	2.17	customer transitioning from slide rules to software
9	5	6	1	4.49	0.00	heavy Scoville Units
10	5	5	1	14.99	1.89	financial planning
NULL	NULL	NULL	NULL	NULL	NULL	NULL

Figure 11.23: Verifying the existence of the rows

2. Delete the items as a transaction:

```
START TRANSACTION;

DELETE FROM orderitems
WHERE OrderID = 5;

#    COMMIT;
ROLLBACK;
```

By doing this, you should be able to rollback your changes.

WHAT NEXT?

Now that you've mastered the fundamentals of SQL, continue to build your knowledge and advance your career with one of our other Workshops...

THE PYTHON WORKSHOP

- Learn how to write clean, concise code with Python 3
- Automate essential day-to-day tasks with Python scripts
- Tackle entry-level data science problems and create engaging visualizations
- Get started with predictive machine learning models

THE APPLIED SQL DATA ANALYTICS WORKSHOP

- Experiment with data analytics using basic and advanced queries
- Interpret data through descriptive statistics and aggregate functions
- Study advance analytics, including geospatial and text analytics
- Integrate your SQL pipelines with other analytics technologies

THE JAVA WORKSHOP

- Write clean and well-commented Java code that's easy to maintain
- Use third-party libraries and software development kits (SDKs)
- Learn how to work with information stored in external databases
- Keep data secure with cryptography and encryption

...or search online for "Packt Workshops" and browse the rest of our range for inspiration.

PLEASE LEAVE A REVIEW

Let us know what you think by leaving a detailed, impartial review on Amazon. We appreciate all feedback – it helps us continue to make great products and help aspiring developers build their skills. Please spare a few minutes to give your thoughts – it makes a big difference to us.

Index

About

All major keywords used in this book are captured alphabetically in this section. Each one is accompanied by the page number of where they appear.

www.ingramcontent.com/pod-product-compliance
Lightning Source LLC
Chambersburg PA
CBHW080631060326
40690CB00021B/4884